Mental Health Disorders on Television

Representation Versus Reality

KIMBERLEY MCMAHON-COLEMAN
AND ROSLYN WEAVER

McFarland & Company, Inc., Publishers
Jefferson, North Carolina

DEC 0 6 2022

Library of Congress Cataloguing-in-Publication Data

Names: McMahon-Coleman, Kimberley, author. | Weaver, Roslyn, 1979– author.
Title: Mental health disorders on television : representation
versus reality / Kimberley McMahon-Coleman, Roslyn Weaver.
Description: Jefferson : McFarland & Company, Inc., Publishers, 2020. |
Includes bibliographical references and index.
Identifiers: LCCN 2020015191 | ISBN 9781476672151 (paperback: acid free paper) ∞
ISBN 9781476640204 (ebook)
Subjects: LCSH: Mental illness on television.
Classification: LCC PN1992.8.M46 M37 2020 | DDC 791.45/6561—dc23
LC record available at https://lccn.loc.gov/2020015191

British Library cataloguing data are available

ISBN (print) 978-1-4766-7215-1
ISBN (ebook) 978-1-4766-4020-4

On the cover: Front cover: Sofia Helin in the 2011 series
The Bridge (Filmlance International AB/Photofest)

Printed in the United States of America

*McFarland & Company, Inc., Publishers
Box 611, Jefferson, North Carolina 28640
www.mcfarlandpub.com*

For our families, with love and thanks

Acknowledgments

In a long-term project such as this, there are people whose support and encouragement make an enormous difference. Thanks must go to conference audience members and journal reviewers whose feedback has both enriched this work and given us the momentum to continue. Thanks also to Rosser Johnson, Ed Janak and Ludovic Sourdot, who graciously granted permission for some previously published works to be revised for this book (McMahon-Coleman, *Doc Martin*; McMahon-Coleman, *Little Professors*).

We would also like to acknowledge and thank our colleagues at the University of Wollongong's regional campuses and at Western Sydney University.

Kimberley would like to thank Tony, Jamie and Robert Coleman, and she promises to try not to overload her metaphorical plate this badly in the future. Thank you for your ongoing encouragement and belief, which we reciprocate in spades, particularly towards the academic endeavors of Jamie and Robert at our alma mater, UOW. To Grace, Yeovany and Trinidad; Dany, Viviana, Sofia and Iker; Ellyn, David, Emma and Carter—the Coleman clan is so grateful to you, your families, the fates and AFS for bringing you into our lives. Special thanks also to the other members of a wonderfully diverse adoptive family: godsons Jackson and Charlie and their mum, Jody; the Draisma clan; Josh Peters; Cathy O'Brien; Jo Evans and the younger Js three; Phoebe Zeller and Nick and Alex Hawley; and our Relay family. Thank you to Wendy Church for your continued efforts to convince me to apply some mindfulness and self-care strategies to my own life—please see above promise to Tony, Jamie and Robert. A very special thank you is owed to Roslyn herself as well as her lovely parents and extended family. Sharing accommodations to save on conference costs fifteen years ago has led us through these dangers untold and hardships unnumbered; we have fought our way through libraries, boats, and theaters across three continents, to the theme park castles beyond the goblin cities of procrastination and writers' block, for our will is strong, and our kingdom is great. I can't wait to see what adventures the next fifteen years bring.

Roslyn would like to thank her parents, siblings and their families, aunt, and friends and colleagues in far flung parts of the globe who have variously encouraged, cajoled, and prodded her into continuing with the academic lark even when moving outside the world of academia, all while moving multiple times geographically across several continents as well. Thank you particularly to Kimberley for this shared, somewhat epic, journey towards the Mount Doom of completing this project and casting the metaphorical ring into the fire at last—a journey that has required a patience and friendship in the mold of a Sam and Frodo, or a Harry and Ron and Hermione, on an admittedly smaller scale. To paraphrase C.S. Lewis: "Friendship is born at that moment when one PhD student says to another, 'What! You too? I thought I was the only one.'" From shapeshifters to maternal figures and now mental health, our shared research areas have taken us in many different directions, but ones that we always trust are of interest to others as well and we humbly hope that will in this case add something of use to the increasing dialogue around mental health representations in this field.

There are not words to express our gratitude to our interviewees, who agreed not only to discuss their own mental health diagnoses but also to watch programs depicting mental illness, both tasks with potential to be uncomfortable. We value your time and honesty, which added a critical element to this book.

Table of Contents

Preface

The idea for this book was first tossed around in a distant time when we were feeling euphoric about the completion of our first co-authored adventure with McFarland, *Werewolves and Other Shapeshifters in Popular Culture*. That book contained a chapter on disability, illness and mental health, and given that Roslyn was working in medical humanities at the time and Kimberley was teaching academic language and literacy to students with disabilities, it was one of the easier chapters to write. We felt instinctively that there were many more examples of mental health disorders on our screens that did not include supernatural shapeshifters. We were haunted by the findings of a 1995 study that found that people with diagnosed mental illness were both more likely to critically analyze stereotypes (the example given being the idea that people with schizophrenia are violent) because they had firsthand experience with the illness but, conversely, were also likely to self-stigmatize or feel pressure and disappointment that they were not doing as well as fictional characters whose recovery was mediated by scriptwriters rather than real-world expert treatment (Philo, Secker and Platt).

This project has remained a labor of love despite both of us experiencing changes in employment, Roslyn moving across the world (twice!) and various other distractions in our personal and professional lives. Some of Kimberley's distractions have been related to living in a multi-diagnosis household, so concerns around stereotyping, stigma and misconceptions are more than just an academic pursuit. Images on our screens matter: we invite them into the intimacy of our living rooms, sometimes on a regular basis and for years on end. It is therefore important that they do not perpetuate negative and unhelpful stereotypes that continually re-marginalize individuals when they are most vulnerable. Over the past decade, we have seen some more realistic and responsible representations of disorders listed in the DSM-5; equally we have seen some that appear determined to cling to outdated or even incorrect ideas.

We hope that this book will at least encourage scholarly conversation about representations of mental health disorders on television, and we encourage you to join the conversation online. We can be found on Twitter @ KMcMahonColeman and @roslynweaver and at our blog: shapeshiftersinpopularculture.wordpress.com.

Introduction

One man from Norway wrote me a 20-page letter about his life living with Asperger's. It was so touching. I also got letters from the Asperger's Society in Sweden. They are happy, because she is not judged just because she is different—she is the hero. Actor Sofia Helin, cited in Khaleeli 5

In 2012, media reports around new Scandinavian television series *The Bridge* highlighted the social awkwardness of the lead character, Saga Norén (played by Sofia Helin), linking it with autism and Asperger's Syndrome and noting how the representation had been praised by individuals on the spectrum as well as support groups. As with so many other television characters, a diagnosis is never made explicit to viewers of *The Bridge*; instead audiences are encouraged to "read" mental illness diagnoses into particular characters and to identify certain behavioral traits as belonging to specific mental health and developmental disorders.

In recent years, representations of mental health and development disorders and difference are increasing on television, with mixed results. Some television programs explicitly position characters as having a mental health disorder, assigning particular diagnoses to the characters, as is common in crime shows. Indeed, a number of contemporary television series incorporate a range of characters with mental health disorders into their storylines, where the disorder may play a major role in the plot, as is the case with *Monk*, *Homeland*, and *Glee*. As with *The Bridge*, in many series it is increasingly a main character who exhibits symptoms of a disorder, even when no diagnosis is made. Saga Norén joins eponymous series lead Doc Martin, *The Big Bang Theory's* Dr. Sheldon Cooper and *Bones'* Dr. Temperance Brennan as characters who are routinely read by audiences and critics alike as having autism spectrum disorder (ASD), even when the shows' producers deny the diagnoses. Other characters such as Erin Silver in *90210*, Carrie Mathison in *Homeland*, Ian Gallagher in *Shameless*, and bothersome brothers Billy Chenowith (*Six Feet Under*), Marty Fisher (*Shameless*) and Sean Tolkey (*The Big C*) are represented—with varying degrees of success—as having bipolar disorder. From the criminalization of mental illness within police procedurals such as the *Law and Order* franchise to the institutionalization of an allegedly schizophrenic Buffy, on-screen representations are often negative, although in series such as *Buffy, the Vampire Slayer*, this negativity is mitigated by rather more sensitive handling of topics such as fear, depression, social alienation, schizophrenia, kleptomania, psychosis, and a host of other related issues.

Significant changes to the television industry have also had an impact on in-narrative diagnostic representation in recent years. The so-called "Netflix Effect," which has seen a shift away from mainstream content towards personalized in-home viewing, has changed the landscape of film and television production. Since 2013, Netflix has been producing its own content, which now makes up 85 percent of its available programming (Morgan). As many within the industry have noted, this means that programs with lower anticipated audiences than was traditional are now being produced (Gunsberg Podcast; Shepard, *Kutcher*; Shepard, *Bryant*). Whereas traditional television programs needed to pull in audiences in the millions in order to be viable, Netflix is prepared to run shows with viewerships of around seven hundred thousand (Shepard, *Bryant*). This has led to the development of a number of shows that meet "underserved audiences" (Shepard, *Kutcher*) or which involve storylines that may have previously been deemed too risky. The immediacy of reactions being conveyed to program executives via social media can also lead to more responsible depictions of mental health issues, with programs such as Netflix's *Atypical*, for example, making significant changes in its representation between seasons.

However, as with *The Bridge* and its ilk, we still see series that avoid naming diagnoses for their characters, instead relying on certain unusual behavior or personal quirks as code for particular disorders. Thus, the socially awkward character or mathematical genius is understood to have ASD. An unstable personality represents dissociative identity disorder (DID). The violent criminal has schizophrenia. Wrist injuries are shorthand for a character involved in cutting and self-harm. As the public becomes more aware of the range and scope of mental health issues, we grow ever more adept at "diagnosing" on-screen characters for ourselves.

Television's interest in illness is not new, nor unexpected. As others have noted, the medical world often involves spectacle: Chapman describes as a "spectacle of surgery" events in Australia when a cancer fundraiser auction included the chance to watch a surgery (Chapman 283). Bonner similarly writes that medical documentaries provide viewers with a "spectacle of the real" (Bonner 110), where the images "carry the stamp of authenticity" (Bonner 114). Meanwhile, van Dijck calls on the work of Guy Debord regarding our culture as a "society of the spectacle" to discuss how medical documentaries recall earlier freak shows in their use of fascination and discomfort (van Dijck). There is a complicated relationship between fiction and reality, where these images of health can almost seem to become the "reality." Indeed, the proliferation of images of medical practice might be usefully understood in the framework of Baudrillard's work on simulacra and simulation or Debord's more politically-charged analysis of a society substituting lived reality for its representation (Baudrillard; Debord). Perhaps for some viewers, the incessant models and images and reflections of mental health disorders in the form of television mean that, in one sense, the public "knows" about mental illness even without personal experience because they have already seen it so many times on television. Indeed, Belling argues that for most viewers of medical documentaries, it is more important that the documentary has the appearance of reality rather than faithfully reproducing the real (Belling).

This duality of representation and reality relating to mental health disorders on television is at the heart of this book. Representations of particular characters with mental illness, diagnosed or otherwise, tell us much about how we as a Western society see people with mental health disorders, and in this book we are interested in untangling some of the ways in which two distinct, yet related, aspects of television come to bear on our cultural understanding of mental health. In the chapters that follow, we analyze a range of popular television programs for how they conceptualize mental health and how they construct characters who exhibit symptoms relating to mental health disorders. These images form the representation side of our book; the reality aspect is drawn from interviews with viewers of the programs who have a mental health disorder to explore their perceptions of how television can influence not only their own identity but also public attitudes to mental illness.

Mental Health: Changing Concepts

It is particularly timely to consider these issues when we reflect on the shifting medical classification of mental health disorders in recent years. The well-publicized and at times controversial revisions of the *Diagnostic and Statistical Manual of Mental Disorders* (DSM) draw attention to the flexible boundaries of what constitutes mental illness. The manual is produced by the American Psychiatric Association and guides clinicians, health professionals, policy makers, insurers and other groups in making and understanding psychiatric diagnoses. The DSM covers a vast spectrum of clinical, developmental and intellectual disorders, relating to mood (for example, bipolar, depression), anxiety (agoraphobia, obsessive-compulsive, post-traumatic stress), addiction (drugs, gambling), development (autism, Asperger's), eating (anorexia, bulimia), personality (paranoia, narcissism), psychosis (hallucinations, delusions, schizophrenia), impulse-control (kleptomania, pyromania), sleep (insomnia, sleepwalking), and sexuality (pedophilia, sexual sadism), among others.

The manual has evolved over the last sixty years, from its origins in 1952 to the major revisions in the current iteration, the 2013 DSM-5, including new disorders such as binge eating, changed diagnostic criteria, the removal of some specific disorders (such as some schizophrenia types), and refining categories for disorders (such as Asperger's Syndrome no longer being a distinct disorder but rather included as a component of the autism spectrum), among other changes. Such revisions have been met with public concerns from health professionals and others, about over- or under-diagnosis, with accusations ranging from a belief that the changes will result in a proliferation of mental health diagnoses, thus greatly increasing the proportion of the general population diagnosable for mental health disorders, to fears that a one-size-fits-all approach to autism spectrum disorders will be detrimental to those previously diagnosed with Asperger's Syndrome.

Regardless of the legitimacy or otherwise of such concerns, the revisions do highlight one important point relating to how we classify and understand mental health diagnoses, and that is how such "definitions" can change over time. Unlike physical illness, which is comparatively straightforward in terms of diagnosing physical injuries and maladies, mental health has always been subject to more scrutiny and suspicion around its diagnoses, its patients, and its practitioners. Historically, those with mental illness have been ostracized and physically isolated from the rest of society: confined in mental institutions away from public sight and attention, feared and even persecuted by others in society. Broadening diagnostic criteria and disorders has the likely effect of further collapsing the boundaries between "normal" and "different." Thus, in conjunction with a rise in activist and support groups campaigning for greater government funding and public recognition related to various mental health disorders, it is both important and timely to expand our understanding of these areas.

Public Perceptions of Mental Illness

Society's treatment of those with mental disorders goes far beyond official guidelines for diagnostic criteria and has much to do with public perceptions of mental illness and those with mental health disorders. These perceptions are often influenced by images produced by the media. Representations of mental illness inevitably have some influence on how society sees people with mental health disorders and how they see themselves. People with mental health disorders are often stigmatized for their difference in society, and, in part, such stigmas can develop because of patterns in how popular culture portrays mental health disorders.

Mental health is an area of study that is gaining attention with respect to the cultural understanding of mental health disorders and illnesses. Previous studies show that negative portrayals of mental disorders can not only influence people's beliefs (Livingston; Pirkis et al.) but also impact the identity of people with mental disorders (Hinshaw; Philo, "Changing Media") and affect the chances they will seek or continue treatment because of the associated stigma of identifying with a mental illness (Corrigan; Stuart). Indeed, research suggests that portrayals of people with mental disorders in popular texts across film, television and other media are often negative (Hinshaw; Pirkis et al.; Wahl and Roth, "Television Images"). For instance, studies have found that characters with mental disorders on television are usually more violent than other characters (Diefenbach; Hinshaw; Wilson et al., "Mental Illness Depictions"), whereas in reality, people with mental illness were not only more likely to be victims of violent crime than perpetrators but also more likely to be victimized than the general population (Hinshaw). Elsewhere, a study of madness and the Joker in *The Dark Knight* showed the perceived links between danger and mental illness (Camp et al.). Film and television often perpetuate stigmas by associating mental illness with several negative stereotypes, including homicidal maniacs, dangerous seductresses, or narcissists (Hyler et al.). Other stereotypes on television include characters with mental health disorders being shown as simple, unpredictable, asocial, or untrustworthy (Wilson et al.). Where college-age students self-cited television as their primary source of information regarding mental illness, there was a clear positive correlation between the number of hours watched per week and the extent of their stigmatizing attitudes (Granello and Pauley). Even children's television consistently presents negative associations of mental illness and includes pejorative language that suggests mental disorders involve loss of control; such practices can socialize children into accepting these stereotypes (Wilson et al.). Other stereotypes might be more positive, where those with mental illness are shown to be caring or empathic (Wilson et al.), but negative images predominate. If fictional images are not negative, they are often inaccurate. For instance, Draaisma and also Hyler both note that popular media often links autism with special talents and abilities (Draaisma; Hyler), yet the incidence of such abilities, such as savant syndrome, is in fact uncommon, despite famous fictional characters such as Raymond Babbitt in *Rain Man* and *The Good Doctor's* Shaun Murphy contributing to perpetuating such links (Treffert).

Wahl and Roth found in 1982 that little had changed with regard to screen representations of mental health disorders since the 1960s, with most depictions being predominantly negative (Wahl and Roth). In a later publication, Wahl cites studies from the late 1970s and early 1980s which found that psychiatric disorders were consistently the most commonly depicted disability in film between 1919 and 1985 (Wahl, "Mass Media Images"). Despite calls for more positive representation (Jorm; Pirkis et al.; Vogel and Kapalan; Wahl, *Media Madness*) and an apparent increase in the public's literacy around mental health (Schomerus et al.), attitudes towards mental illness have not changed appreciably.

A 2010 report commissioned by Shift (a UK government initiative designed to reduce the stigma associated with mental illness) and conducted by the Glasgow Media Group at Glasgow University found an over-representation of television depictions of characters with mental illness as violent or as engaging in self-harm and an oversimplification of some disorders, with bipolar disorder being prominent within the predominantly British programs analyzed (Philo et al., *Making Drama*). This oversimplification was seen in representations of some mental health problems, such as "a character with bipolar disorder being portrayed as 'up and down,'" but the researchers noted that other programs "provided a more nuanced approach" (Philo et al., *Making Drama* 4). The authors found that accurate representations of mental illness have the potential to challenge stigma and prejudice and that programs did not need to be serious in order to deal with mental health issues with compassion. Drama, however, can play a positive role; for example, the process by which a character becomes increasingly ill leading to diagnosis can provide dramatic potential and is thus often well-handled within certain narrative sub-genres (Philo et al., *Making Drama*), although representations around medication and recovery were also often over-simplified. As one of the authors of the report, Professor Greg Philo, summarized in an interview, "[g]reat progress has been made in recent years, but we've got some way to go before we see more of the everyday realities of living with a mental health problem properly represented and stereotypes like the axe-wielding maniac take a back seat" (BBC News Health).

As the Shift study noted, almost half of all fictional characters with mental illness diagnoses have storylines depicting them as violent or posing a threat to others, and some 63 percent of all references were "pejorative, flippant or unsympathetic" (Philo et al., *Making Drama* 47–53). Commentary published around this time noted that television series did not often recognize that medication and treatment for issues such as bipolar disorder can lead to a reduction in symptoms or even remission (Mullen; Tartakovsky). Research has also recognized that representations of mental illness within the mass media are critical because they are a key source of information for both the general population and those with diagnoses (Hinshaw; Tartakovsky) and called for more responsible and accurate portrayals (C. Davies; BBC News

Health; Corderoy; Edwards; Mullen; Tartakovsky). Mindframe, an Australian partnership between mental health organizations and screenwriters, has
produced a number of guides for stage and screen writers that offer advice on
how to more fairly represent characters with mental illness. They point out
that individuals can manage and live with mental illness; "it is not 'traumatic'
every day" (*Mindframe* 7). Yet these guidelines are voluntary, and the Australian television industry produces only a very small proportion of what is seen
around the world, so on-screen anomalies continue.

Given that many studies noted the impact of language on stigmatization and self-stigmatization, we have also given consideration to the matter
of people-first versus disability-first language. We understand that language
can involve a political choice; for example, some people on the autism spectrum prefer to refer to themselves as being part of an autistic community. In
a written text such as this we have obviously not been able to cater to readers'
individual language preferences and have thus opted for people-first language
in the belief that it is less likely to reduce an individual to their medical diagnosis. In other words, rather than referring to a person by their illness, such
as referring to a character as "schizophrenic," we have instead chosen to refer
to characters as having schizophrenia, which is only one aspect of that person
as whole. We also recognize that the terms "illness" and "disorder" are themselves imbued with negative connotations and, in some contexts, will have a
limiting effect. While acknowledging these concerns, we have chosen to use
the most current clinical terms at the time of publication.

Much of the work done in this general area comprises smaller studies
published in journal articles. While there are several books which deal with
mental health and television representations, these are largely written from
a clinical perspective. For example, Gary Morris' *Mental Health Issues and
the Media: An Introduction for Health Professionals* explores the subject for
the purpose of equipping health practitioners with knowledge about media
images of mental health. Lesley Henderson's *Social Issues in Television Fiction*
canvasses some of the ideas outlined here, but it includes a much broader
range of social issues than just mental health and has a large number of examples from Britain and from the 1990s and earlier, whereas our focus is
solely on mental health in contemporary television series primarily from the
American industry. Works such as Stuart Murray's *Representing Autism: Culture, Narrative, Fascination* covers similar ground but examine one particular
health disorder across a range of media. More recently, Sharon Packer and
Lawrence Rubin have edited collections that examine mental illness across
a range of popular media. Here, we propose to analyze a range of mental
health disorders within the recent history of one medium with a large reach:
television.

We chose to focus on television for several reasons. As noted earlier, television is seeing an increase in the numbers of programs featuring characters with a mental health disorder, including protagonists. This is particularly important because of the media available to the general public; television remains the most popular medium with far-reaching appeal and influence. Thus it is critical to pay attention to these contemporary representations of mental health.

Our motivations for writing the book, therefore, begin with addressing this gap in research: our goal here is to provide a full-length critical examination of these topics as represented in popular television. We also share an interest in the area of mental health and popular culture because of our previous work in both the fields of inclusive education and medical humanities. In our previous book, *Werewolves and Other Shapeshifters in Popular Culture*, writing our chapter on mental health and fantasy texts provoked us to think more generally about how society, and particularly television, is dealing with mental illness and mental health (McMahon-Coleman and Weaver, *Werewolves*). In some of the texts we examined for that project, the fantasy genre was used as a means to explore how disability, mental illness or more supernatural "conditions" could be viewed as a gift or a source of strength; for some characters, it provided a means of overcoming limitations and rigidity of identity. Rather than exploring one genre or even one television program in detail for its construction of mental health, however, we decided here to take a broader approach to assess multiple series in order to gain a more complete picture of mental illness in popular culture. Further research revealed the importance of television in constructing perceptions about mental health and mental illness, provoking discussions about the impact on the identity, self-esteem and education of those with diagnoses.

Our overarching aim in this book is to explore several main areas relating to mental health: what these representations are saying about mental health disorders; how particular programs may impact audiences; the impact of normalizing Othering language; and what effect these factors may have on the identity formation of those with a mental health diagnosis of their own.

Thus, we employ two strategies to answer these questions, in line with our focus on representation and reality. Rather than focusing solely on the text and not the audience, we have chosen to support textual analysis with audience research, reaching beyond how such programs represent these topics to understand how people experience their reality of living with a mental health disorder. Drawing together these two areas of representation and reality provides a significant contribution to our understanding of mental health disorders in contemporary society.

As Pirkis et al. note, what constitutes a positive portrayal involves some level of subjectivity, since commentators may disagree in this point. We have therefore chosen to include in our analysis perspectives from viewers who have mental health disorders or are close to someone who does. These are the people most likely to be immediately impacted by popular (mis)representation. Combining the elements of textual and audience analysis is not particularly common in studies of television programs but including the experiences and reflections of viewers in our study of representations is fitting, as it speaks to the importance of understanding popular culture. Analyzing these representations is only one aspect and must be accompanied by exploring how viewers respond to these images on television. How do these representations influence their self-perceptions and the perceptions of others? Examining both these strands has the potential to offer a more complex picture of representation and reality.

Scope of the Book

Our choice of television programs is pragmatic and reflects our own interests as well as practical aspects relating to availability and accessibility of television recordings. The series chosen for analysis cover a range of genres: crime, fantasy, drama, and comedy.

Most television programs we discuss are American. This reflects the fact that the United States is the largest producer and exporter of television programs globally and that many other nations consume American television programs in significant numbers. Given this global reach of the American industry, it is likely that our findings will have some relevance and transferability in many Western nations. However, we do include some programs from other television markets, such as *The Bridge* (Sweden-Denmark), *Offspring* (Australia), and *Doc Martin* (the UK).

We include analysis of programs that explicitly name a diagnosis alongside those that do not, in recognition of the fact that in many cases viewers will be making their own "diagnoses" anyway, or that in some cases producers or writers will acknowledge the implications of their characterization outside rather than inside the program. Although at some points we discuss diagnostic criteria in relation to characters, our goal is not to play a game of diagnosis but instead to expand knowledge of our societal understanding of mental health by examining cultural constructs of mental health.

Our analysis of the specific programs is guided by several main questions: how do the programs conceptualize mental illness and mental health? What role does the character play within the series, and how are their differences treated by other characters? What discourses are evident around the different mental health disorders of the characters?

In line with John Fiske's work, our analysis of the programs acknowledges that meaning is created in television in several ways. Fiske describes three codes on television that combine to construct discourses: reality, representation, and ideology. Basic elements such as acting, costumes, and the characters' speech comprise social codes of reality. A second code is representation and relates to technical aspects including dialogue, setting, camera work, lighting, music, and editing. These two codes together create the third level, which is that of ideology, where we might consider such elements as race, gender, and class. In our reading of these television programs, we are interested in how the different pieces of television storytelling are placed together to give a picture of mental health disorders in society.

Although we aim to cover a fairly wide range of programs and mental health disorders, we do not intend to provide an exhaustive catalogue of television series or mental disorders. In addition, in many cases we have chosen to focus on specific episodes or story arcs rather than entire seasons of the selected programs. Our interest is in highlighting several key examples to explore in more detail to add to our knowledge of how our contemporary society conceptualizes, represents, and reads mental health disorders through the lens of popular media.

Accordingly, our analysis is organized not by program but by types of mental health disorder, although within the chapters we do discuss the programs individually. It is inevitable that there is some crossover in the topics and series discussed over the chapters; however, we have organized our sections around several key points related to different aspects of mental health representations.

The Chapters

Chapter One focuses on the autism spectrum of disorders (ASD), in line with increasing public awareness of the disorder (including the syndrome formerly known as Asperger's). ASD is a particularly useful place to begin our analysis of mental health disorders on television because it encapsulates the complex relationship between reality and representation. Although there remains ongoing debate as to how to define ASD with regard to mental health (with some researchers referring to it as a developmental delay, rather than a mental illness), we are taking a broad approach in line with the DSM and thus we discuss these disorders which are becoming more commonplace on television, but which are not always acknowledged within the series. *Parenthood*'s Max Braverman is one of the first characters to have been diagnosed on screen. In contrast, *Bones* creator Hart Hanson has said that the lead character, Temperance "Bones" Brennan, does have the syndrome but that this is never mentioned on screen in order to reach a larger audience. Similarly, *The Big Bang Theory*'s Bill Prady describes Sheldon Cooper's behaviors as "Sheldon-y rather than Asperger-y" (Waldman) in order to avoid the responsibilities inherent in portraying the condition accurately. *Doc Martin's* co-creator and actor Martin Clunes denies that the character has Asperger's (*LA Times*), even though most of the audience reads him that way and the series' lead writer has said in interview that he wrote him as "Aspergic" [sic] (Minghella). Fox's *Touch* presents a character with clear symptoms of autism, yet the word does not appear in the promotional material and it is a diagnosis which the character's father outright rejects early in the narrative. Audiences have also linked the representation of Saga Norén in *The Bridge* with ASD. This chapter will explore these programs and why the disorders on the autism spectrum, in particular, are so often not labeled in popular representations, and will contrast them with recent, niche programs that embrace their characters' diagnoses, such as *Atypical* and *The A-Word*.

One of the most popular anxiety disorders on screen that is commonly treated for comedic effect is obsessive compulsive disorder (OCD), and this is the subject of Chapter Two. *Glee's* Emma Pillsbury and the eponymous Monk are both characters whose obsessive-compulsive behaviors have been front and center in the development of their characters. Emma's OCD, in particular, is often played for comedic value and discussed in disparaging tones, at least by the glee club's nemesis, Sue Sylvester, a character who arguably displays symptoms of mental ill health—in the form of megalomania—herself. Although Monk's OCD is also the subject of humor and is a barrier for him in living a "normal" life, it is at the same time one of his particular strengths because it gives him an attention to detail that benefits his detective work.

Chapter Three explores two disorders commonly confused with each other: schizophrenia and DID. Joss Whedon's fantasy series *Buffy, the Vampire Slayer* includes one episode, "Normal Again," in which series protagonist Buffy Summers is caught between two identities and must determine which is "real": a superhero who is destined to save the world from evil supernatural creatures, or a young woman with undifferentiated schizophrenia who is incarcerated in a mental institution and is only hallucinating her superhero persona. The scenes in this episode reflect many contemporary images of mental health facilities and their patients: the institution is cold and isolated, and the patients display stereotypical traits of "crazy" characters. Yet assigning this and other mental health disorders to the popular main characters in this series does offer somewhat of a departure from the usual treatment of schizophrenia as violent. Similarly, DID representations in popular media tend to focus on violence and unpredictability, yet somewhat alternative examples are found in an episode of *Criminal Minds* and the series *United States of Tara*, where the depictions are for the most part sympathetic and almost appear to suggest (unconsciously or consciously) the failings of society rather than the characters.

Chapter Four focuses on the psychotic mood disorder bipolar disorder. A common misconception with regard to bipolar disorder is that all patients will rapid cycle from extreme highs to extreme lows on a daily basis, which is rarely the case in reality. This chapter examines recent screen depictions such as those on *90210, Homeland* and *Shameless* to explore what messages they send about the disorder to members of the general public and how these may potentially lead to public misunderstanding. It also highlights the strengths of these portrayals, which are rather more positive than historical on-screen representations of individuals with bipolar.

In our fifth chapter, we turn to anxiety, depression and traumatic disorders on screen in dramas (*Offspring*) and comedy (*The Big Bang Theory, You're the Worst*). This includes symptomatic social awkwardness such as selective mutism, which is explored in television shows such as *The Big Bang Theory*. This chapter explores the efficacy and impact of such representations on those who are afflicted by them; particularly in shows which present the disorders largely for their comedic value. When a mental health disorder is the subject of humor, can this be seen in a positive sense of normalizing the disorder and making it visible, or does it denigrate those people with the disorder and contribute to stigma? In the case of *You're the Worst*, how can a comedy successfully negotiate the serious issues of clinical depression and post-traumatic stress faced by their lead characters?

We recognize that our reading of these texts may be different to others' interpretations, and to add a further dimension we include in our sixth and final chapter the perspectives of television viewers who identify as having a mental health disorder or those close to someone with a disorder. Including audience responses and reflections on the programs is important not only in acknowledgment that there are multiple interpretations of these programs and characters but also to give voice to those who have so often been excluded and marginalized in society. These audience insights are based on interviews we have conducted for this book project. Following approval by the University of Wollongong human research ethics committee, we asked participants a range of semi-structured questions around their viewing of particular shows and their thoughts on how television treated mental disorders generally and how such images affected them individually. Using thematic analysis to interpret the qualitative data from our participants, we have organized their responses into our final chapter that essentially asks the question: what impact do these representations have on the reality for these people? To respect and protect their confidentiality and privacy, we have assigned pseudonyms to all participants, removed any identifying details from their text responses, and presented their reflections in this chapter with only basic demographic information and with only minimal interpretation or commentary from us.

Informed by the six chapters, our Conclusion argues that popular television representations of mental health and mental illness deserve critical attention because of their historical tendency to represent mental health disorders negatively or inaccurately. We do not, however, suggest that this is the case for all televisual representations, and our analysis shows that some programs are using mental health disorders in more complex, sensitive ways. The concluding chapter also aims to consider the impact of such depictions on the subset of the viewing audience who share diagnoses with the fictional characters they see on screen. This is particularly relevant given the number of recent and seminal popular television texts which deal with this subject matter.

Moving beyond the immediate textual analysis of our programs in this book, we might consider broader questions about this area of research. Is television solely responsible for how society understands mental health disorders? Will people with mental disorders find their identity constructed primarily or even partly through television images? Although we do not attempt to argue this is the case, we do contend that television does play some role in reflecting and shaping our cultural beliefs and attitudes; that the stories that are popular in society tell us much about that society; and that even unconsciously we can absorb some of the un/intended messages within television programs. The participants in our study provide strong evidence that this is indeed the case. Thus, critical attention to televisual representations of mental health is crucial.

Accordingly, we hope that this book will not only contribute to our knowledge of how society understands mental illness but also will suggest more avenues for research and provoke further discussion among viewers, clinicians, and those people who have a mental health disorder, or know someone with one, as we continue to reflect on and refine our ideas about mental health in our society.

ONE

"I don't pick up on signs"
Autism Spectrum Disorder

In this chapter we consider recent popular television representations of autism spectrum disorder in terms of responsibility and authenticity. Televisual representations of characters that are implicitly or explicitly understood to be on the spectrum will be examined and critiqued. We have identified a number of trends in these portrayals and note that while representations are improving over time, the movement towards nuanced, authentic representations of autism spectrum disorder (ASD) has been painfully slow.

Included for analysis are shows wherein characters are explicitly diagnosed on screen; those who ignore or refute the possible diagnosis, even as other characters discuss the possibility openly and, in some cases, definitively; and those where the character's symptomatic behaviors are explained away by important people behind the scenes as merely being quirky. We posit that part of the reason for the latter two attitudinal trends is a concern around accuracy and responsibility in portrayal. The lack—or outright denial—of an on-screen diagnosis abrogates show runners being obliged to engage with frameworks like the Mindframe guidelines, or to speak with experts and/or those with lived experience in order to construct a fair representation. In the case of comedy shows, in particular, relegating behaviors to "quirks" of a character is likely to be more palatable to an audience than the notion of laughing at a person's disorder.

In characters who are both formally diagnosed on screen and those who are not, we sometimes see "bingo card syndrome"—whereby a character will not have just a few symptomatic behaviors, but a full range that would be highly unlikely to appear in any one individual. Again, however, this is arguably more prevalent in the depictions that have not engaged meaningfully with expertise around responsible and accurate portrayals.

Background: What Is ASD?

Symptoms of autism spectrum disorder are found in popular television characters so often that particular characters are often read by audiences as being on the spectrum, regardless of whether their creators acknowledge the possibility of a diagnosis, name it outright, or flatly deny the possibility. Autism spectrum disorder, often known by its acronym of ASD, is a continuum of neurodevelopmental disorders that impact social interaction, communication and behavior (Adreon and Durocher); misunderstandings around social interactions and communications are a mainstay of situational comedy, and all television narratives are based, to a greater or lesser degree, on the relationships depicted within them, so "autistic" responses to on-screen situations will necessarily impact those narratives. As Diane Adreon and Jennifer Durocher note, symptoms of ASD "can occur in any combination and can range from very mild to very severe" (Adreon and Durocher 272). Autism spectrum disorder is defined in the *Diagnostic and Statistical Manual of Mental Disorders-IV* (DSM-IV) as "[p]ersistent deficits in social communication and social interaction across multiple contexts" (American Psychiatric Association 50). This kind of descriptive language in the most-widely accepted definition of autism is a significant factor in its continued representation as a deficit disorder, rather than one wherein individuals have unique strengths (Graetz). Others note that clinical accounts even reframe positive aspects of the syndrome in terms of deficit language: "Intense curiosity became *perseveration*. Precociously articulate speech became *hyperlexia*. An average score on a test became a *relative deficit*—evidence of an *uneven cognitive profile*" (Silberman 432). Clinical psychologist Professor Tony Attwood has provided an alternative to this deficit language, by going so far as to suggest that Asperger's syndrome may even represent a next stage in human evolution (*Found in Translation*).

There are many people in the wider community who do not really understand what autism is, and for some, news reportage of violent events such as the Port Arthur massacre (1996), Colorado theater shooting (2012), and Sandy Hook school massacre (2013) that focused on the perpetrators' autism has led to a misconception that autism inevitably leads to violence and should thus be feared. Psychopathy is not a symptom of ASD; rather, autism is a lifelong developmental disorder characterized by marked difficulties in social interaction and communication, behavioral and sensitivity issues and restricted and repetitive interests. Autism is a behavioral impairment rather than a psychotic mental illness. Still others have knowledge limited to their understanding from popular culture, as opposed to popular news media; and will argue with an individual with ASD that their clinical diagnosis must be incorrect if their behaviors do not closely align with the prevailing cultural images of autism, such as Raymond Babbitt from the 1989 film *Rain Man*.

In the 1940s, American child psychiatrist Leo Kanner and Austrian pediatrician Hans Asperger both wrote papers about a form of autism typified by a need for sameness and a resistance to change. Perhaps unsurprisingly in this period of history, it was Kanner's paper that was widely circulated and cited, while Asperger's went largely unnoticed until Lorna Wing brought it to the world's attention in the early 1980s. A recent book by Steve Silberman alleges that Kanner was aware of Asperger's paper (that had been published a year earlier), but failed to cite his work. It seems unfortunate that it was Kanner's version that was circulated, given that he promoted the idea of toxic parenting and "refrigerator mothers" as being the cause of high functioning autism; Asperger, on the other hand, noticed that the range of patients and symptomatic behaviors was diverse, and began designing a school that would play to their different cognitive strengths (Baron-Cohen, "Book"). It may also be worth noting that despite concerns that existed for many years about the political viewpoints of Asperger, who was living in Nazi-occupied Austria, he was a vocal opponent of eugenics laws (Attwood, *Complete Guide*; Silberman).

The DSM-IV (American Psychiatric Association) identified Asperger's Syndrome as a discrete subset of autism spectrum disorders. These were children characterized with some of the following unusual social capabilities:

- difficulty making friends or subject to teasing
- difficulties with conversational aspects of language
- advanced but often pedantic use of language
- unusual prosody—oddities in the pitch, tone, and rhythm of speech

Asperger also noted a tendency to intellectualize feelings and that self-help and organizational skills were not commensurate with those of peers. Clumsiness of gait and sensory sensitivity are also identified indicators (Attwood, *Complete Guide*).

Controversially, Asperger's Syndrome and other subsets of ASD were removed from the DSM-5 in 2013 (American Psychiatric Association). Not only did this cause issues around identification, as "Aspies"—as people diagnosed with Asperger's often nicknamed themselves—identified as a community, but it also made it more difficult to arrive at a diagnostic threshold. The DSM's criteria are, in fact, the only recognized standard for diagnosis, since there are no laboratory or other diagnostic tests (Kulage et al.). The mutability of autism from Kanner's Infantile Autism in the third edition; to a spectrum including Asperger's in the fourth; and a spectrum but without subsets like Asperger's in version 5, has contributed to difficulties with maintaining accurate statistics around prevalence in the population.

ASD in the Media

Arguably the seminal screen representation of autism remains Barry Levinson's iconic 1988 movie *Rain Man*. *Rain Man* was a phenomenal success and won multiple awards, including Academy Awards for Best Picture, Best Actor in a Leading Role, Best Director and Best Original Screenplay. It brought a cultural awareness of autism that had previously not been seen on screen. It has become a touchstone of the autism spectrum to the point where programs that explicitly diagnose their characters as being on the spectrum reference it (*Parenthood*; *The A-Word*; *Atypical*; *The Good Doctor*), as do programs that do not explicitly diagnose their characters, yet wish to signal to their audiences that they understand the characters are being read as on the spectrum (*Bones*; *The Big Bang Theory*; *Community*).

Despite its commercial success, what *Rain Man* did not do at all well was articulate that autism is a spectrum disorder. Consequently, Dustin Hoffman's depiction of Raymond Babbitt became, for many, the defining representation of autism. Indeed, even Steve Silberman—who would later write an award-winning work about autism—notes that there was a time when all he knew about the spectrum was learned from the 1988 film, and that, as far as he knew, "autism was a rare and exotic neurological disorder, and savants like Ray were even rarer than that" (Silberman 4). This singular and somewhat restrictive depiction has retained a cultural resonance that has proven problematic for others on the spectrum; the title of the film has become something akin to a profanity to people on the spectrum and their families, carers, teachers and medical practitioners, since it has profoundly limited society's understanding of this very complex disorder.

Played by Dustin Hoffman, Raymond Babbitt is an institutionalized, middle-aged man on the autism spectrum. Younger brother Charlie Babbitt, a yuppie businessman with big aspirations and even bigger financial troubles, was not even aware of the existence of Raymond until the death of their father. Charlie learns that his childhood imaginary friend, "the Rain Man," who used to sing to him when he was sad or scared, was, in fact, Raymond, whom he had since forgotten. In a buddy road trip with a twist, the pair bonds as Charlie receives a crash course in the preferences for routine and stability that are typically present in persons on the spectrum, set against the premise of a cross-country drive which is, of course, full of change. Even the road trip itself is the result of Ray's rigidity and prodigious memory, for he steadfastly and famously refuses to fly with anyone but QANTAS, citing their competitors' less impressive safety records.

When Barry Morrow wrote the first draft of the script, he had never heard of autism (Silberman); instead, Ray was based on a friend of his, Bill Sakter, who had an intellectual disability. Morrow intentionally flipped the

Pygmalion myth to have Charlie learn about what was important about life from interacting with Ray, rather than having Ray be "cured" of his disability; it was Steven Spielberg and Dustin Hoffman who would later make the call to change the intellectual disability to autism spectrum disorder, and this idea was retained when Spielberg left the project. Hoffman would eventually combine elements of Sakter's behavior with those of Kim Peek, Joe Sullivan and Peter Guthrie; all people on the spectrum with whom he consulted. Peter Guthrie was the source of one of Ray's favorite phrases, "Uh-oh," while Ray's ability with large numbers and fear of loud alarms came from Joe Sullivan. It should also be noted that all four of these men were living their lives outside of institutions. While Ray became the ultimate representation of autism, he was an amalgam of several people, all of whom lived more independently than their on-screen counterpart (Silberman).

Echoes of *Rain Man* continue to be prevalent in screen representations of autism. It has become such a benchmark that other series featuring characters on the spectrum, or often read by viewers as being on the spectrum, invoke the *Rain Man* standard. In the British TV series *The A-Word*, a medical professional with an autistic nephew creates a teaching video about what she terms "Joe-type autism," suggesting that many of her colleagues would miss his autism since the two known stereotypes are an unspeaking child in distress, or Rain Man. In *Community*, Abed Nadir is referred to as "Rain Man" by his peers and teachers alike; his friend Pierce even refers to Abed "playing the *Rain Man* card" late in Season 3. In those programs that do not offer their characters an on-screen diagnosis but about whom there is debate that they may be on the spectrum, invoking *Rain Man* has become a way of demonstrating an awareness of the off-screen debate; for example, Temperance ("Bones") Brennan in *Bones* (2005–2017) uses Rain Man's oft-repeated line "I'm an excellent driver" at numerous points throughout the series. Like "I don't know what that means," this line from *Rain Man* becomes a catch phrase for Brennan in *Bones,* and her partner, Booth, even remarks in Season 4, "Thank you, Rain Man." Even the most recent televisual representation of ASD at the time of writing, the American series *The Good Doctor* invokes *Rain Man* just a few minutes into the pilot episode, despite a thirty-year gap in production.

Programs such as *The Good Doctor* create characters that sit uneasily on the spectrum, sharing traits of Raymond Babbitt to denote the diagnosis, and yet otherwise having so-called "higher functioning" forms of ASD; in many cases, the characters are highly educated, highly intelligent, and very successful in their career fields. It should also be noted, however, that this kind of language is also inherently problematic. Not only does it suggest a hierarchy within the disorder, but it also does not adequately reflect that an individual may be high functioning in some areas or at some times, but highly symptomatic in other areas or when under duress. Nevertheless, it is true that most media representations of ASD depict those who would be classified as Level 1, or "requiring support" under the DSM-5 criteria (American Psychiatric Association 50–51), as opposed to Levels 2 ("requiring substantial support") and 3 ("requiring very substantial support"). They typically do not appear to have a co-morbid intellectual disability and are typically highly verbal. This is likely a function of the need for narrative arcs and character development in episodic television; characters with challenges around verbal communication offer script writers very limited narrative scope.

Because autism represents a spectrum of behaviors, two individuals on the spectrum might behave in radically different ways (Bradshaw). Most televisual representations, however, share certain key characteristics: autism tends to be portrayed visually through rocking and "stimming" (repetitive, comforting behaviors) such as hand wringing; through staring into space to denote a problem with eye contact; and through an unusual prosody of voice. Characters who are not diagnosed on-screen but who are understood to have autistic traits, however, may in some cases have less overt symptoms and might instead be gruff or emotionless, incapable of understanding humor or sarcasm, and have difficulties with simple facial expressions—both interpreting those of others, and replicating them themselves. Finally, these programs have become, over time, self-referential; key catch phrases, special interests, and behaviors that came to be read as symptomatic from earlier programs such as *Bones* and *The Big Bang Theory*, now appear in more recent ones such as *Community* and *Atypical.*

In the first decade of the 21st century, the trend seemed to be for characters to not have an official "diagnosis," but to share so many of the characteristics of autism that they were widely interpreted by audiences as being on the spectrum. These include *Bones* and *The Big Bang Theory* (from the United States) and *Doc Martin* (from the United Kingdom). Another trend that developed was for one significant creator of the character to endorse this reading, while another denied it. The prime examples of this are the long-running comedies *Doc Martin* and *The Big Bang Theory.* Over time, representations have evolved to include those that discuss a diagnosis on screen (*Community*), to those that explicitly diagnose the character in-narrative (*Parenthood, The A-Word, Atypical*).

"Take two aspirin and insult me in the morning": ASD in *Doc Martin*

Whether or not the lead character in *Doc Martin*, Dr. Martin Ellingham, has the form of autism that was, until relatively recently, known as Asperger's

Syndrome, has long been a contentious issue. Certainly, the character has no recognizable bedside manner; he is terse, blunt, and often monosyllabic in his responses. He shows little to no affect and remains stony-faced even during emotional life events (including his proposal to Louisa as well as their wedding). He often vocalizes that he does not know the socially acceptable thing to say in particular situations and is very routine-bound. He does not have any particular stimulatory behaviors (stims), but his hobby of restoring clocks seems somewhat intense, as is the work ethic which sees him combine reading to his infant son with a need to review the latest edition of *The Lancet*.

Debates rage in the blogosphere as to whether or not Martin Ellingham is on the spectrum, with lengthy threads being devoted to it (Bollard; Kinder; Doc Martin an Aspie; Jacobsen). Some contributors have offered a checklist of character traits as compared with the DSM; others have stuck to very literal thinking in the form of citing a Martin Clunes interview in which he said that the "Asperger's thing … was quite weird…. I just made the guy up, you know; none of that stiffness and malfunction was ever really on the page" (*LA Times*). Still others cite the blog of Dominic Minghella, the writer who created the character (and for whom Ellingham, an anagram of Minghella, is named) and who seemed to take a rather different view in a blog post published the very same month, April 2012. When asked if he was aware of the character's autistic tendencies, he replied in the affirmative: "It was deliberate. I seem to be surrounded by people with Aspergic [sic] tendencies" (Minghella). Within the program the diagnosis is flatly rejected when Antony Oakwood, a senior lecturer in applied psychology, comes to town and approaches Martin to be a case study in his proposed new research project about people on the spectrum who have successful careers, *You Don't Have to Be Mad to Work Here*. Martin furiously rejects the idea that he has Asperger's Syndrome, despite his knowledge of the syndrome and its symptoms, which as Antony points out, may include "bad communication skills, [and] no sense of humor"—attributes to which Martin admits in other episodes. Interestingly, *Doc Martin* readily acknowledges the character's hemophobia, but hedges its bets as to whether Martin's social awkwardness is related to "nature" or "nurture"—his behavior could also be plausibly attributed to a lack of care from parents who are depicted as truly awful, selfish human beings.

Susan Dodd notes that proper social etiquette requires understanding social distance, vocal quality, knowing how to start, maintain and finish a conversation, knowing how to request assistance and how to obtain someone's attention; and also identifies that these requirements place a great deal of stress on people on the spectrum (Dodd). Throughout the series, Martin struggles to understand social niceties, and is almost incapable of replicating them. This is often shown to great humorous effect in his relationship with local schoolteacher Louisa Glasson and later, their son, James Henry. At the end of Season 1 after an overnight medical emergency, the couple shares their first kiss, prompting Martin to ask Louisa about her dental hygiene routine. Later, during a discussion with Louisa about his behavior, he responds with great honesty and no small amount of bafflement: "I'm sorry. I have absolutely no idea what it is you want me to say." When Louisa returns to the village visibly pregnant some months after they call off their wedding, he dispassionately tells her that it is probably a bit late for an abortion. When she encourages him to read six-month-old James Henry's favorite book about a talking fire engine, Martin replies that it is "highly unlikely that he can grasp the concept of a fire engine, let alone one that's sentient." All of these responses, while amusing, also seem extremely rude to a neurotypical person. To a person on the spectrum, however, this is merely a sharing of truthful and therefore likely beneficial information. In the words of Tony Attwood, "Their allegiance is to the truth, not people's feelings" (Attwood, *Complete Guide* 77).

Elsewhere, Martin is shown to have great difficulties in making conversation with his patients. He often replies to questions with an emotionless, monosyllabic response. When a young girl in his surgery asks in great fright, "Am I going to die?" he replies, "Yes, you are. Everyone dies," before remembering himself and hastily adding, "But not today." In another instance with an elementary school aged child who becomes ill on a school field trip, Martin diagnoses her with an illness that he characterizes as "serious and potentially fatal"—in front of her entire class. When Louisa tries to reassure a peer that the girl will not die, Martin insists that she might: "There's a significant risk of a coronary artery aneurism, not to mention the risk of a heart attack," causing mass hysteria among the girl's schoolmates. These vignettes suggest that the character has many of the issues with social etiquette that Dodd identifies, including aloofness and a lack of awareness about the impact of behavior or speech on others (Dodd).

"My mother had me tested": ASD in *The Big Bang Theory*

Labeling around autism spectrum disorders is also at the forefront of debate around the popular American situation comedy *The Big Bang Theory*. It focuses on four nerdy friends—Dr. Sheldon Cooper, Dr. Leonard Hofstadter, Dr. Rajesh Koothrappali, and Howard Wolowitz. All four work in a University, have high IQs and low EQs; that is, standardized test scores would indicate high intelligence, but their on-screen behavior suggests that their emotional quotients, or abilities to discriminate and label feelings appropriately, would not be commensurate. Of these four characters arguably the most profoundly socially impaired is Sheldon, a savant who began studying for his first doctorate at the age of 14, but who struggles to develop meta-cognition, particularly as it applies to social rituals. He often demonstrates that whatever social niceties he understands have been rote-learned, such as when—on numerous occasions throughout the series—he offers his friends a hot beverage, and will not accept a polite refusal, citing that that is what one must do when someone else is upset. Sheldon has a number of key and intense hobbies, such as a love of trains, comics and flags; the former two are shown to be long-running interests, established in the prequel *Young Sheldon*, and the latter appears in his on-screen YouTube channel, "Fun with Flags." Tony Attwood uses this specific example of an obsessive interest in national flags when describing the intensity of autistic "special interests" in his seminal guide (Attwood, *Complete Guide* 194).

Sheldon is generally read by audiences as being on the spectrum. Indeed, the actor who plays Sheldon, Jim Parsons, is aware of the rampant conjecture, responding in interviews when asked whether Sheldon has Asperger's: "good grief, he certainly has a lot of the traits!" (Bianculli); "he couldn't display more facets of it" (Collins); and the "majority" of what he read in *Look Me in the Eye*, the autobiography of John Elder Robison (a person with Asperger's), "touched on aspects of Sheldon" (N. Murray, Interview: Jim Parsons).

Yet Parsons is also quick to point out that the writers have repeatedly stated that Sheldon is not on the spectrum (Bianculli; Collins; N. Murray, "TV Club Interview"). Series co-creator and lead writer Bill Prady has been quoted as saying that Sheldon's actions are "just Sheldon-y," and is emphatic that "[w]e write the character as the character. A lot of people see various things in him and make the connections. Our feeling is that Sheldon's mother never got a diagnosis, so we don't have one" (Waldman). This response is somewhat disingenuous, however, given that the character in his late thirties and early forties over the show's run; it is perfectly understandable that a person of this age would not have been diagnosed with Asperger's Syndrome or High Functioning Autism as a child, since such diagnoses were virtually unheard of at the time.

Prady also allegedly told Alan Sepinwall of the *New Jersey Star-Ledger* that "calling it Asperger's creates too much of a burden to get the details right" (Sepinwall). This seems pertinent, given that Sheldon displays the full gamut of high functioning autistic behaviors on screen, effectively creating a kind of *uber*-Asperger's identity; the "bingo card syndrome" to which we earlier alluded. In reality, an individual with a diagnosis of high functioning autism would display a number of the associated traits, but not all of them. Responses to Prady's assertions have been mixed, particularly among the ASD community. A review of the online ASD discussion space *Wrong Planet* shows that some agree with the arguments put forward by show runners Chuck Lorre and Bill Prady as reasons for not diagnosing Sheldon: firstly, that to laugh at the symptoms of a disorder or exaggerate a disability for comedy would be in poor taste; and secondly, that the official diagnosis would constrain the writers as there would be an increased need for accuracy and responsibility in the portrayal. Some forum members write the show off as offensive parody. Others worry that it will lead to an increase in unofficial amateur diagnoses as well as increased stereotyping, with comments about not needing another *Rain Man*.

Sheldon's difficulty with sarcasm is an ongoing personality trait and a significant source of humor throughout the series. The extremely literal thinking we see in characters like Sheldon Cooper or *Bones'* Temperance Brennan are often written as coded signifiers of ASD, because they cause difficulties with interpreting social context. "Mindblindness" is a term coined by Simon Baron-Cohen (Baron-Cohen, *Mindblindness*). It represents the difficulties that people on the spectrum may face when trying to interpret nuances, gestures and gazes, in order to understand how another person is feeling. Tony Attwood describes a series of tests which are used to ascertain an individual's ability to determine what someone in a story might be thinking or feeling. Some, such as the questionnaire developed by Baron-Cohen and Sally Wheelwright, also measure the time taken to deduce an answer (Baron-Cohen and Wheelwright). In this way, the clinician can judge whether a correct response was intuitive or arrived at by correcting applying a learned, logical response.

The exaggerated facial expressions of Sheldon Cooper, for example, are designed to telegraph to the viewer that his responses are achieved through intellectual analysis and rote learning. Forced smiles which could more accurately be described as grimaces, and lines of dialogue wherein Sheldon explains the thinking behind his responses, are designed to telegraph to the viewer that he is largely incapable of empathizing with how another person might feel in any given situation. This is particularly noticeable in his romantic relationship with Amy Farrah Fowler, which remained unconsummated for five years. When Amy confronts Sheldon about the frustrating lack of pace or intensity within their relationship, he is repeatedly unable to see things from her point of view. When Amy alludes to the irony of his obsession with the fast-moving Flash in Season 8, he tells her that "irony is not really [his] strong suit," but that he has been "getting better at sarcasm," then appears ironically oblivious to her sarcastic response.

Sarcasm has been an ongoing struggle of Sheldon's since the first season. In an early episode, Sheldon reorganizes the apartment of his new neighbor, a waitress named Penny whose life is somewhat chaotic. He is oblivious to her rage at sequential *faux pas* that include breaking into her apartment at night without permission, going through her things, and leaving a note on how to maintain his preferred standards. This demonstrates that his desire to help is very much tied to the physical, not the social world; he appears unaware throughout the entire process that invading Penny's personal space is considered to be a significant social violation, let alone one of which most people would deny all knowledge. Penny attempts to point out the extent of the social transgression by articulating it for Sheldon: "[You were i]n my apartment. While I was *sleeping*." Sheldon takes the mention of sleep as an opportunity to steer the conversation in a direction which he sees as important, informing Penny that she was snoring and should see a specialist to rule out sleep apnea. A furious Penny asks Sheldon which kind of specialist will be required to remove her shoe from his backside, and Sheldon responds to the question very literally, telling her that "depending on the depth, that's either a proctologist or a general surgeon." At this point, Leonard holds up a piece of card on which he has hastily scribbled, "SARCASM." In Season 4, it is revealed that Sheldon keeps a monthly count of how often he accurately identifies instances of sarcasm—less than a third of the time, but he is encouraged by this limited success.

Concerns around missing social subtleties like sarcasm and irony are contributing factors to the higher levels of anxiety often experienced by those with ASD. They also typically do not cope well with change, and so structure becomes an important coping mechanism. This rigidity is also reflected in the unusually intense focus of which people on the spectrum are capable. As Tony Attwood notes, this is different to a hobby in that the intensity is abnormal and of clinical significance. Indeed, one of the traits which often leads parents to seek a diagnosis is a child researching a special interest in astonishing depth, and then recounting it at length and often *in lieu* of more socially acceptable conversations (Attwood, *Complete Guide*). Sheldon's lifelong love of trains is a case in point, but we also see a more adult equivalent when he becomes unusually focused on work problems.

For one specific example of this, when Sheldon is conceptually stuck trying to determine why electrons have no mass when they move through a graphene sheet, he takes to using items such as peas and corn to kinesthetically reconstruct the ways in which carbon atoms move. His levels of frustration and complete focus are such that he cannot sleep and breaks into an indoor children's playground in order to access a ball pit, reasoning that the balls are of a more appropriate scale for representing carbon atoms. For some viewers, however, the scenes involving Sheldon in the ball pit appeared to be yet another codified reference to ASD, since ball pits are often used in sensory rooms as a means for overstimulated and introverted people with autism to retreat from the pressures of social conformity and take control of their environment by choosing sensory stimulation which is palatable to that individual. Further, the mall security guard who calls Leonard (rather than the police) confides that he made that decision because his sister has a "kid who is special." Certainly, the scene has become so iconic as to become a highly self-referential in-joke among shows with similar characters. In *Community*, Abed pops up from beneath a pile of lost Frisbees and greets Jeff with "Bazinga," a Sheldon catchphrase that he used repeatedly in the ball pit when diving in and out of the balls to evade Leonard's attempts at extracting him from the playground.

As *The Big Bang Theory* develops, however, Sheldon develops better understanding of various social situations. His rote-learned reactions to social conventions such as comforting others with hot beverages, and demonstrating empathy via scripted, practiced responses eventually develop into an increased awareness of his own behaviors, and an occasionally eloquent ability to express this. He confides in Howard's wife, Bernadette, that as a child, he found life "confusing and chaotic," and that his autistic interest in trains stemmed from a desire for the order they represented: "I could line them up and categorize them, control them. I guess you could say that they gave me a sense of calm in a world that didn't." The obsession with trains is repeated in other series, such as in Netflix's *Atypical*, when Christopher, a young man on the spectrum demands to know how much longer Elsa will be staying as a guest in the spare room, which he refers to as "my train room."

Sheldon also exhibits the relatively rare symptom of synesthesia ("Autism; Synaesthesia") blithely remarking to colleague Raj, "you know how when you see prime numbers they're red, but when you see twin primes they're pink and smell like gasoline?" This is reiterated in the prequel, *Young Sheldon*. A then-nine-year-old Sheldon is paid by his father to help older brother and classmate Georgie with algebra. Sheldon is unable to teach him, attempting to use strategies that apparently only work for his somewhat unique way of thinking. He suggests that Georgie close his eyes and visualize the Math problem, but the teenager can only visualize Elle Macpherson. Sheldon, on the other hand, matter-of-factly recounts his own synesthetic response: "Quadrant one is red. Quadrant two is soft and blush; quadrant three smells like lavender. And quadrant 4 is overlaid with a Fibonacci spiral." Sheldon believes Georgie to be "weird," but the audience understands that it is Sheldon's visualization that is atypical.

"I don't understand. And I am not used to not understanding": ASD in *Bones*

The character of Dr. Temperance ("Bones") Brennan on the American series *Bones* (2005–2017) was also widely read as being on the autism spectrum. As with Drs. Cooper and Ellingham, Brennan is a highly intelligent, highly skilled and highly educated character, who displays difficulties with social nuances and demonstrates that she is actively learning responses to particular social interactions. She is also a female character, meaning that if she is on the spectrum, she would be what has sometimes been termed as "Aspergirl" (Simone), or a "subculture within a subculture" (Simone 13). For some time, it was thought that ASD only affected boys, given that they were the focus of both Kanner's and Asperger's studies. More recent statistics place the referral rate of males to females as 10:1, but there is now a school of thought that the number of diagnoses may not accurately reflect the prevalence of the syndrome in girls (Attwood, "Pattern of Abilities"). The prevailing thinking is that girls and women may be better able to mimic adaptive behaviors and camouflage their areas of difficulty, meaning that parents are less likely to seek a diagnosis and clinicians may be reluctant to make one (Attwood, *Complete Guide*; Attwood, "Pattern of Abilities"; Simone).

Brennan, played by Emily Deschanel, is a world-renowned forensic anthropologist and best-selling crime fiction writer who can, by her own admission, "read bones, not people." She is vocally dismissive of psychology and puzzled by the interest of others in motives for murder; for her, science is all-important, and the means of murder all-encompassing. In Season 1, she is shown to rely heavily on her boss, Dr. Goodman, to tell her what her social obligations are with regard to work. When he is replaced at the beginning of Season 2, Brennan—who is objectively the best qualified member of the team—wonders aloud why she was not chosen to be the replacement head of the unit. Her partner Booth replies frankly: "My guess? People skills." Over the series' 12-year run, however, Brennan comes to understand both her strengths and her limitations, and when a new Head needs to be appointed in the series finale, she recommends the appointment of a colleague rather than herself, so that Brennan can continue to spend the bulk of her time conducting forensic investigations.

Like Martin Ellingham, Brennan's in-story narrative about her childhood provides a plausible in-story alternative to the typically assumed ASD diagnosis. Both parents disappeared when Brennan was a teenager, and she was then a foster child. Throughout the narrative, however, it becomes apparent that Brennan's prodigious memory, high intelligence, and unusual interest in death, dying, and the decay of bodies, long predated these events. Conversations about her younger childhood suggest that she was odd, bullied and alone.

Brennan's thinking is particularly literal, and this extends to all areas of her life. When asked if she believes in love, she tells Booth that she believes in "dopamine. And norepinephrine simulates euphoria because of certain biological factors like scent, symmetrical features." When she fosters a baby, she assures the crying infant that there is "no need to fuss" before becoming alarmed by the appearance of his toy: "elephants are not purple. This is wrong." This theme is revisited several seasons later, when she is pregnant with her own daughter and announces that she will not be encouraging her child to play with teddy bears· "Do you have any idea how many fatal bear maulings occur in North America every year?" She also fails to understand that Booth might like to be at the sonogram appointment where she learns the sex of their baby, reasoning that "ultrasounds are poorly pixelated and in black and white. You only like movies that are in color."

Throughout, Brennan displays noticeable aspects of mindblindness, articulating her thought processes and learnings around social interaction. For example, when Booth is distressed, she tells him that she would like to say the right thing, but usually she asks him what that is; she recounts that she has learned that lying is sometimes a gift and that she is "hazy on the rules" but that the person being lied to will understand that it is being done out of love. When she leaves for a year-long overseas expedition in Indonesia and her colleague Dr. Jack Hodgins, an entomologist, gives her a laminated list of poisonous animals in the area, she responds with an uncharacteristically warm "I love you, too" before admitting, "Booth informed me that the proffering of overly solicitous advice is indicative of love."

"I'm not unstable, I'm just different": ASD in *The Bridge*

Another female character typically read as being on the spectrum is Saga Norén from the Danish/Swedish noir police drama, *The Bridge*. Saga is a detective in the Malmo Police, whose highly data-driven approach solves cases, but often offends colleagues and families of victims of crime. Her stims appear to be largely sexual in nature, and her inability to break bad news gently produces some darkly comedic moments on screen, as when her partner Martin Rohd warns her, "Next time you ask if someone's daughter has done porn, be more gentle." Her need for routine is reflected in her actions, as is her choice of a long jacket, leather pants and a shirt, worn as a virtual and somewhat enigmatic uniform throughout all four seasons. Her attempts at mimicking social norms typically fail—her idea of small talk, for example, is to ask deeply personal questions about her colleagues' love lives. Saga is, in some ways, remarkably self-aware, telling her boss that sensitivity training would be a waste of time, since she knows her limitations and that her emotions never affect her work. She also tells both of her Danish partners, Martin and Henrik, that she is able to not think about things that are upsetting to her.

Like Ellingham and Brennan before her, Saga Norén has a traumatic childhood backstory that might offer at least a partial explanation of her lack of affect; both Saga and her now deceased sister, Jennifer, were impacted by their mother's Munchausen by Proxy, leading to Jennifer's suicide while still a teenager. When Martin asks if there were any signs of Jennifer being depressed, Saga replies matter-of-factly: "I don't pick up on signs." Later, she tells Martin that Jennifer was not like her, but "normal. Quite popular."

Also like Brennan, Saga reduces complex human emotions like love to their chemical components. She tells her partner Henrik: "When you're in love the brain's reward system releases neurotransmitters such as serotonin and dopamine. There's also an increase in the hormone oxytocin…. Oxytocin can affect the memory. Serotonin can lead to insomnia."

She then applies deductive reasoning to her own recent and uncharacteristic memory lapses and reasons "I think I'm in love with you."

Like Brennan and Booth, Saga and Henrik face an unplanned pregnancy storyline that involves the person presumed to have ASD making decisions that exclude the other parent. In *The Bridge* storyline, however, the father has been denied knowledge of an abortion, rather than participation in an ultrasound. Because Saga has already decided that parenting is a "form of empathic interaction [that] is not [her] strong suit," they agree that Henrik (whose wife and daughters have been missing for a number of years, presumed dead) will raise the child, and she will distance herself. Saga reneges when she comes to understand that she loves Henrik and would prefer to continue their relationship than continue with their parenting agreement. Unfortunately, she neglects to discuss any of this with him before acting on her epiphany. At other times, however, Saga is able to demonstrate significant insight. In the season finale, after Henrik has been reunited with one of his missing children and as Saga, now in therapy, attempts to explore a life outside of the city of Malmo and the police force, she tells him that they have "managed quite well, considering [their] psychosocial difficulties."

"Sometimes the hardest prisons to break out of, are the ones without locks": ASD in *Community*

Dan Harmon's quirky series *Community* features a character, Abed Nadir, whose status on the autism spectrum is heavily hinted at from the opening lines of the pilot episode. In his very first scene, he recounts that classmate Britta had told him that she has a relative with a "disorder that I really should look up." Abed speaks very quickly, but shows little to no affect, and clearly has a prodigious memory, recounting his previous conversation with Britta in such great detail that the Machiavellian leading man, Jeff Winger, who is interested in dating her, tells Abed: "I see your value now." Somewhat disturbingly, Abed calls after him, "that's the nicest thing anyone has ever said to me." Later in the pilot, Abed expresses his disappointment in Jeff's behavior using popular film as a touchpoint, remarking that he is "like Michael Douglas in any of his films." Jeff's childish retort is "Yeah? Well, you have Asperger's." Another member of the study group, Annie Edison, help-fully explains: "it's a serious disorder." Abed, for his part, does not seem to comprehend this exchange in any meaningful way; it does, however, set up a key trope of the series, which is that Abed navigates the world by applying patterns that he has learned from film and television.

Unlike Martin Ellingham, who vehemently denies an ASD diagnosis on screen as vehemently as Martin Clunes does off screen, or Sheldon Cooper, who also denies the possibility of a diagnosis by reiterating that his mother "had [him] tested" (even as the actor who portrays him agrees with those audience members who believe him to be on the spectrum), Abed seems to be aware of his symptomatic behavioral patterns and while other characters name it as ASD, the label never quite appears to register with Abed himself. Indeed, in a Season 2 episode wherein the characters all play Dungeons and Dragons, he is given the title of "Abed, the Undiagnosable." Abed also has noticeable mindblindness, as when he asks a girl with whom he later has a relationship, "Is that a judgmental face or a happy face?" or when his friends learn that he has placed geo-tracking devices on them so that he can keep track of their whereabouts, "You guys are all changing your faces. Are you mad at me, or hungry?" Interestingly, while Abed is never officially diagnosed on screen, his creator, Dan Harmon, has noted in media interviews that it was while researching ASD in relation to the character that he discovered that he shared a number of symptoms, leading to his own diagnosis (Eldred-Cohen; Lyons).

Understanding sarcasm is something with which Abed struggles. Abed finds that would-be actresses from within the student body are sending him muffin baskets in misguided attempts to flatter him into casting them in his movies. Abed tells his peers that Meryl Streep has two Oscars because of her baking, but immediately shifts the initial humor of the line to be at his ex-pense, by explaining, "Oh, that's sarcasm, but I forgot to inflect." At a nar-rative level, this suggests that Abed's funny lines must be unintentionally so because the character is supposed to be lacking in self-awareness owing to his presumed diagnosis, while also demonstrating that Abed is consciously learning strategies in an attempt to meet social and conversational norms.

In *Community*, Abed finds comfort in the predictable structures of ep-isodic television and popular movies. He is able to use them as reference points, because he understands their internal structure. He even claims to have been raised by TV. He co-opts these structures in order to understand social situations and communicate with those around him, although not al-ways successfully, as when he begins narrating their study group and Jeff has to remind him that it "makes the group uncomfortable when you talk about us like we're characters in a show." Abed is able to use his discomfort about some televisual techniques in order to articulate his own social difficulties, such as when he remarks that he dislikes bottle episodes because they feature "wall to wall facial expressions and emotional nuances" and notes that he "might as well sit in the corner with a bucket over [his] head."

Community, with its almost-diagnosis of Abed, is the forerunner of a new trend that emerged in the second decade of this century: programs in which a character would be explicitly diagnosed and named on screen as being on the spectrum. In some cases, this has led to more realistic and sympathetic portrayals; in others, it has merely replicated stereotypes. In truth, most probably fall somewhere in between.

"He's smart and he's beautiful and there's so much potential and hope": *Parenthood*

Parenthood is widely credited with being the first prime time television program to depict autism (Diament; Holton; Orley). Based on the 1989 film starring Steve Martin, the show aired between 2010 and 2015. It focuses on the Braverman family, which includes four siblings, Adam, Sarah, Crosby, and Julia, as well as their partners, parents and children. The series traverses separation, infidelity, co-parenting, adolescence, retirement and career changes as well as two significant story arcs about medical diagnoses: breast cancer and Asperger's syndrome. Both of these directly impact the family's oldest and arguably most responsible sibling, Adam; his wife Kristina undergoes breast cancer treatment, and his son Max, played by neurotypical child actor Max Burkholder, is diagnosed with Asperger's. Both storylines were inspired by events in the life of executive producer Jason Katims.

The family's developing understanding of Max's condition bookends the show's six-season run, with the first episode focusing on his unusual behavior on the baseball field and in his elementary school classroom, and the final shot of the finale showing the Braverman clan once again on a baseball field, and Max participating. It is likely that this focus on Max was deliberate, given that the character's storyline was based on Katim's own experiences as the parent of a child on the autism spectrum. An educational psychologist at the school suggests that the family seek a diagnosis, an idea that Adam rejects strenuously: "I've seen autistic kids! The Lessings' kid, with the hand-flapping?" Even when they explain to Max that the specialist clinical psychologist he will be seeing is the "Bob Dylan of Asperger's," Max responds unemotionally but with factual logic and an unusual propensity for trivia, noting that Bob Dylan never had a number one record.

Throughout the seasons, Max is shown to struggle with metaphor, puns, and physical affection. Initially, he merely argues against the sense or logic inherent in the metaphor, as in the Bob Dylan example above, or when

Adam cheerfully announces that Max is "using his noodle," and Max retorts that there is no noodle in his head, only a brain. Max is shown to have a number of behavioral interventions, with a behavioral therapist in addition to regular advice via Dr. Pelickan as well as a period in a specialized educational setting, Footpath Elementary. Max's behavioral therapist, Gaby, is shown establishing a token economy with Max, which is an evidence-based practice used to establish ideas around natural consequences and the certainty of consequences (Rogers; NYU Steinhardt). It has been found to be effective in a range of environments and for a range of ages (Klimas and McLaughlin). Food is often chosen as a powerful and tangible reinforcer (Doll et al.), and this is something that the Bravermans often use with Max long after Gaby leaves their employment—Kristina keeps a range of candies for this purpose; cousin Amber uses Tootsie Rolls to reward Max when he effectively role-plays apologizing; and Skittles become such an incentive that at one point Kristina blurts out that word in an attempt to quickly change Max's course of direction as he tries to show her his progress through puberty.

Over time, Max is better able to articulate his feelings, as we would expect to see from a child being offered appropriate interventions to learn about social situations and interactions. Max is able to tell his mother that he does not like being hugged but allows her to continue when she offers this kind of support after a particularly bad middle school field trip. In the Season 2 finale, Max finds it demonstrably difficult to put the needs of others before himself; becoming impatient that the pancakes he was promised have not materialized because of an unexpected period in a hospital waiting room, after his cousin Amber is seriously injured in a motor vehicle accident. Adam carefully explains to Max the importance of family, and of being there for family in times of crisis. Max responds by dispassionately asking for more whipped cream on his pancakes (although he does later apologize to Amber's mother). By Season 4, however, when Kristina is diagnosed with breast cancer, she is desperate for him to attend the school dance, fearing she might never see him go to such an event. Max categorically does not want to attend the dance, nor wear a collared shirt, but when Adam asks him to do it because it is important to Kristina, he announces to her that his father has promised to bring him home after thirty minutes, "so that's what we're going to do."

As we will see in other representations of young people on the autism spectrum, Max's relationship with his sibling Haddie is of particular interest. Max's single-mindedness and the family's increasingly difficult schedule as they attempt to implement behavioral interventions, as well as the financial burden of these, impact the resources that are able to be devoted to older daughter Haddie. When Adam attempts to apologize for the recent changes,

Haddie points out that Max's behavior, even before his diagnosis, has always led to him receiving more attention; citing the example of her tenth birthday party being "ruined" by him knocking over the cake because the candles triggered his phobia about fire. While this is recounted with all the drama one might expect of a teenaged character in a television drama, it does align with Tony Attwood's observation that the siblings of young people on the spectrum may be aware—even before diagnosis—that the young person is unusual and that they "may have been compassionate, tolerant and concerned about any difficulties, or embarrassed, intolerant and antagonistic" (Attwood, *Complete Guide* 29).

In Season 5, Max develops a working friendship with his Aunt Sarah's former love interest, Hank Rizzoli, a socially awkward photographer. Hank had previously gifted Max his first camera, saying that it would allow him to see people without looking directly at them. When the shutter jams, Max arrives at Hank's shop asking if there is a warranty. Hank encourages Max in his hobby, and Max spends some afternoons in the shop. Over time, as Max becomes increasingly estranged from his middle school friend, Micah, he declares Hank to be his best friend, since he spends more time with him than any other non-family member, and they have a shared interest. In fact, for his middle school graduation, Max demands a brown suit because Hank has a brown suit. After Max has a meltdown in Hank's shop, Adam offers Hank the loan of a book about autism. As he reads it, Hank finds that the descriptions resonate, to the point where he, too, begins to see Dr. Pelickan. Katims has explained that this storyline was inspired by attending a conferences and meeting two fathers who had been diagnosed only after their children were identified as being on the spectrum (Orley). The phenomenon of adult-diagnosis of a parent after a child's diagnosis appears to be quite common, and a significant contributing factor to recent rises in diagnosis rates (Attwood, *Complete Guide*; Silberman; Simone).

Parenthood closes with the demise of the patriarch, Zeek Braverman. The family honors his wishes to have his ashes spread on a baseball field, and then plays a game together. This montage is intercut with images of Zeek's children and their families in future years, showing extra grandchildren and great-grandchildren. As the Bravermans leave the field, most are in a close gaggle, many hugging each other. Max is further behind, stopping to pick up the bat from home plate. As the camera zooms up and out, Max is seen to be catching up to his family, until he is part of the large group, the baseball bat slung across his shoulders. Visually, in this final scene, he is no longer an outsider, but part of the extended Braverman clan in a way that he arguably had not been previously.

"A puzzle I love": ASD in *The A-Word*

Another program that deals with autism in young children, and the impact on families, is the British series *The A-Word*. An adaptation of the Israeli series *Yellow Peppers*, it focuses particularly on the family dynamic and how it changes when five-year-old Joe is diagnosed. The program suggests that communication issues are prevalent throughout Joe's extended family—from his gruff and politically incorrect grandfather, Maurice; to his aunt Nicola, who dislikes metaphor; to his father, Paul, who learned to deflect with humor when dealing with his own learning difficulties; and to his mother Alison, who is fiercely protective, and determined that her son not be labeled within their local community. The director, Peter Bowker, has stated that this focus on communication was deliberate, because a drama that was solely focused on autism "could have been full of angst" (DVD Extras). Nevertheless, the family's initial resistance to the diagnosis drives much of the narrative in Season 1.

Joe is often seen listening to music through headphones. His special interest is 1980s rock and he recites metadata about songs—artist, title, year of release, and writer. His other stim is to sing along. Both of these strategies appear to be variations of the common ASD symptom of echolalia. Echolalia, or the repetition of the speech of others, is a defining feature of autism and, until recently, was thought to serve no communicative function; more recently, it has been argued that there are contextual and interactional aspects to its function (Sterponot and Shankey). Joe also demonstrates more conventional echolalia in times of high stress; for example, when his mother shouts, "That's enough!" he replies by shouting it back at her. After she apologizes, Joe reverts to singing the Human League's "Don't You Want Me, Baby?" Within the narrative, Joe's therapist explains that singing or reciting the metadata is a means of self-preservation for Joe, since he knows the rules of engagement and it does not answer back. As his uncle Eddie surmises, "he's a kid who can't make himself heard in a family of loudmouths."

Joe's routine includes walking along a local road every morning, a quirk that is well known and understood by the workers at his grandfather's factory, who routinely pick him up and bring him home. Strangers who come across a five-year-old boy strolling alone in England's Lake District, however, find this to be noticeably more disconcerting. Arguably Joe's most noticeable stim is to play with doors, opening and shutting them repeatedly before he will himself pass through, and wanting to be the last to leave. He also has a penchant for roofs, climbing onto the roof at school on more than one occasion, as well the roof of the restaurant his father is building. At one point another child follows him, causing even more chaos at the school, but Joe's grandfather sees this as progress: "at least Joe had a mate up there with him this time."

Once Joe is diagnosed, significant questions around how best to assist him are raised. Of particular interest is the notion of schooling. Alison insists that she will home school him, despite Nicola's sensible suggestion that the best cure for social isolation may not be more social isolation. Paul begins to investigate schools for specific purposes, but Alison has concerns over Joe's advanced ability in mimicry and protests: "He'll come out more autistic than he went in!" Ultimately Joe attends a special unit within a mainstream school, which, as the most inclusive environment in which he can cope at that time, is a sound decision, and in line with the agreed principles of the United Nations Convention on the Rights of Persons with Disabilities; specifically, that students should be educated in the most inclusive environment that is suitable for their needs (UNESCO). Joe's new school is in Manchester, however, leading to a separation of the nuclear family unit during the school week, which creates problems of its own.

In the background to this, Joe's older sister Rebecca is in her final year of high school, navigating a complex relationship with her boyfriend and an even more complex one with her biological father, Stuart. Rebecca characterizes Joe as "just a kid. A normal lad," yet later confides in Nicola that she has "binned" her university offer because she is needed at home. She tells her parents she understands that one day she will be the only person Joe has in the world, and she understands that, and him, and includes him—but they do not. While the sentiment that Rebecca includes Joe in family and social activities in a way that no one else does is true, the suggestion that he will one day rely on her is troubling. There is nothing to suggest that Joe has an intellectual disability or any other indicators that might limit his independence, prevent him from securing employment, or make a future relationship unlikely. Indeed, when he is first diagnosed, the specialist comments that he is "polite" and "affectionate"; Maurice notes that Joe "smiles, he talks, he looks you in the eye"; later, testing for his entry to the special unit at school indicates that Joe has "a spiky profile." Queries around the ways in which such profiles are determined or judged are also raised, as when Max's Uncle Eddie decides that he will teach Joe how to ride a bike, since not being able to do so is an indicator on an assessment tool. Eddie rages that the test is reductive, and focuses on what the child cannot do, as opposed to what he can. Joe, for his part, turns the bicycle upside down and is mesmerized by the relationship between the pedal and the wheel. Rebecca watches on and asks, "Is this him still processing it, or telling us he doesn't want to ride the bike?" It is a very pertinent question. Central coherence is an ability to synthesize information from different schematics in order to build a *gestalt* meaning (McMahon-Coleman and Draisma); people on the spectrum often have a cognitive style that is known as weak central coherence. This means that they tend to focus on the details, rather than the overall picture. The examples that are typically given to explain this way of thinking include opening and closing the doors on a toy vehicle, or focusing on spinning the wheels on them, rather than the more typical imaginative play that features using the toys in a conventional manner by using them on an imaginary road system (Dodd).

"I don't like the idea of living at an angle": ASD in *Atypical*

Netflix's series *Atypical* deals with an older child, Sam Gardner, and his family. The program first aired in 2017, and almost immediately came to our attention anecdotally via the praise of teachers working in specialized units for teaching secondary students on the autism spectrum, who enthused that it was an accurate depiction. The response online, however, particularly from those who share a diagnosis with central character Sam, has been quite critical (Aswell). Sam is a high school student, supported at school by his neurotypical sports star sister, Casey, and later, his girlfriend, Paige; at home—and to an extreme extent—by his mother, Elsa, at work by his friend and co-worker Zahid, and professionally by his young therapist, Julia, on whom he develops a rather unhealthy crush. His inability to understand social cues ultimately and unwittingly is the catalyst for destroying Julia's *de facto* relationship.

To their credit, with the 2018 release of the second season, Netflix and the show's creators have addressed some of these concerns; working with author David Finch (who is himself on the spectrum) to ensure a more accurate representation, and adding five new teenage characters with autism, all played by actors on the spectrum (Diament; Luterman). Christopher from the support group, played by Anthony Jacques, had been the only actor on the spectrum in Season 1. In another step towards inclusive representation, the young people in this group are exploring their post-school transition options and these are not all in the fields of science or maths, as is often typical (as in *The Big Bang Theory* or *Bones*). Sam is exploring options around art, and his peers' career aspirations include dentistry or working as an EMT. This shift has been well received by critics, and particularly by critics who are themselves on the spectrum (Luterman).

Sam is depicted as an intense but intelligent young man. His key stims or comforts are rhythmically flicking a rubber band on his wrist and reciting the four types of penguins that can be found in Antarctica. The continent and its fauna are his special areas of interest. Like Joe, Sam often wears noise-cancelling headphones, but it appears that in his case it is to directly limit aural overload, whereas Joe uses the output of the music to mask other aural distractions. When distressed, Sam has a favorite hooded sweatshirt on which he relies. He may also opt to pull his bed out from the wall and pace around it. When he "elopes" or flees a situation, he will hide under a bench or seek out another small space; like the hooded sweatshirt, this limits sensory overload and the confinement is soothing. At times, his sister Casey or another family member will replicate this by joining him in the space or hugging him from behind. Casey also chooses to comfort Sam, at one point, by reading to him from the Wikipedia page of the famous Antarctic explorer, Ernest Shackleton.

Sam's relationship with Casey appears to be very authentic. In the pilot, Sam remarks in voiceover that his sister will not let anyone beat him up ... except herself. This arguably universal sibling dynamic is mitigated by Sam's autism diagnosis, which sees Casey often acting as an older sibling; advising Sam and looking out for him. Sam does indicate, however, that he is cognizant of this, sometimes making his point quite eloquently, as when he buys her new pencils for her first day at a new school and declares, "I'm your big brother. I can take care of you, sometimes, too." Casey's protective role does not preclude her from taunting Sam, however; she claims that in so doing, she has "adequately prepared him for the real world." Casey appears to vacillate between the two sibling stances identified by Attwood; sometimes being compassionate, and sometimes antagonistic. Each sibling calls the other annoying on a regular basis, yet their peers all know to call Casey in a crisis. In Season 1, the siblings' friend, Beth, calls Casey in the middle of her interview for a sports scholarship to an elite private school to say that Sam is missing; Casey takes the call, explaining to the interviewer, "it's kind of my job, as his sister." In Season 2, Sam is at work when he realizes that he has lost his painstakingly compiled art portfolio for his application to the Rhode Island School of Design. Zahid tells him that everything is under control, and promptly calls Casey. Together, they vow to scour the town until the missing portfolio is located. In the very same season, however, Casey taunts Sam by moving his toothbrush from its usual location to increasingly odd places around the home, contributing to Sam having a meltdown of epic proportions.

One of Sam's coping mechanisms is to build a mental library, as is described by Temple Grandin and Tony Attwood, among others. In her own concept formation, Grandin would associate words with single exemplars. For example, "cat" would represent a particular cat, not all felines. Over time, as she added exemplars to her library and could see their commonalities, she would gain a more pluralistic understanding of meaning (Jordan). Attwood notes that many people on the spectrum apply this strategy to social experiences and social rules (Attwood, *Complete Guide*). In *Atypical*, Sam is shown to use this as a strategy for understanding idiomatic phrases. When Paige tells him that it was good to hear information "from the horse's mouth," Sam asks, "Is that an insult or a phrase?" and is then shown studiously adding it to a list that he carries.

As with the other characters discussed here, Sam does not always understand social conventions or react as one might expect to certain stimuli. The program sensitively debunks the myths that people on the spectrum do not feel emotions, and more specifically, do not feel empathy. Sam's missing art portfolio is a case in point. He had matter-of-factly announced to his peer support group that he was applying to the design school but that he had researched artists and learned that many of them died penniless and alone. Another participant, Amber, had become so distressed at the idea of Sam dying in such a state that she had taken his portfolio in order to prevent that happening. Throughout both seasons that had aired at the time of writing, the voiceover technique—which typically then cuts to Sam speaking with a therapist—allows him to articulate the feelings he would be unlikely to admit to other characters. Sam has significant insight into his autism and how it manifests, noting, "People think I don't know when I'm being picked on, but I do. I just don't know why. Which is worse," and that he is especially bad at lying, "which is funny, because people lie to me all the time. They think because of my autism, I can't handle things." Ultimately, however, Sam comes to surpass his mother's hopes for him upon diagnosis as a young boy—that he find a friend, do OK in school, find something he loves to do, be able to safely leave the house, and be able communicate clearly. In addition, he demonstrates the ability to liken his family and friends to other mammalian "packs" critical for survival, graduates high school, is accepted into college, and even overcomes his fear of public speaking and steps in to read Paige's valedictorian speech on her behalf when she is unable to do so.

Like Max Braverman attending the school dance to appease his mother, Sam agrees to attend a school disco with his girlfriend, Paige. Despite articulating that he does not like dressing up or dancing, he concedes that it is important to her and what a boyfriend should do. This storyline humorously depicts Sam's literal thinking—when Zahid tells Sam that he looks "like a million bucks," Sam comments that that represents a "really good return" since the tuxedo rental was only $99—but it also shows Sam's unusual but nevertheless strong ability to empathize, as he goes to extraordinary lengths to make amends with an offended Paige; retrieving her lost necklace from the school swimming pool, despite not liking being in water that other people have touched, and wearing his rental tuxedo. For all the angst of this tortured teenage relationship, Paige has also demonstrated great care for Sam through organizing an inclusive, silent disco. This allows him to wear his headphones—as everyone else does the same—and to maintain some control over an otherwise overstimulating sensory environment.

"He's not Rain Man!": ASD in *The Good Doctor*

A recent television iteration of ASD is found in *The Good Doctor*, which began broadcasting in the fall of 2017. Despite a gap of thirty years, *The Good Doctor* explicitly links Freddie Highmore's Dr. Shaun Murphy with Dustin Hoffman's *Rain Man* character.

Indeed, early responses to the series trailer also referred to the iconic film, with Ethan Anderton noting, "Medical dramas are a dime a dozen on network television, but this one has a concept that feels like *House* meets *Rain Man*, and that might just be enough to make it interesting" (Anderton). Elsewhere, critic Daniel Fienberg watched the trailer and concluded, "I'm wary" (Fienberg), noting, "We've had decades of eccentric, socially awkward procedural heroes whose place on the autistic spectrum was left unspoken, so this trailer feels both kinda progressive and really dated. Too much felt on-the-nose." Ben Travers and Steve Greene were more enthusiastic, describing the premise as being "a doctor who uses his unique outlook on the world to assist in medical diagnoses" and likening it to *House* noting that the "title card with the phrase 'from the creator of *House*'" encourages the comparison. They suggest that the creators are "toeing the line between presenting a thoughtful depiction of his condition and using his perceptive abilities as a kind of secret weapon"—a line that is well worn in these shows (Travers and Greene).

In the opening scenes, Dr. Shaun Murphy is seen getting ready for the day, and using perseverative behavior to do so—washing his hands and brushing his hair more than once, and straightening his collection of Rubik's cubes. When Shaun leaves the house, his trajectory is superimposed on the ground, already suggesting the "different abilities as superpowers" narrative. Shaun is also shown to be unaware of typical social interactions, as when an errant soccer ball lands at his feet and he does not respond by returning it until prompted. Instead, the viewer sees a disturbing flashback to him being kicked by a gang of peers on a soccer pitch; an incident that ends with the intervention of a smaller child, later shown to be his neurotypical younger brother, Steve. Present-day Shaun continues his journey to the bus and later, airport, where he witnesses a horrific accident in which a young boy has his jugular severed by a falling sign. Shaun is not the first responder, but corrects the doctor who assists, announcing, "You're killing him," and explaining that while the pressure being applied would be suitable for an adult, it is hampering the breathing of the child. Throughout this scene, Shaun stares into space, and speaks in a sing-song, robotic voice. Lack of eye contact and vocal prosody are both symptoms of autism spectrum disorder but may not always be this pronounced. Adults who are university educated, for example, will often learn to ameliorate such symptoms except when under extreme duress, but Shaun continues to display these behaviors well beyond this particular emergency, and so constantly throughout the first season that it is reasonable to suggest that these become integral to the characterization.

Distracted by an injured child, Shaun fails to attend a panel interview with the hospital's Board of Directors, who had convened a meeting specifically to question the wisdom of hiring a surgical intern with autism. Hospital president and Shaun's friend Dr. Aaron Glassman goes to bat for the absent intern, declaring, "he's not Rain Man! He's high functioning; he's capable of living on his own. Capable of managing his own affairs." Glassman is passionate in his defense of Shaun, explaining that the intern also has savant syndrome: "genius level skills in several areas: he has almost perfect recall. He has spatial intelligence and he sees things and analyzes things in ways that are just remarkable and ways that we can't even begin to understand. Those are assets, undeniable assets for any doctor—particularly a surgeon."

The main irony here, of course, is that the *Rain Man* narrative very specifically articulates that Ray, too, has savant syndrome; and Freddie Highmore's depiction of Shaun draws heavily on the stereotypes and behaviors established in *Rain Man*. This is not to say that people on the spectrum do not have these symptoms, in reality; however, it would be unlikely for so many symptoms of this level of severity to consistently and obviously co-exist in a professional person. Further, in later episodes Glassman decides that Shaun is not capable of managing his own affairs, after all, and attempts to employ a carer for him.

Conclusions

Early television depictions of what is widely thought to be ASD denied the characters' diagnosis; it is only in the last decade that we have seen characters with a diagnosis, beginning with *Parenthood*'s Max Braverman. Whether explicitly diagnosed, implicitly diagnosed, or denied a diagnosis in conversations about the character, these representations have typically made the characters over-symptomatic.

Despite aberrations like *The Good Doctor*, which has not really moved past *Rain Man*-esque interpretations of autistic behaviors, there has been noticeable improvement in terms of consulting with people on the spectrum, and including autistic actors, leading to more sensitive representations. In Chapter Six, we will examine the impacts, positive and negative, of these popular representations on cultural understandings of ASD, as understood by viewers on the spectrum.

Two

"It's a gift and a curse"
Obsessive Compulsive Disorder

As we have seen with ASD, some disorders have seemed to be used for comedic purposes in popular media more than others, and among them is obsessive compulsive disorder (OCD). This is in contrast to other mental health disorders—such as schizophrenia or DID (see Chapter Three)—that are commonly represented on television in dramatic ways that link the illness with danger and uncontrolled violence. In this chapter, we examine two characters with OCD from prime-time television in recent years, Adrian Monk (*Monk*) and Emma Pillsbury (*Glee*), with a focus on how the programs deal with the impact of the disorder on the characters' social and professional lives, and specifically the concept of the condition as both gift and curse.

There are several reasons why *Monk* and *Glee* offer fertile grounds for analysis. First, both productions are mainstream, popular television series of recent years, yet sit within two different genres (detective and school/musical), thereby offering two ways of examining how OCD has been conceptualized in popular culture and its effect on social and professional lives of those with the disorder. Second, OCD is experienced by the main character of one program (*Monk*) and a supporting character of the other (*Glee*), a difference which may mean the disorder has more scope for variations in its depiction—by which we mean to say that giving a disorder to a main character is more likely to involve emphasizing its positive ennobling qualities rather than giving OCD to a secondary character, which may potentially play more to cliché and one-note characterizations. Finally, the eponymous Monk and *Glee*'s Emma Pillsbury are both characters whose disorder has been front and center in the development of their characters. To contextualize the analysis of *Monk* and *Glee*, we begin with a summary of OCD itself, followed by a brief survey of general representations of OCD in the media.

Background: What Is OCD?

OCD is a mental health disorder that affects more than 1 percent of the population, with an average age of 20 years at onset; around a quarter of people with OCD first experience the disorder by the age of 14 (American Psychiatric Association). Risk factors associated with developing OCD include family history, and childhood physical or sexual abuse or other trauma (American Psychiatric Association).

After being categorized under Anxiety in previous editions of the DSM, OCD was removed in the DSM-5 from the anxiety disorders section and separated into the new category, Obsessive-Compulsive and Related Disorders, which also includes other disorders such as hoarding, body dysmorphic disorder, trichotillomania (hair pulling) and excoriation (skin picking). OCD was not the only disorder to be removed from Anxiety; a further separate category was also created for Trauma and Stressor-Related Disorders, which includes post-traumatic stress disorder (PTSD, discussed in Chapter Five), among others.

Based on the DSM-5, diagnosis of OCD relies on the following components:

- the person experiences obsessions, compulsions, or both
- the obsessions or compulsions are time consuming (e.g., more than 1 hour a day) or cause clinically significant distress or impairment in social, occupational, or other important areas of functioning
- symptoms are not caused by another drug, medical condition, or mental disorder (e.g., excessive worries as in anxiety disorder, repetitive behaviors as in autism spectrum disorder)

The experience of OCD is different for different people, as with all mental health disorders, but the usual pattern includes four main components (NHS), as described below.

Obsession	A repeated and unwanted, intrusive thought or idea or impulse.	Examples might be fears about illness or harm or injury, whether to yourself or someone else, fears about getting things wrong or being incorrect about something, or fears about dirt and infection.
Anxiety	Caused by the obsession.	Examples include intense anxiety, or intense distress.

Compulsion	A repetitive behavior caused by the anxiety in an attempt to relieve it.	Examples of the repetitive behavior might be repeatedly washing, cleaning or counting, or hoarding. For instance, if someone has an obsessive idea of their house being burgled or broken into, the anxiety arising from this fear may then lead to a behavior of obsessively checking locks.
Relief	The compulsive behavior brings relief. However, this relief is only temporary, and the cycle begins again at step 1, with the obsession.	For example, checking locks may temporarily relieve someone with OCD who fears their house being burgled, but the obsession can then continue if and when the unwanted thoughts or ideas or impulses return, which can then lead to anxiety, followed by the compulsive behavior, and so on.

Given that the concept of "being OCD" has been somewhat hijacked in popular culture—as we discuss more in the next section—it is important to note that the obsessions and compulsions are not typically enjoyable elements for people with OCD. For example, an obsession about contamination by infection may be unwanted, severely distressing, and lead to compulsive and repeated cleaning, behavior which itself is also distressing—contrary to the popular and erroneous belief that people with OCD "love cleaning" (OCD UK).

It should be no surprise, then, that OCD can be severely disruptive to daily routines and normal functioning. People with the disorder typically avoid any situations, settings, people, or objects that may trigger the obsession and compulsions. Someone with a fear of contamination may avoid public places to minimize exposure, or someone who experiences the urge to harm others might avoid social interactions (American Psychiatric Association) Clearly, OCD can seriously affect quality of life and in some cases the ability to work and to have relationships. Furthermore, comorbidities are common, and can include anxiety disorder (occurring in more than three-quarters of people with OCD), depressive or bipolar disorder (almost two-thirds), and tic disorder (around a third) (American Psychiatric Association). People with OCD and depression may also experience suicidal impulses (NHS); around half of people with OCD will have suicidal thoughts and a quarter will attempt suicide (American Psychiatric Association).

Nearly half of those with OCD onset in childhood or adolescence will experience remission by early adulthood (American Psychiatric Association). Outcomes improve with treatment. Without treatment, OCD can be chronic and few adults with the disorder will experience remission (American Psychiatric Association). Treatment is typically a combination of antidepressant medication (selective serotonin reuptake inhibitors [SSRIs]) and counseling (NIMH). Counseling usually involves a type of cognitive behavioral therapy (CBT) called Exposure and Response Prevention (ERP) therapy (International OCD Foundation), which comprises exposing the patient to the thought or impulse that initiates the obsession (exposure) and then a decision to not initiate the compulsive behavior (response prevention); over time, anxiety can lessen (habituation). Treatment can help people with OCD manage symptoms and improve quality of life (NHS).

OCD in the Media

OCD has gained traction in popular culture over the last decades. Paul Cefalu has written that the increased incidence in depictions of the disorder can be linked to greater understanding of the disease: where OCD was once poorly understood, considered rare, and believed to be difficult to treat, advances over the last decades in diagnosis and treatment have changed perceptions of OCD to the point that it is now better understood, more common than previously thought, and now known to be treatable.

As should be clear from the preceding brief review of symptoms and patterns in OCD, the disorder can be a very distressing and serious experience for those who have it, which can lead to social isolation, impaired work and familial and romantic relationships, and in some cases, suicidal tendencies and/or attempts. How, then, is the disease portrayed in popular media?

In comparison to other disorders which have received negative depictions overall, OCD is more likely to be portrayed fairly positively (Ma; Siegel). In an analysis of 11 films that include a character with OCD (labeled or apparent), including *The Aviator, Nim's Island,* and *Matchstick Men,* Dustin E. Siegel found that OCD was portrayed more positively than mental illness generally, but still has depictions of violence, and little is shown on the effect of stigma (Siegel).

Another study on OCD and film by Fennell and Boyd reported mixed findings, including positive representations alongside more negative elements (Fennell and Boyd). The study involved content analysis of popular media, covering OCD as portrayed in 39 characters in 34 films, as well as the television program *Monk*; the authors also interviewed 54 viewers who identified as having OCD and/or hoarding. Fennell and Boyd reported that the images were complex, in some cases reinforcing common stereotypes of mental disorders (e.g., people with OCD are aggressive, unpredictable, unreliable) and in other cases challenging others (e.g., people with OCD are functional and able to contribute to society). Other findings included that characters were not always explicitly labeled as having OCD, displayed symptoms not aligned with formal diagnostic criteria, and were victimized by medical professionals; such issues can be problematic, contribute to stigma, and impair someone's willingness to access medical help (Fennell and Boyd). The authors concluded that images of OCD in the films and in *Monk* do impact the mental health literacy of viewers, noting that their participants did in fact use such representations for "self-diagnosis and informative purposes. They recognized the power of the media as a source of information for themselves and the community" (Fennell and Boyd).

This potential for television to provide information about mental health disorders has also been also raised by other researchers in their work, who variously note the potential may be realized in positive or negative ways. For instance, a dissertation on OCD in television by Sam Martin describes the dangers of an "OCD trope [that] emphasizes the compulsive behaviors associated with the illness while ignoring the obsessions that drive them" (S. Martin)—that is, viewers may be at risk of thinking OCD is simply about unusual behaviors without understanding the preceding disruptive obsessive thoughts or urges, and accompanying fears and anxieties. As Martin—who begins the thesis with an autobiographical discussion of experiencing OCD—acknowledges, this is to some extent inevitable with televisual media, which lacks the ability to easily show thoughts compared with actions. Martin also critiques certain depictions of OCD which emphasize specific compulsions such as cleaning, suggesting that it reinforces stereotypes that OCD is (only) about "being germ conscious. The implications of this assumption are damaging" because it implicitly threatens the legitimacy of other forms of OCD—that is, people who have OCD marked by obsessions about harm, or anything other than germs.

In their research into OCD and social media, Pavelko and Myrick write that OCD can be trivialized in three ways: oversimplifying symptoms and causes, skepticism about disease severity, and using humor or mockery to describe it (Pavelko and Myrick, "That's So OCD"; Pavelko and Myrick, "Tweeting and Trivializing"). Such depictions can potentially result in ambiguity and misinformation, although the potential exists for social media to also provide a space for advocacy and education (Pavelko and Myrick, "That's So OCD"). This is obviously not constrained to social media. So it is, too, with television and other popular media, which can similarly perform an advocacy or educational function—or misinformation and trivialization. In the case of mental health, how society understands illness is, in part, shaped by the stories we tell ourselves in our popular culture, by the ways that television and film and literature frame disease. In terms of OCD, Cefalu writes that the growing use of OCD in popular culture may have a positive side of raising the profile of the disorder and making it more understandable and removing fear about it.

Similarly, several authors have noted that reality television programs on OCD may have positive educational benefits for the general public. Two examples illustrate this well· ten years apart, dealing with British and American programs respectively, both reviews compare an OCD-focused reality program with the *Big Brother* series, and both conclude there are educational aspects of the OCD programs that can serve the public well. A review in *British Medical Journal* in 2005 discussed the British program *The House of Obsessive Compulsives*, a show in which three people with OCD were placed in a house and treated with ERP therapy (Dosani). The reviewer highlighted the educational aspects and concluded the program to be "a fine stab at enlightened educational entertainment" with "an inspiring and informative angle that is missing from the *Big Brother* house" (Dosani). Ten years later, a published article from authors Miller and colleagues describes their study in which they assigned 77 young adults to watch two episodes of either *Big Brother* or *The OCD project*. *The OCD Project* was an American reality series of one season in 2010, which features six people with OCD living in a house and who receive ERP therapy; their specific symptoms vary from fears of contamination to fears of becoming a psychotic killer. The *Big Brother* episodes used in the study similarly featured people living in a house, but no mention of OCD nor ERP was made. Miller and colleagues found that the 35 students assigned to watch *The OCD Project* had significantly fewer negative beliefs about exposure therapy than the 42 students watching *Big Brother*. The authors concluded that reality television offers the potential for a "modest psychoeducational benefits" which could be "used to change attitudes about mental health problems and their treatment" (Miller et al.).

Beyond this opportunity to inform—whether accurately or otherwise—the general public about OCD, television is also prone to depicting OCD with comedy, in contrast to other mental health disorders such as schizophrenia, which are often portrayed in popular culture with drama that effectively associates the disorder with unbridled danger and violence. It is increasingly common to hear anyone in the general public jokingly and dismissively refer to themselves as "being a bit OCD." As researchers Pavelko and Myrick have noted, "A quick search for the hashtag "#OCD" on Twitter results in screens full of content related to benign events like highlighting in a book or organizing pencils— far from behaviors that would merit a clinical diagnosis. As the frequent use of "#OCD" on Twitter indicates, this misrepresentation of the disease has seeped into the public vernacular" (Pavelko and Myrick, "Tweeting and Trivializing").

To some extent this is not unique to OCD; people without any form of mental illness might also (jokingly or otherwise) refer to themselves or others as being "bipolar" or having "multiple personalities" without actually meaning this in the true sense at all. Yet such remarks generally treat OCD in comical and positive terms (in the sense that "being a bit OCD" usually just implies someone is very clean or organized, which are hardly problematic issues for people who do not actually have OCD), while other disorders tend to be treated in more critical and negative terms (in the sense that saying that "so-and-so has multiple personalities" would generally imply they are behaving unpredictably and badly, by anyone's standards).

As noted earlier, Paul Cefalu described the rise in popularity of OCD representations in popular culture as attributable to better medical understanding and treatment of the disease. What is less clear, Cefalu writes, is why those representations so frequently rely on "levity and humor"—which may go beyond humor to cruel mockery—to portray the experience of OCD, where people with OCD are typically protagonists in "comedies or [...] tragicomedies": "How can we explain, then, the extent to which recent literary and cinematic portrayals of obsessive-compulsive disorder suggest that sufferers of OCD can always be counted on to make us laugh? Recall Jack Nicholson's compulsive sidestepping of those dangerous cracks in the sidewalk in *As Good as It Gets*" (Cefalu).

To this may be added the comedy film *Matchstick Men*, which was included in a list of "best movies about mental health" on the website of the National Alliance on Mental Illness (Greenstein), or the comedic take on Jodie Foster's character with her various repetitive and obsessive behaviors in *Nim's Island*. Exceptions exist, of course; for example, OCD in the television series *Girls* was not treated as comically as it has been elsewhere, but they are exceptions to a norm.

It is clear, then, that OCD is commonly represented with comedy and humor in popular culture. For Cefalu, the link between comedy and OCD is, in part, due to the incongruity theory of humor which relies on cognitive dissonance: "The incongruity and, arguably, comic element in such cases [of compulsions such as scrubbing hands] is a conventional mix of the high and low, a tragic foreboding tied to what most would consider inconsequential behavior" (Cefalu). Other potential reasons may include the childlike repetition or machine-like behaviors of OCD that can prompt humor (Cefalu). The outcomes of this link between OCD and comedy are complex. Humor can conversely reduce stigma but simultaneously trivialize the condition by reducing OCD to "a personality trait or quirky habit" (Fennell and Boyd). There is, then, a risk of trivialization and over-simplification, as others have highlighted. Yet it must be reiterated that not all popular texts use humor in relation to OCD, and even those that do rarely treat OCD solely as humorous, as Fennell and Boyd note in their survey of the field.

One point from Fennell and Boyd's study is worth considering further. They reported in their analysis that most of the characters associated with OCD were able to function well in society:

> In contrast to media stereotypes of those with disorders as outcasts and social fail-
> ures, characters [...] were relatively well-functioning. Although over half experienced
> problematic thoughts/ideas/urges, symptoms were sometimes perceived as a boon.
> Characters were largely shown moving about in society in their everyday lives rather
> than in institutions. When "symptoms" (whatever the potential disorder) were at their
> worst, 25% of characters were completely unable to function, and 27.5% seemed as
> competent as other characters. When "symptoms" were at their best, only 5% were
> completely unable to function, while a majority were as competent as others. Unlike
> images of mental disorders where characters are shown to be a burden on society,
> only a minority of sample characters never demonstrated an ability to hold down a job
> [Fennell and Boyd].

It is well worth pausing here to emphasize that there appears to be a marked
distinction between popular media understandings of OCD and of other
disorders: stereotypical depictions of OCD, with order and cleanliness and
organization, appear to be more conducive to media depictions of high levels
of functioning in society than is seen with other disorders, which may, in
contrast, be seen to involve disorder and danger and confusion. As such,
comedy may be perceived as more appropriate.

Orienting ourselves around these twin points of humor and of relatively
high functioning ability, then, in the following analysis we want to take a
closer look at two comical characters in popular television, to examine specifically how the television programs conceptualize OCD as it relates to professional and social behaviors, and what implicit meanings are being made by
such representations—both positive and negative.

"I couldn't fix the whole world, I knew that, but I could fix little pieces of it, one little piece at a time, put things back together": OCD in *Monk*

Monk remains one of the best-known television examples of OCD portrayals. An American detective series that aired on television for eight seasons
between 2002 and 2009, *Monk* features a private detective—Adrian Monk—
who works as a police consultant for the San Francisco police department. In
the opening episodes viewers learn that Monk was formerly a police detective
who had a breakdown after his wife was murdered; he was discharged from
the force and is now operating as a private consultant while hoping to be
reinstated as a police detective and return to his former career. Given the
length of the series, it would not be feasible to provide a full analysis of the
series within the constraints of this one chapter section and it would be disingenuous to pretend such an endeavor is even worth attempting; instead, we
are necessarily cherry picking certain themes and episodes in *Monk* to serve

a broader purpose of discussing mental health on television. This inevitably entails overlooking nuances and plot developments which would, in their totality, be worthy of a sustained analysis in book form elsewhere.

It is worth considering in some detail Monk's introduction in the Pilot double episode, "Mr. Monk and the Candidate," as well as some key scenes in other episodes and also the conclusion to the series, to make some general points about OCD. OCD is emphasized throughout the Pilot episode and charts the course for the rest of the series, immediately signposting to readers that Monk's unusual attention to detail—which is a proxy for his OCD—is "a blessing and a curse" or "a gift and a curse," as described in many later episodes. In the Pilot episode, viewers are introduced to Monk as he stands in the middle of a crime scene, a murder, surrounded by people watching and waiting for him to speak. The camera moves from a line of officers and detectives to a shot of Monk framed by their shoulders as they stand watching. Background music plays in a minor key as the camera then zooms in on his face as he looks around the crime scene, with the music swelling when he sees the dead body and then pausing as he suddenly looks upwards. These music and visual clues tell viewers he is about to reveal something extraordinary. His first words are "The stove," which the police officers—and viewers—assume is a key clue to the crime, but instead it is a clue to his frame of mind because he corrects them at once: "No, I mean, my stove, I think I left it on"; he is worried he has not turned off his stove at home. Detectives and officers turn to each other, shrugging and raising eyebrows as Monk conducts an anxious conversation with his assistant, Sharona, who attempts to reassure him that the oven is definitely switched off. Rapidly shifting from drama to comedy in just a few moments: this is in essence the telling of OCD according to *Monk*.

At this point in the scene, one of the detectives tells Monk that he thinks it was a burglary gone wrong, and Monk then proceeds to give them his reading of the crime scene, showing an extraordinary attention to details and clues that somehow the entire police team has missed, while all the time displaying behaviors marked as unusual because of the puzzled and confused ways in which the others respond to him as he talks to them while tapping a lamp, or talking again about the stove. Sharona takes him aside and tells him: "Forget about the damn stove, okay? You are on a job here. You're a private consultant. [...] The department thinks you're nuts. You're never gonna get reinstated, you're never gonna get hired again, and we are both gonna be unemployed. Do you understand the importance of what I am saying? Now, pull your twisted self together, concentrate and be brilliant." Monk smiles and turns back to the police team to explain his deductions in more detail, before leaving to check on his stove. As he leaves, the police officers say to each other that Monk is a "living legend," and another adds, bemused, "if you call that living."

Cut to the title credits and this one brief scene has now set the stage for the series that follows. In just a few sentences of dialogue and a few visual and music cues, viewers have now had it established that Monk is a brilliant detective; he has (as yet unnamed) OCD; his OCD hinders his detective work but not enough to stop him; and his OCD also aids his detective work because of his focus on minutiae. Comedy and drama go hand in hand, as do OCD and detection. The next scenes cement this pattern. Viewers see him cleaning, counting while brushing his teeth, and rehearsing what he wants to say to Dr. Kroger his counselor, while he chooses between identical shirts and removes socks from individual sealed plastic bags. As he meets with the doctor, Monk's attempts to convince him that he is ready to return to the police force fail when he becomes fixated on a cushion that has moved out of place and must fix it, the jaunty music accompanying this in stark contrast to his sober words just moments before about his dead wife. Over the course of the episode viewers learn he fears germs, heights, crowds, darkness, and milk, all of which makes him the source of comedy for others (over the course of the series, his fears are numbered at 312). As other characters put it, he's a "defective detective," or "Rain Man," despite Sharona's efforts to legitimize his condition to others as "a form of anxiety disorder." His attention to detail is at once a part of his OCD and a strength of his detective work even as it also isolates him socially and also has stalled his detective career. As Johnson puts it, "The structure of each episode progresses from humiliation to triumph, or from embarrassment to redemptive success, as Monk solves the crime even in the face of harsh critics. His OCD is the means of both his humiliation and his ultimate triumph" (Johnson).

OCD is, then, a pivotal part of this show, not only featuring as a condition experienced by the main character but functioning as a definition of his career as well. Even the DVD advertising puts Monk's OCD front and center, recasting the disorder in a way that suggests it benefits him professionally: the Season One DVD cover uses the letters OCD, with the words for each initial spelled out as Obsessive Compulsive Detective. Then, on the back cover of the DVD, the first line tells readers, "He's ingenious, he's phobic, he's obsessive compulsive," thus linking skill, fear, and OCD all in one combination that seemingly cannot be untangled. The connections seem rather fitting and reflect the plot lines and overall conceptualization of Monk's professional work: his attention to detail aids his detective work because he notices valuable clues that others do not.

The logic behind these links between OCD and Monk's professional work become fairly self-evident when we consider the context of genre, which in this case is detective fiction. Crime fiction is, by and large, is about restoring order from chaos, reasserting control and patterns when a crime has disrupted the status quo. As Peter Hühn writes,

Most classical detective novels start out with a community in a state of stable order. Soon a crime (usually a murder) occurs, which the police are unable to clear up. The insoluble crime acts as a destabilizing event, because the system of norms and rules regulating life in the community has proved powerless in one crucial instance and is therefore discredited. In other words, the narrative incapability on the part of society's official agents, their inability to discover and tell the story of the crime, thus threatens the validity of the established order. At this point the detective takes over the case, embarks on a course of thorough investigations, and finally identifies the criminal, explaining his solution at length. Thus, through the development of the second story, the absent first story is at last reconstructed in detail and made known. By reintegrating the aberrant event, the narrative reconstruction restores the disrupted social order and reaffirms the validity of the system of norms [Hühn].

The congruence with OCD is clear enough. Obsessions and the accompanying fear and anxiety disrupt a person's stable mental health. We can then read compulsions as being efforts to restore a sense of order and pattern when the obsessions have disrupted and destabilized a mental state of stable order. And just like long-running detective series, the restoration of order is never complete; there is temporary relief before another crime (obsession) occurs to disrupt the re-established (mental) order, another cycle must be repeated, another effort to restore order is required.

The restoration of order is a key theme in the series. Monk himself alludes to this in the third season, in which he links detective work to restoration: "I never appreciated how much the job meant to me, I feel lost, nothing … fits. […] I had a great job, I was a cop, that's all I ever wanted to be. I couldn't fix the whole world, I knew that, but I could fix little pieces of it, one little piece at a time, put things back together." This obsession with "fixing" society, "putting things back together" is a restoration of what is broken, a return to order, which parallels the gradual return to order for Monk himself. He begins the series having lost his police job after a breakdown and, at one point in the series, also temporarily loses his private detective license because of his OCD behaviors, and in various scenes performs compulsions that hinder him, such as letting a suspect escape when he is paralyzed by acrophobia on a ladder; he is as much broken as the societal order he is attempting to restore.

Monk's focus on "fixing" things and "putting things back together" in society thus reflect his ongoing obsessions and anxieties. In this sense the program does represent the stages of OCD with some accuracy; Monk is not simply performing repetitive external behaviors such as checking locks, but his internal obsessions and anxieties are performed via dialogue and his acting. As viewers saw in the very first scene, his fears about the stove kept interrupting his attempts to explain the crime scene to other people, which demonstrates the intrusive nature of obsessive thoughts. He is made unhappy by his condition; when Sharona tells him that he is "going straight to hell" for his insistence on fishing his house keys from a dead man's coffin during the funeral service with a paper clip and roll of dental floss from above, Monk replies "I am in hell"; when he learns he has not been reinstated to the police force early in season one because of his OCD behaviors, the acting and music and camera work paints a picture of despair, and at regular points over the series this despair is reiterated. The "curse" of OCD has interrupted his cherished professional work, and his fears are a constant interruption to his ability to fully perform his role.

Interruption, yes, but cessation, no. Despite his intrusive anxieties, and despite his inability to return to the police force for years, Monk is nonetheless able to continue his work and successfully solve crimes at least in a private capacity, with the assistance of Sharona and later Natalie. Even when Monk does win his way back onto the police force, he quickly realizes he prefers operating in the capacity of a private detective. Sharona describes him as a "zen Sherlock Holmes," and this is apt: his gentle, unassuming personality is often attacked by others and his theories are denounced and meet with rejection and laughter ("This isn't police work, this is, this is vaudeville!") yet he ignores their skepticism and shows a remarkable and peerless crime solving ability that speaks for itself and invariably proves him right. Even his former partner and now police supervisor, Captain Stottlemeyer—who is responsible for denying Monk's return to the police force in the first season—begrudgingly admits, "There is only one Adrian Monk" and later becomes his greatest advocate. Monk connects cases that others think have no connection, and he sees patterns that others do not; in a visual representation of this the program hammers this point home in the first episode when Monk literally pieces together clues when he re-orders shredded paper. As well as the crimes in each episode, Monk is also intent on solving his wife's murder as well as undergoing his own rehabilitation as a person so he can rejoin the police force: he is at once seeking a professional and personal restoration, a fitting together of puzzle pieces on several levels.

Another reading of this preoccupation with order aligns it with the obsession of hygiene itself, as an attempt to "sanitize" society from an infecting crime, as Johnson notes:

> Monk is destined to be a detective because of his unique personality. One of Monk's hallmark OCD symptoms is his obsession with order. Seeking order is not in itself pathological, but Monk pursues orderliness with a zest that disrupts his social functioning. In one characteristic example, Monk is asked to identify a suspect in a police line-up. He is unable to concentrate on the task and instead insists that the men behind the glass exhibit a neat appearance and order themselves according to height. It is this personality trait, this excessive zeal for order, which enables his remarkable skill as a detective. Monk's obsessions with sanitizing his home and his hands are directly correlated with his desire to sanitize society from its criminal elements. His driving passion is to "order" society according to a perfect rationality where crime, the ultimate unpredictable and chaotic event, is exorcized. This obsession with order gives

Monk a special vision, enabling him to see details and draw connections that others would miss. What is in normal social life pathological—the inability to see the "big picture" for an obsessive focus on minor details—is the greatest asset for a detective [Johnson].

Johnson goes on to discuss *Monk* in the context of a control society, theorizing that traditional exclusionary discourses of madness as Other have been replaced by the reframing of madness as one's identity. According to Johnson, this new concept of illness as identity has transformed madness into capital, an importance resource in a consumerist society which sells products by pretending that purchasing the product will establish or reinforce one's identity; the links with *Monk* are in Monk's obsession with specific branded products, whether bottled water or so on. Ironically, Monk's obsession with hygiene is almost his demise when his hand wipes are poisoned by someone attempting to kill him.

The portrayal of OCD in *Monk* has met with mixed responses from commentators and researchers. Some mental health disorder advocacy groups have received the program well. A *Variety* article noted that, at the start of the series, then-director of the OCD Foundation Patricia Perkins had said, "It's very funny. I have OCD, and that's my sense of humor" (North), while the then named Anxiety Disorders Association of America (ADAA) considered it sufficiently positive to use the show in a campaign called "Treat it, don't repeat it," which featured *Monk* actor Tony Shalhoub, executive producer David Hoberman, and ADAA president Jerilynn Ross for a public service announcement (Anxiety and Depression Association of America). Ross herself has praised the show for its utility in raising awareness: "Even as a comedy, the show demystifies this mental illness respectfully and makes people aware of what someone suffering from OCD experiences. It also lets people know that if they have OCD, they are not alone and they can get help" (North).

As Hoffner and Cohen note in a study, Hoberman received a Career Achievement Award from the Substance Abuse and Mental Health Services Administration for his work on *Monk* and was also a board member of the ADAA (Hoffner and Cohen). The study examined the reactions of 142 *Monk* fans, of whom about half reported having a mental illness (and half of that number specifically reported having OCD), exploring the parasocial relationship (the emotional bond between audience and a character) and its effects relating to OCD. They found that forming a parasocial relationship was associated with lower stereotypes and lower social distance from people with OCD, while people with OCD and a high parasocial relationship felt the show helped them cope with OCD.

Not all agree with the positive reactions; the varied published responses to the program from web commentators identifying as having OCD have ranged from supporters who consider the show to have "provided some hope and relief to see a character with my illness portrayed in a positive light" (Standley) to critics denouncing *Monk* as *"the worst portrayal of mental disability and psychiatric treatment I've ever seen,* in any form of media [...] irresponsible and dangerous [...] horrifyingly misguided" (Wortmann; italics in original). Criticisms chiefly center around the idea that OCD is unrealistically portrayed and is simply a "gimmick" without showing the anxiety and fear that accompanies the condition (Wortmann). It is easy to point to several troubling depictions of medication and therapy to support a negative reading. For instance, Monk has extremely limited experiences with any medication, either refusing to take any kind of OCD medication at all or having such extremely negative reactions that he is better without them, such as one example when a drug successfully removed his OCD symptoms but also his detective abilities. His counseling experiences also appears to chiefly consist of talking rather than therapeutic strategies such as ERP, with hypnotism, and aversion therapy among the rarely mentioned options, neither of which Monk undergoes. In these ways the program could be argued to be propagating the false idea that there are no medications nor therapeutic strategies that can aid a person with OCD, when in reality both elements may have some success in treating the disorder.

As with web commentary, responses from those in the research community are also worlds apart. Johnson argues that the program is unhelpful because OCD, not crime, is the chief interest of *Monk* and as such Monk becomes defined by his OCD: "the suspense derives from Monk's personality rather than the crime proper. [...] Monk's OCD personality is central to the plot of the show: the series centers on the connection between Monk's identity and his occupation. Detecting is not simply Monk's job, but a fundamental part of who he is" (Johnson).

Martin, however, disagrees, arguing that *Monk* escapes this conflation of illness and identity by making his condition simply part of his personality:

> The central character of the show, Adrian Monk, is a detective living with OCD, and though the disorder has a significant impact on every area of his life, the story of Monk doesn't necessarily treat his diagnosis as the central point of conflict. [...] This treatment of a character with OCD as a part of a personality rather than the primary characteristic or identity illustrates an example of how this OCD trope can be subverted to a message that is more positive and potentially influential in challenging the hegemonic discourse of stigma and appropriation of Obsessive-Compulsive Disorder in media [S. Martin].

In Martin's reading of the program, *Monk* successfully escapes the OCD trope by allowing Monk to be a "complete character" where he is not solely defined by his condition.

It cannot be denied that the series is preoccupied with Monk's behaviors, yet OCD is rarely named explicitly. And despite the behaviors, Monk is not seriously impaired by his condition professionally. His social impairment may be more serious but given the series portrays him as devoted to his wife's memory and intent on identifying her murderer, his success in the social realm or lack thereof is for the most part inconsequential; it has little value in this world because only his professional skills matter. And his professional skills, regardless of the intrusions of his OCD, are unparalleled in the world of *Monk*, even when it is outside the official police role. Moreover, it would be doing a disservice to the program to insist that there is no sense of fear or obsessive anxieties experienced by Monk, as the dialogue, music, and acting do attempt to demonstrate this in numerous ways across the entirety of the series—as Monk describes it, his condition makes life "unbearable" and he regularly confesses how "tired" he is of the disorder and its effect on his life.

Whatever difficulties there may be with the depiction of OCD in *Monk*, then, the character of Monk performs a crucial, valued role in his profession and in society itself, and as such, OCD is seen relatively positively because the condition does in some ways aid that work, and, as such, aids other people. The most obvious point is that OCD has been given to a likeable main character of the program, not to a villainous caricature or hapless sidekick. OCD is portrayed as a "curse" to some extent because of its delimiting role on Monk's social relationships and even on his policing and his career, but its "gift" to Monk in the skills it gives him is, by far, the greater. By the end of the series, Monk has not conquered OCD, but he does function so successfully that he wins his way back onto the police force, even if he decides to continue instead in a private capacity. He also solves the murder of his wife, Trudy, and establishes a positive relationship with her daughter, Molly; arguably the greatest restoration of order possible for Monk both professionally and domestically. The closing episode of the series includes a pivotal scene with Molly, in which Monk refers yet again to his gift and curse. Molly corrects him, telling him instead that "it's not a curse. It's a gift." Above all else, Monk is not unable to function in society because even with his limitations outside of police officialdom, he is still the vital player ensuring that crimes are solved, that criminals are captured, and that the world is, in some ways, "fixed" with much more of the broken bits "put back together" and order restored.

"I will fix you": OCD in *Glee*

Glee was an American television program that aired for six seasons from 2009 to 2015. It is a comedy about the members of the William McKinley High School glee choir and their teacher, Will Schuester. Although primarily focusing on Will, several choir members, and their nemesis the football coach Sue Sylvester, *Glee* also includes a number of important supporting characters, one of whom has OCD and is the focus of this discussion: McKinley guidance counselor Emma Pillsbury. Although we primarily consider the first episode to assess how Emma and her OCD are introduced to viewers, two other episodes are also worth noting for their handling of OCD: "Born This Way" and "Asian F."

In the Pilot episode, Emma's introduction highlights a mysophobic obsession with hygiene. Viewers first see Emma when she walks into the staff kitchen and exchanges friendly greetings with Will and another teacher—and less than friendly greetings with *Glee* villain Sue—and the camerawork alternates between their conversation and Emma's behaviors, using camera techniques to signpost to viewers that her behaviors are unusual: the camera highlights her putting on plastic gloves, cleaning the apparently spotless table, then pans from a shot of her hands cleaning the table to Will's bemused face as he watches, and then shows her lining up neatly organized boxes of food. This scene is bookended by her attention to cleanliness and so too is her next, where she walks into frame and gasps in horror when she steps on a piece of gum, turning a terrified face to Will who stops as he passes and cleans her shoe. At this point her condition remains unnamed. Instead she simply tells Will, that "I have trouble with things like that, you know, the—the messy things." Her next scene depicts her carefully cleaning a pencil. Next: cleaning a car door handle.

Based on this introduction and some of Emma's scenes in later episodes, it is tempting to immediately dismiss this representation of OCD and say that Emma's OCD is the focus of all her scenes, and she does not exist without it. Indeed, there is something to be said for this view, which was put forth by Martin, who critiques the program's conflation of identity and illness arguing that unlike Monk, Emma is defined solely by her OCD with little other plot value. As Martin (who reads Sheldon in *The Big Bang Theory* as having OCD) puts it, "The reduction of an entire character to a diagnosis dehumanizes the condition and, much like Sheldon, creates a character that is a problem to be managed rather than a peer to interact with or relate to" (S. Martin). However, it could also be argued that an alternative way to consider this is that aligning this particular character to a diagnosis may actually *humanize* a condition because Emma is "one of the group," one of the valued supporters of the glee choir, and OCD therefore cannot be simply Other because it is now an in-group condition.

A closer view shows that Emma's role in the television series is not simply as a diagnosis, but far more. Some of her scenes, particularly as the series progresses, have no verbal or visual reference to OCD; and even the ones that do are still generally telling a story that is greater than simply her condition. In her first scene, Emma is the one who mentions that the existing glee choir director has been fired, an innocent observation which prompts Will to ask for the position in the very next scene. And in her second scene—the shoe cleaning scene—she is interacting with Will, who asks for her advice after experiencing a turbulent start to his glee club reign. Emma gives him valuable suggestions for how to recruit students for the glee club, advice that he puts into practice—albeit more dishonestly than she may have meant—and which prove successful. The scene ends with Emma encouraging and validating Will by commenting that he cares about the students. The scene is intercut with another scene between Will and Sue, where Sue is offering him the opposite advice, discouraging and dismissing him, and is followed later in the episode with an argument between Will and his then-wife Terri, who wants him to quit teaching and earn more money as an accountant. Emma encourages him to remain a teacher. Terri refuses to act as chaperone to the glee choir when Will asks; Emma volunteers and in a later episode even takes the glee choir to sectionals in Will's place when he cannot; she becomes the club's "good luck charm." In this opening episode and across the series, Emma is Will's biggest supporter—and by extension the glee club's biggest supporter—and becomes his confidante and eventually his wife and mother of his children by series end. Emma's support of the glee choir is undoubtedly emblematic of her attraction to Will—which in some ways is an unhealthy fixation or obsession in itself, as signified by her wide-eyed staring at Will in their early scenes—but her empathy extends to other scenes that show her caring for the students. For instance, whether in her guidance counselor capacity or more informally, she attempts to help Rachel with her crush on Finn and Artie deal with his disability, and when she takes over from Will for sectionals, she defends the glee club against opposing choir teachers who cheat the McKinley students; she is also shown supporting Kurt at the hospital as he waits for news on his father's illness. As such, Emma's role and value in the *Glee* world transcends simply a diagnosis.

In these ways Emma is much more than simply her condition. She is also, in other important ways, portrayed as far more "normal" than most other characters. Like Monk, she is portrayed as a gentle and quiet personality; Emma's encouragement and support of other people and her easy interactions with everyone around her are a stark contrast to Sue's bullying and the poor social skills of virtually every other character in the series, adult or otherwise. Notably, she is also depicted as entirely "normal" compared with Will's first wife, Terri, whose increasingly bizarre and histrionic behavior, which includes faking a pregnancy, probably warrants its own diagnosis. At one point, Emma refers to both herself and Terri as "crazy," but this is difficult to justify given that the show frames Terri as a villain by undermining Will and Emma as a heroine for supporting him.

"Normal" Emma might be shown to be in contrast to other characters, but nonetheless her condition does affect her emotionally. Martin points out that Emma's portrayal highlights the fear and anxiety that accompanies OCD in a way that is lacking in other depictions, such as in *The Big Bang Theory*.

> While Sheldon is marked as "other" as a result of his compulsive behavior in his inter-actions with his friends, Emma is primarily designated as OCD because of her unre-lenting phobias. This emphasis of the cognitive distress rather than simply identifying specific behaviors does add a level of nuance in her character as her greatest battles are fought against herself. Though Emma is overly simplified to the point of being a walk-ing diagnosis, her experience of OCD is one that consists of the fear and anxiety that characterize the disorder [S. Martin].

It must be said that this sense of fear and anxiety is not at all evident in her first scene. Unlike Monk's obvious anxieties and obsessive thoughts which keep impinging on his scenes, Emma appears calm and unaware of her unusual behavior, devoid of anxiety; she also seems perfectly content indi-vidually cleaning each grape in a scene of the second episode. More distress is evident when she steps in gum in the Pilot episode but initially at least her behaviors are more usually treated as a joke, played for comedy value, and discussed and dismissed in disparaging tones, at least by the villains such as Sue, or Terri—who says "I guess being crazy has its benefits"—or by other characters such as Ken, who promises "I'll put up with all your crazy" when he attempts to woo her. If not ridiculed, her obsessions are dismissed as en-dearing by Carl, her fiancé at the time in the series, who says "Oh I love that look of instant panic every time I try to change your routine! Adorable!"; Will also mentions she is "so cute about it [the OCD]" even as he describes it as a severe anxiety disorder that stops her enjoying life.

Yet *Glee* appears to attempt to take OCD more seriously as the series progresses. The opening episodes of the series pictured Emma in denial of her condition: "I don't have a problem," she insists to Will in the second epi-sode, saying instead, "I have a little trouble with messes, but it's not like it's a problem." Will asks her if she has seen a therapist, but Emma dismisses the notion saying, "it's completely manageable." By the second part of the first season when Emma and Will are dating, Emma is now admitting that she has a problem and that it is not, after all, manageable but instead is negatively affecting her relationships, and she shows emotional distress when she admits to Will, "I just haven't found the right person, you know, someone who won't reject me when things are really hard with my—with my problem." By the end of the next episode Will gives Emma the details of a counselor and encourages her to seek professional help for her condition. He also points out that OCD is triggered by stress and she makes the telling comment "At what age are you allowed to look back on your life with nothing but regret? Is thirty-two too young? I actually believed that I'd have a handle on my OCD by now. It's just been so long and I'm so tired," words that in part mimic Monk's as noted ear-lier. These scenes are not typically played for laughs but instead rank among the many that the producers use for drama and depth—along with Rachel's loneliness, Kurt's isolation, or so on.

By the second season episode "Born This Way," which heavily emphasizes ideas of self-acceptance, Emma has arrived at a pivotal point in her OCD. The episode ends with the glee choir characters taking to the stage wearing tee shirts that proudly broadcast their point of difference, whether looks or sexuality or otherwise: Rachel has a shirt that says "Nose"; Finn has "Can't Dance"; Mike "Can't Sing"; Kurt "Likes Boys"; Sam "Trouty Mouth"; Brittany "I'm With Stoopid" while Puck has "I'm with Stupid" (varying only by the spelling and part of their anatomy the arrow is pointing towards). Emma's says OCD; it is framed as a crucial moment given she is now publicly acknowledging the condition. It must be said that the whole concept wilts under closer inspection if viewers pause to realize that the producers are essentially equating big lips or stupidity with OCD, and as such it is a significant trivialization; the inability to sing well or dance well may have its challenges in life but it is difficult to see how that could compare with the experience of OCD. However, this theme of self-acceptance is in fact a sham: the episode is not about accepting OCD at all as a quirky part of her personality; instead it is about Emma admitting she has a problem that she has to address, that OCD is actually *not* who she is but it stops her from being who she is. While other characters may simply need to accept big lips or poor vocal skills and move on, Emma cannot. As such, this discourse directly counters any conflation of illness and identity and implies that Emma is a character defined not simply by OCD—she was not in fact "born this way"—but one who wants something else for herself and is now empowered to move towards that. Indeed, she is later shown in the episode meeting a therapist who tells her that mental illness, whether bipolar or OCD or depression, is subject to stigma in the U.S. yet is "very treatable" and she will feel better; she is prescribed a low dose SSRI and therapy. From this point on she makes gradual steps towards recovery as she takes her medication and finds it helpful.

Earlier in this chapter we noted Monk's desire to "fix" the world around him. It is in this context—as well as the broader conceptualization of mental illness as disorder—that *Glee* provides another interesting take on OCD in a third season episode called "Asian F." The episode includes a memorable scene when Emma is upset about her OCD when a visit from her parents—who mockingly call her "freaky-deaky"—triggers her symptoms and Will sings her the Coldplay anthem "Fix You" as she prays and cries, which prompts broader questions about popular understandings of OCD as both something that may gift special insight but is also something that must be "fixed." Neither medication nor Will can easily "fix" her OCD, however, at least not quickly; in a later episode when Will proposes to her, Emma explains that she is taking her medication but has good days and bad days when it comes to her symptoms. Indeed, her attempts to plan their wedding again trigger her anxiety and, unable to cope, she jilts him at the altar, putting paid to any idea that there is a quick fix to OCD. She later explains to Will, "my therapist says that I use my OCD to control the uncontrollable." Yet when they do finally marry, the theme of being fixed is repeated when she describes Will in her wedding vows as making her feel "clean" and "whole again," reinforcing the concept of restoring something that is broken. Unlike many early episodes, therefore, over the series there appears to be an increasing attempt on *Glee* to move away from simple comedy to instead show the complexity and also suffering associated with OCD.

Despite the distress Emma is shown to feel and these connotations of brokenness, Emma nevertheless appears, for the most part, entirely functional in her professional capacity, because viewers see little evidence of her symptoms having an impact on her actual job, a point also made by Will when he remarks that she functions very well despite her disorder. The impact is instead primarily social and specifically romantic, as she struggles to overcome her fears around sex, but even in the social sphere she is well liked among other teachers—the contempt of Sue notwithstanding which is, it must be said, extended to everyone—and accepted by the glee choir students, and is able to marry Will and become pregnant with their first child.

One final point about *Glee* relates to setting and genre. If one considers OCD in the context of the high school setting, Emma's preoccupation with order and patterns and restoration seems, perhaps, somewhat fitting, and suggests Emma's value to her setting. High school can be a difficult, anxious, and confusing environment for many teenagers, with adolescence a time of trying to chart one's course through a world that can seem chaotic and upsetting at times. Emma's role as a guidance counselor is, in theory if not in practice, a position that helps her establish order in chaos, as she helps steer students through high school towards their future goals, and in doing so removes some of the anxiety from the experience. Her role on the program is not simply to be "fixed" by Will but also to be someone who plays an integral part of "fixing" other people—in her support of Will and the glee choir as well as his dreams beyond glee club. Emma's condition arguably aids her professional work in some ways, if only in that it could be seen as giving her more empathy, helping her professionally in her guidance counselor career even as it complicates her romantically.

Similarly, the musical genre is worth a brief mention in passing for its relation to OCD. *Glee* also uses very conventional, familiar pop music that relies on repetition and patterns, repeated verses and choruses, and catchy hooks that repeat themselves in one's head endlessly, which in some ways, links to OCD and Emma's attempts to bring order and patterns to her world. And most tellingly, in the opening scene of the *Glee* Pilot episode, Will is shown arriving at the school, walking through the parking lot and interacting with students, and then stopping to stand in front of a display cabinet for awards. While the song "Shining Star" plays, there is a close up of the 1993 trophy for first place in the "Show Choir Championships," a pan to a woman's photograph on a plaque with her name, Lillian Adler, 1937–1997, and a quote which reads, "By its very definition, Glee is about opening yourself up to joy." Joy is the very opposite of the intense anxiety that characterizes Emma's OCD. Her growing involvement in the Glee choir and her relationships with its director and members are portrayed as key factors in her path away from anxiety and fear and towards joy. And yet even in this, as in so much else, Emma again appears more normal than most: in the Pilot episode Will himself bemoans Terri's behavior to Emma, saying that "she used to be filled with so much joy"; the irony is that despite her phobias, Emma is shown to have more joy than Terri, and the program shows that this only increases as she accepts her OCD and seeks treatment. The series ends with scenes of Will and Emma married with children and—even if not entirely "fixed"—not only significantly improved from her opening state of mind but also apparently thriving.

Conclusions

As with popular representations of other disorders such as ASD (see Chapter One), OCD has been depicted in *Monk* and *Glee* in comedic ways because of the difficulties in the social realm experienced by the individuals. Furthermore, and similar to some representations of ASD (e.g., the Rain Man trope), OCD also provides special insight that sets the characters apart from other people, particularly in the case of *Monk*. Thus, there is a contradiction at work in the two programs wherein OCD is a barrier to functioning in social settings yet may also be an advantage in the professional world because of that insight. In the case of *Monk*, OCD has been used in the way of some mental health disorders before: it is a gift that can aid Monk in his professional career; his obsessive attention to detail is linked to his OCD and is undeniably an aid to his detective work. It is, at the same time, a curse that can cause him serious problems with navigating the world. Similarly, in the case of *Glee*, OCD is a gift that can aid Emma's insight and empathy as a counselor but is a hindrance to her romantic and social relationships. Although Emma is ridiculed for her OCD behaviors by some, she is also notable for her empathy, which is implicitly linked to her experiences of OCD, and this aids her position as guidance counselor.

Both programs use the language of "fixing" as a proxy for professional work (detection and counseling) even as the direction of their professional endeavors differs significantly: Monk's intent is to "fix" the world and restoring it "one little piece at a time" in tandem with others—via his detective work, restoring order to a world broken and destabilized by murders—while Emma is focused on "fixing" people—via her guidance counselor work, restoring order and direction to her students and to other teachers—and she is also the subject of a project to be fixed herself. As such this restorative work is portrayed sympathetically and positively, on the whole, because both Monk and Emma are functioning members of a society who are making valuable contributions to that society, wherein the value is dictated by the setting—policing and education. As such, perhaps the greatest irony of these two programs is that despite the themes of restoring order to what is broken, on "fixing" things and people, on showing the difficulties experienced by a mental health *disorder*, neither character appears truly broken. Quite the opposite: both characters function very well and even excel in their profession.

Returning, then, to the questions raised earlier in this chapter about comedy: while it is inarguable that these television programs contribute to raising the profile of OCD in the general public, does the use of comedy to do so in fact trivialize a condition that can be seriously debilitating and distressing for those who have it? The answer is not entirely, precisely because of the reasons outlined above. The use of comedy to make these representations is not as suspect as it might be otherwise, for neither Monk's nor Emma's character is reduced to simply a comical lead or played-for-laughs minor character, but instead both characters are integral and valued members of their societies who perform a productive role skillfully. They at once succeed in raising the profile of OCD while also potentially misinforming uncritical viewers about OCD by not fully showing the attending anxiety and obsessions of the compulsive behaviors—or very much about possible treatment—but instead showing two highly functional people. Yet given the limitations of television as a visual medium, and the fact that everyone's experience of OCD is different anyway, these do not appear to be fatal flaws.

The very term *disorder* implies a schism, a breaking of order. The focus on order, patterns, and repetitive behaviors is perhaps one reason OCD is treating humorously in some media—as Cefalu suggested—and we might also extend that to the tendency to portray ASD in comical ways too—both disorders are extremes of behavior that are perhaps seen as "safe" precisely because of the limits and boundaries to behaviors. It is predictable, it is rehearsed. It is perceived as being contained within the individual with little effect on others. Put another way, it is controlled madness. As such, it is "safe" to laugh about it. This is in contrast to the extremes of behaviors seen in other disorders we discuss in this book: DID, schizophrenia, and bipolar disorder. Those are usually treated seriously, and the behaviors portrayed as "unsafe" because of the lack of limits and boundaries, because the behaviors are unpredictable, unrehearsed, "unsafe"; they are uncontained and can spill over into the lives of others and endanger them. They signify uncontrolled madness. In the next chapter, we begin to delve deeper into what television has portrayed as the darker side of mental health disorders: DID and schizophrenia.

THREE

"Tell me who I am"

Schizophrenia and Dissociative
Identity Disorder

In this chapter we break with our approach in most other chapters by exploring not one but two different disorders: schizophrenia and dissociative identity disorder (DID). The rationale is both conceptual and pragmatic: the disorders are so commonly mixed up by most of the lay public (and thus by extension on television, even in the episodes we discuss here) that it seems more prudent to acknowledge this from the outset and directly discuss some of that confusion, even if some may argue that doing so may contribute to that confusion. To mitigate that, the structure of this chapter still divides the two disorders into discrete sections, while opening and closing with a brief discussion of both. As with our other chapters, before discussing the television programs, we first define each disorder and provide a brief summary of media depictions.

A secondary reason for combining these two disorders is even more pragmatic: despite a wealth of depictions of schizophrenia on television—and to a lesser extent DID—there is, on the whole, very little that is nuanced about those depictions. More typically represented in ways far removed from the comedy often used with ASD and OCD, both schizophrenia and DID are most usually portrayed in simplistic terms and linked with danger and violence in individuals, particularly in crime programs. We instead attempt to locate a few key depictions that depart from this practice.

Schizophrenia is the better known of the two disorders, although it must be immediately noted that better known does not mean better understood; instead, it is commonly confused with DID. Schizophrenia is typically misunderstood as being characterized by split or multiple personalities—with an obvious reason being the Greek roots of schizophrenia literally mean split mind (McNally). DID, meanwhile, does actually refer to multiple personalities and was formerly (and even currently) known as multiple personality disorder; to further confuse matters, DID is the subject of ongoing debate within the psychiatry profession with a range of stances about its nature, causes, treatment, and most importantly, its legitimacy as a disorder itself. Both disorders are, then, almost impossibly entwined within popular understandings and at the same time are probably less well understood than most other disorders discussed in this book.

Schizophrenia

To make several points about televisual representations of schizophrenia, we survey how it is conceptualized in *Buffy, the Vampire Slayer,* a popular fantasy series of the late 1990s about a teenage vampire hunter called Buffy Summers. Although schizophrenia has appeared in multiple television series, as noted earlier it is usually rather simplistically associated with violence and crime and relegated to villains and minor characters. As such, the *Buffy* representation offers somewhat of a departure from this by allowing its popular main character to be (temporarily) associated with schizophrenia via an alternate reality plot device.

Background: What Is Schizophrenia?

Estimates of the prevalence of schizophrenia vary, but generally suggest a lifetime prevalence of less than one percent (Simeone et al.). Generally presenting in the late teens to mid–30s with peak age at onset in the 20s, schizophrenia involves a range of symptoms rather than a single defining one, with the experience of schizophrenia varying between people. This variety of possible symptoms is reflected in the DSM diagnosis, which primarily involves the following main elements:

- at least two of the following, each present for a significant part of a one-month period (or less if successfully treated), with one of the first three mandatory:
- Delusions
- Hallucinations
- Disorganized speech such as incoherence
- Grossly disorganized or catatonic behavior
- Negative symptoms (i.e., diminished emotional expression or avolition).
- low level of functioning (compared with prior to onset) in one or more major areas, such as work, interpersonal relations, or self-care

- continuous signs of the disturbance persist for at least six months
- schizoaffective disorder and depressive or bipolar disorder with psychotic features ruled out
- not attributable to a substance (e.g., a drug of abuse, a medication) or other medical condition
- if there is a history of ASD or a communication disorder of childhood onset, the additional diagnosis of schizophrenia is made only if prominent delusions or hallucinations, in addition to the other required symptoms of schizophrenia, are also present for at least one month (or less if successfully treated)

The course of the disorder is favorable in only around one in five people with schizophrenia; few recover completely and most require either formal or informal support; others experience chronic symptom remission and relapse; still others experience progressive decline, although the DSM also notes that psychotic symptoms typically lessen over time (American Psychiatric Association). Genetic factors appear to play a role in risk for schizophrenia although few people have a family history of psychosis. Quality of life is generally negatively affected with significant difficulties in functioning, and approximately one in five people with schizophrenia attempt suicide. Substance-related disorders are a common comorbidity, as are anxiety disorders; OCD and panic disorders are also higher in people with schizophrenia (American Psychiatric Association).

Given that the causes of schizophrenia are not yet fully understood, treatment is symptom based and includes antipsychotic medication and therapy such as CBT, illness management skills, rehabilitation and family education as well as treatments targeting some comorbidities, such as treating substance abuse (NIMH). Despite the common association of schizophrenia and violence in the public, people with schizophrenia are more likely to be the victims of violence than its perpetrators (NIMH).

Schizophrenia in the Media

Although schizophrenia has appeared in many programs, an early episode of the classic cozy crime program *Murder, She Wrote* is perhaps best at encapsulating popular understandings of the disorder. In the first season episode "Hit, Run and Homicide," the following dialogue takes place between bestselling mystery writer/ small-town amateur sleuth Jessica Fletcher and one of her friends, Daniel, who is falsely accused of murder.

DANIEL: I keep wondering somehow if I could have done it and not remember. Maybe I'm a schizoid? Jekyll and Hyde?

JESSICA: I doubt that.

[...]

DANIEL: The lawyer Tony got wants me to undergo a psychiatric examination. I think he's laying the groundwork for a plea of temporary insanity.

Here we have a neat summary of the themes most beloved of television writers when it comes to schizophrenia: a mix up of schizophrenia and DID, and the notion that the disorder (either one, it hardly seems to matter in this case) can and is used in the criminal justice system as a justification or explanation of a violent act (usually murder), whether real or not—not to mention the concept of "temporary insanity," which is perhaps not the actual lived experience of all people with schizophrenia.

Schizophrenia is one of the mental health disorders that has typically not fared well in media depictions, whether news media or fictional media. For instance, a study of 1,196 articles published in five UK national daily newspapers in 1996 and 2005 found little had changed in the decade with reporting still low quality and prone to stigmatizing descriptors (Clement and Foster). A more recent study examining use of the term "schizo" in an Italian newspaper from 2001 to 2015 reported equally negative findings: although the term was used less over time, of the subset of articles using the term that were actually related to mental health, one in three reinforced negative stereotypes (Pingani et al.). A recent UK study also reported decreased use of "schizo" in newspapers but noted that the adjective "schizophrenic" was commonly used; and frequently to describe someone who had committed a violent act; the authors concluded that the media "still use a range of graphic language to present people with a diagnosis of schizophrenia as frighteningly 'other' and as prone to violence" (Bowen et al.).

In fictional media, study findings do not suggest much has changed. A study of 41 films released between 1990 and 2010 with a main character with schizophrenia found most characters experienced delusions, auditory and visual hallucinations; most were violent; almost a third murderous; around a quarter committed suicide (Owen). Some films in particular have raised the ire of advocacy groups, such as *Me, Myself, and Irene* (2000), in which the lead character has a schizophrenia diagnosis but actually has multiple personalities (Baron-Faust). Not all portrayals are negative, however; the semi-fiction/biographical films *A Beautiful Mind* (2001) and *Shine* (1996) show exceptionally gifted people with schizophrenia, although there is also criticism of films such as *Shine* sacrificing veracity to instead dramatize events in a simplistic way (Rosen and Walter). In light of these findings, it is worth turning to how a popular young adult television series has used schizophrenia in both positive and negative ways.

"She believes she's some type of hero":
Schizophrenia in *Buffy, the Vampire Slayer*

Inspiring devotion in fans and many academics alike, the cult series *Buffy, the Vampire Slayer* about a teenaged vampire hunter called Buffy Summers screened for seven seasons between 1997 and 2003, and led to a vast array of media spinoffs, accompanied by countless articles and book-length treatments of various themes within the program. Previous work has highlighted a range of mental health issues that intersect with Buffy and creator Joss Whedon's other works—including madness (Peeling and Scanlon), gothic fear (Davis), psychoanalysis (Kromer), mental manipulation in *Dollhouse* (Ginn), and even the use of *Buffy* or other vampire films as a therapeutic tool (Priester; Schlozman),and vampirism in psychiatry (Mac Suibhne and Kelly). Research suggests that some viewers can find watching *Buffy* cathartic in some ways, because of its ability to convey "important psychodynamic concepts" (Schlozman 49).

This attention to mental health is warranted to some extent, given that the program includes various plots that involve mental health challenges for many of the main characters. For instance, characters find that their anxieties come to life in "Nightmares," and again in "Fear, Itself" (see Chapter Six for this theme highlighted by one of our interviewees). When Buffy is brought back to life, twice in the series, her behavior changes and she feels depression and disconnection (Season 6). The dangers of abusing alcohol are portrayed in Season Four's "Beer Bad," and Riley experiences an addiction akin to substance abuse when he starts visiting a vampire nest—equivalent to a crack house—seeking the high of being fed upon by prostitute-like vampires. Buffy, Joyce, and Tara suffer symptoms of mental disorders because of supernatural events (Season 5), and Dawn's storyline includes self-harm and kleptomania (Seasons 5 and 6). By giving mental illnesses to main characters, and by regularly including storylines referencing mental health issues, the series has the potential to normalize mental health as an important aspect of adolescent life.

Buffy's powers might be supernatural, superhuman, but the series begins with the message that she simply wants to be normal. In the first episode of the program, "Welcome to the Hellmouth," Buffy tells Giles, her Watcher (mentor), that she has "retired" from vampire slaying. Her reluctance to take on her supernatural responsibilities stems from very natural concerns: wanting to fit in, to make friends, to belong and "be like everybody else." Although Buffy goes on to accept her slayer role, the normal and the supernatural exist in an uneasy juxtaposition throughout the series. When Giles demurs at the prospect of Buffy becoming a cheerleader, her answer encapsulates this dilemma: "I will still have time to fight the forces of evil, okay? I just want to have a life; I want to do something normal. Something safe." This juxtaposition of extraordinary and normal informs the dialogue at many points, as when a visiting exchange student tells Buffy, "You must teach me everything about your life. I want to fit in, Buffy, just like you, a normal life," to which Buffy grimaces and replies, "One normal life, coming up." In this instance, both exchange student and Buffy are more than they appear—the student is an Incan mummy, Buffy a superhero slayer—reminding viewers that appearance does not tell the whole story. Each season concludes with a climactic supernatural battle, and each season begins with Buffy attempting to find her way "back to normal" and find her place in an ordinary world, whether that is high school, college, or the workforce.

Despite her wish for normality, Buffy's responsibilities and her superhuman powers weigh heavily on her psychological state. She faces the stresses of being not only a superhero saving the world but also a human girl who must deal with boyfriends, bills, employment, and (reluctantly) parenting her sister Dawn when their mother dies in Season Five. The pressure and stress she feels lead to catatonia in "The Weight of the World" after Dawn is kidnapped, and Buffy cannot cope with the burden of responsibility: "This is—all of this—it's too much for me." Much of Season Six concerns her struggle to accept her lot after being returned to life from heaven by her friends; Buffy admits, "I've been so detached. … Every day I try to snap out of it. Figure out why I'm like that." Her disconnection is not new; as early as Season 2 Buffy was having difficulty coping with the realities of her supernatural life. When Buffy returns to Sunnydale after visiting her father in Los Angeles following her brief death in Season One's finale, her father also comments on this disconnection: "She was just, I don't know, um … distant … there was no connection. The more time we spent together, the more I felt like she was nowhere to be seen." Buffy's identity as the Slayer is necessarily lonely and, although her friends and eventually the Potential Slayers assist in fulfilling her duties, this theme of isolation provides much of the emotional resonance of the series.

This background is key to understanding the episode discussed here because Buffy's growing difficulties dealing with stress and reconciling her responsibilities and desires culminate in "Normal Again," where Buffy experiences hallucinations of an alternate reality in a psychiatric institution. It is here that she questions if her entire vampire slayer existence is, in fact, an elaborate delusion caused by schizophrenia and must make a choice as to which reality she wishes to belong to. In the episode, a demon's poison causes Buffy to experience life in an alternate reality where she is a patient in a mental institution. In this alternate reality, Buffy's parents are both alive and present, and her sister does not exist. The episode moves between the two realities and provides a rational explanation for the fantastical events of the previous seasons: Buffy has been suffering schizophrenia for the preceding years and has imagined her entire Sunnydale existence: "For the last six years, she's been in an undifferentiated type of schizophrenia.... Buffy's delusions are multilayered. She believes she's some type of hero. ... She's surrounded herself with friends, most with their own superpowers, who are as real to her as you or me." Her alternate reality parents and doctor urge her to reject the Sunnydale delusion and her Slayer identity so she can return to them. Meanwhile, in the Sunnydale reality, Buffy's friends realize she has been poisoned and create an antidote to the demonic poison causing her hallucinations, and Buffy must choose whether or not to take the antidote. Buffy struggles to understand which of her delusions is real and which is not: "What's more real? A sick girl in an institution ... or some kind of supergirl chosen to fight demons and save the world? That's ridiculous."

The on-screen representation of this disorder and how it is managed could be argued to play to the worst of stereotypes about schizophrenia in particular and mental illness in general, given its setting in an institution. It must be noted first, however, that for all the flaws of how schizophrenia and its treatment are portrayed in this episode, *Buffy* entirely avoids the common mix up of schizophrenia and DID. However, viewers would not perhaps find much else that is informative about schizophrenia on the program. We are simply told that Buffy's diagnosis is an "undifferentiated type of schizophrenia" which involves delusions, and based on these scenes, schizophrenia appears to involve convulsions and hitting one's head repeatedly against a wall, and its treatment appears harsh and cruel. Buffy is injected against her will. Her bed has restraints, suggesting she is prone to violence and out of control. Patients in the institution sit staring expressionlessly at nothing; others jerk their arms around in a straitjacket or walk slowly down corridors bent to one side. The institution scenes use cold, blue lighting, and costuming with monochromatic tones. The mental institutions scenes of the alternate reality are portrayed far less favorably than the Sunnydale shots, which have a *mise en scène* that comprises warm, bright, light-filled sets saturated with color, featuring a wide range of people and sounds and interaction across home, campus, and work locations. The jarring music used in the episode to signify cuts between the Sunnydale and institution realities further reinforces the disruption to Buffy's mental state caused by schizophrenia and her delusions.

Even the language around mental illness here is negative, offering a range of synonyms and slang: "cuckoo's nest" and "sick," "twisted brain" and "funny farm delusion," caused by a demon's "crazy juice." Dawn says that Buffy's "fever" is "cooking your brain" to make her believe things that are not true; Buffy's father tells her that her mind is "playing tricks on you." Previous episodes have already established this derogatory attitude to mental illness: "Listening to Fear" gives us "insanity," "madmen," "mental patient," "losing their marbles," "insane wacky," and "crazy." Mental illness is a "sweeping plagues of madness," a "short circuit," and "something wrong." The patients are "bothering," "babbling," a "crazy guy." In "The Weight of the World," Xander calls the mental ward "the vegetable section," and Buffy's catatonic state is equivalent to being "stuck in some kind of loop" when Willow tries to reach her psychically (see Wilcox and also Kromer for more on the language of Buffy generally).

In some ways, this language simply reflects the general irreverence of the dialogue, a disregard for authority that manifests itself in the show's writing as black humor and nonchalance. Yet such language is hardly designed to encourage complex or sensitive portrayals of schizophrenia or other mental health disorders. Given that the characters' wordplay and humorous dialogue is how they interpret, make sense and share meaning with each other, and that this very wordplay is one of the primary sources of enjoyment for many viewers, the characters' use of such negative words seems to ultimately operate as an exclusionary strategy that confirms existing social distinctions between groups. Wilson et al. point to the "vocabulary of stigmatisation" in children's television which can be pejorative, negative, and imply a loss of control (Wilson et al., "Mental Illness Depictions"). Buffy deploys many of these same pejorative terms, and in this sense, the series may be said to contribute to and reinforce the negative stereotypes that can be harmful and hurtful to people with mental disorders.

One of the functions of this institutionalized setting is to suggest that schizophrenia is dangerous and should be isolated from the rest of society rather than treated in community care settings. There is an accompanying suggestion that madness can be controlled by this institutional environment—this is, in fact, one of the favorable elements for Buffy, given the institution's clear and defined boundaries. The unpredictability of mental illness is controlled and oppressed, confined by the order and structure of mental wards and psychiatric institutions. Viewers see patients with mental disorders isolated to particular wards, units, and institutions rather than integrated into society. Perhaps this is a physical manifestation of the social exclusion that Byrne identifies as one of the problems around mental illness, where stigma is "a sign of disgrace or discredit, which sets a person apart from others" (Byrne 65) and can lead to social isolation, shame, and secrecy. But this isolation and confinement is also potentially attractive to Buffy because in the institution she is no longer responsible for her own choices: she is controlled and safe compared to the Sunnydale risks of failing her family, friends, and apocalyptic responsibilities. This portrayal of schizophrenia suggests it can be controlled and managed—but, crucially, this management appears to be only possible in an institution rather than a community setting.

Although Buffy initially decides to reject her Sunnydale delusions and embrace the alternate reality by telling her doctor and parents "I want to be healthy again"; eventually she chooses her Sunnydale life and rejects the alternate institution/schizophrenia existence. As Peeling and Scanlon point out, there are obvious problems of presenting schizophrenia or mental illness as a state of mind that can be escaped simply by choice. There are also implications for how the series approaches mental health because of its genre. Episodes such as "Normal Again" and "Listening to Fear" that use demons or other monsters in connection with mental illness might be seen as problematic because even as they may approach the topic of mental illness sensitively, they perhaps draw on more traditional, negative images of the mentally ill as demonic and possessed (Butler and Hyler; Funk) in ways that some might find offensive.

Yet *Buffy* also opens up a space where such metaphors take on added resonance for viewers and call into question popular images of schizophrenia or other mental health disorders. This is primarily achieved through assigning schizophrenia or other mental disorders to main characters such as Buffy. Given that some mental disorders such as schizophrenia may be more stigmatized than others, therefore, associating Buffy with schizophrenia, even temporarily, may have some positive effects. Peeling and Scanlon similarly highlight this, suggesting that Buffy becomes a positive role model for viewers. Television, after all, can play a significant role in raising the profile of mental disorders, increasing visibility of those with conditions and thereby reducing social stigma as well as normalizing mental health as an important aspect of everyone's lives. Thus, while on the whole there remain some troubling aspects of how schizophrenia in portrayed in *Buffy*, they are mitigated by more favorable elements as well.

DID

Moving to DID, we examine here representations of the disorder on two programs in particular: *Criminal Minds* and *United States of Tara*. These two series are worth examining for their different approaches to DID as well as their different genres. A standard crime series, *Criminal Minds* tends towards dramatic representations that link DID with violence and danger, while Showtime's *United States of Tara* presents Tara as a loving member of her family and society with some comedic overtones. Both are, however, somewhat sympathetic portrayals of individuals who struggle with their identity and understanding who they are. And both, in some ways—unconsciously in *Criminal Minds*, consciously in *Tara*—demonstrate the shortcomings of a society that does not give the suffering individuals the help they desperately need.

Background: What Is DID?

According to the DSM-5, DID affects less than 2 percent of the general population, although other prevalence estimates range very widely. People who have experienced physical or sexual abuse are believed to have a higher risk of DID; the vast majority (90 percent) of people with DID report childhood abuse or neglect (American Psychiatric Association). More women than men present in clinical settings in the adult population, and typically have more acute states such as amnesia, flashbacks, hallucinations, and self-harm; men with DID will be more likely to demonstrate violent or criminal behaviors (American Psychiatric Association).

Diagnosis in the DSM-5 is based on five criteria:

- disruption of identity with at least two distinct identities, or an experience of possession, with associated changes in behavior, affect, behavior, consciousness, memory, perception, cognition, or sensory-motor functioning
- ongoing memory problems (daily activities, personal information, traumatic episodes) beyond normal forgetfulness
- significantly impaired functioning and distress (social, employment, other)
- not part of established cultural and religious practices
- not due to substance use or another disorder

Although popular fictional portrayals show very obvious splits between the identities that anyone would notice about the individual with the disorder, in reality DID may not be observable to other people (Canadian Mental Health Association). Common comorbidities include depression, anxiety, self-harm, substance abuse, PTSD or other mental disorders, and a reported 70 percent of outpatients have attempted suicide (American Psychiatric Association). The effect on daily life may be negligible or significant, but even when people with DID are high functioning in professional spheres, their social and familial spheres may be more affected. With treatment there can be improvement in functioning for some people; for others, treatment is less effective and response may be slow (American Psychiatric Association). The prognosis is worse for those with comorbid mental disorders, delayed treatment, recurrent abuse, and trauma (American Psychiatric Association). There is no anti–DID medication, only medication targeting some of the symptoms of DID, so treatment instead comprises various therapeutic approaches with the goal of aiding patients to safely process traumatic memories, improve coping skills, and integrate the various identities (National Alliance on Mental Illness). Treatment recommendations vary, with the findings of an international survey reporting that most of the surveyed clinicians used a large range of approaches at various points throughout treatment, such as assessment and safety strategies, daily functioning skills, psychoeducation, CBT, trauma-focused work, relationally focused interventions, emotion regulation, and EMDR (eye movement desensitization and reprocessing), and addressing dissociation and working with dissociated identities (Brand et al.). The authors reported that integration or unification of the identities was uncommon in clinical practice (Brand et al.).

It is worth at this point pausing to acknowledge that DID has had a complex and contested history as a mental health disorder, for several reasons. First, there was a change in nomenclature between the DSM-III and DSM-IV, in which the disorder used to be termed multiple personality disorder and then was renamed DID in DSM-IV. The change from multiple personality disorder to DID emphasized the dissociation aspect as a key part of the disorder. Rather than multiple competing different personalities, DID may better be understood as multiple identities within a person, all of which may be seen as part of a whole (Canadian Mental Health Association). Yet even now DID is probably better known to the general population as multiple personality disorder. As Spiegel puts it, "In formulating a more rigorous definition of dissociation and the domain of dissociation, it is helpful to make explicit the conceptual confusion that has often afflicted the construct of dissociation. For example, one observer quipped, 'the term dissociation suffers from multiple meaning disorder'" (Stephen Marmer, M.D., personal communication, Chicago, 1993; cited in Spiegel et al.).

This first point of nomenclature suggests that even more than other disorders, DID is likely to be subject to significant misinformation and confusion in the general population and particularly in popular media. A related and second reason is that the confusion about DID is not simply because of this shift in terminology in the academy but also because DID is often confused in the lay population with schizophrenia, with a common misperception being that people with schizophrenia have multiple personalities. Schizophrenia does, after all, literally mean a split mind but this splitting refers to a psychotic break with reality rather than a split identity within a person (Canadian Mental Health Association). Third, and to further complicate the situation, DID is also often misdiagnosed as bipolar disorder (usually bipolar II), although mood shifts are typically—but not always—more rapid in DID than in bipolar disorder (American Psychiatric Association).

Finally, and perhaps the most significant source of confusion, the very legitimacy of the disorder itself is still contested within the psychiatry profession. Perhaps it seems rather fitting that this "multiple personality disorder" has generated its own schism within the academy about the legitimacy of DID. Unlike more established diagnoses such as depression and schizophrenia, DID has been called into question by those who suggest that there is no such disorder as DID but instead it is attributable to suggestible patients influenced by therapists and popular media. Over the last decades, there are two broad camps that have steadily maintained their position. On the one side are those who claim the legitimacy of DID (e.g., Spiegel et al.). On the other are those (e.g., Spanos) who claim it is illegitimate, for reasons that have been variously rejected (Brand et al.; Gleaves; Şar et al.) and reiterated or expanded by others (Boysen and VanBergen; Lilienfeld et al.; Lynn et al.).

The main approaches can be broadly summarized as follows, with one view considering DID legitimate and the others seeking reasons why it is not. As others have described these views:

- The traumagenic/ trauma model perspective views DID as real and usually caused by a (real) severe and chronic childhood trauma, akin to PTSD (Reinders).
- The iatrogenic perspective sees DID as a construct that has been caused by psychotherapeutic treatment. This may include the creation of identities and false memories of a trauma; it may be caused by the psychologist's own suggestions. Within this perspective, the patient may consciously simulate DID or the simulation may be unconscious. In either case the therapist plays a role, because a conscious enactment of DID takes place to satisfy the therapist and an unconscious enactment of DID takes place because the therapist convinces the patient that they have DID (Reinders).
- The pseudogenic perspective sees DID as being simulated consciously without the provocation of psychotherapy and for the purpose of gain (whether seeking attention, legal benefits such as not being held accountable for a crime because of the disorder, or other reasons) (Reinders).
- The fantasy model understands dissociation as a cognitive trait which causes fantasies of past trauma (Loewenstein).
- The sociocognitive model views DID as a product of culture, specifically the North American popular media focus on childhood sexual abuse, memory repression, and multiple personalities (Loewenstein).

North traces the history of DID classification, describing the conflicts and pointing out that there was a rapid surge in reported cases of DID after the publication of *Sybil* and these were primarily in the U.S. and among limited authors who referenced each other (C. North).

Disputes among academics are inevitable and ingrained in any field of academic study, but the published literature on DID seems particularly vir-

ulent and should dispel for lay people any notion that the psychiatric community is at all united in the diagnosis, let alone conceptualization of, mental
health disorders. It is also, it must be said, difficult to resist using puns about
split personalities when considering the vastly opposing arguments laid forth
by the opponents in passionate defense of whatever they believe. This same
split extends, of course, to the inclusions of DID in the DSM-5, with various critics (e.g., Paris) opposing its inclusion and suspecting politicking on
the part of Spiegel, which has not unnaturally provoked recriminations from
Spiegel and others (Brand et al.; Ross).

However entertaining the conflict within the academy may be for ob-
servers, it has more serious and unfortunate consequences for those individuals with a DID diagnosis. As Floris and McPherson note, "when professionals
cannot agree, harm may be done to patients because their already fractured
sense of self is damaged further by the continual questioning and doubt about
their memories of trauma, past symptoms, and here-and-now experiences"
(Floris and McPherson 492). As the authors point out, "Whatever the debate
over the causes, the true extent of abuse, or the proper label for the behavior
and symptoms, there is an imperative to provide care" (Floris and McPherson
491).

Any further investigation into the disputes within the psychiatric academy about this particular disorder are beyond the scope and interest of this
present examination, and in this case we can say no more than Boysen and
VanBergen—"it seems any critical evaluation of DID research opens up a
philosophical gulf, across which communication is unlikely" (Boysen and
VanBergen). Instead, we move from the variations of DID in the academy
to variations of its representations in televisual media broadly, before a more
detailed analysis in two case studies.

DID in the Media

We need look no further than several classic dual personalities to understand how popular media commonly portrays DID: Jekyll/Hyde, Sméagol/
Gollum (*The Lord of the Rings*), Bruce Banner/The Incredible Hulk, to name
only a few of the better-known examples from cinema or television. While
DID is rarely named in these characters and other popular ones like them,
the concept of a break in identity is certainly obvious across all of them and
is therefore something with which many television viewers will be familiar.
In these popular cases, two distinct identities are apparent, and typically the
identities are opposite types. What should immediately strike us about these
examples is they all include a dangerous psychopath as one of the personalities—in stark contrast to the comedic overtones usually associated with other

disorders such as ASD and OCD. The brief examples above show an obvious common link: the alternate personalities depicted in media portrayals are, almost without exception, characterized as violent, dangerous, sadistic psychopaths, while the "real" personality is typically portrayed as quiet, passive, unassuming, and unlikely to harm anyone. The poster advertising for the film *Me, Myself, and Irene* (2000) perfectly encapsulates this stereotype with its tagline "From gentle to mental" and its two-sided face image—while determinedly adding to the confusion even more by giving its multiple-personality character a schizophrenia diagnosis, as we noted earlier. The "gentle/mental" split personalities in that film or in characters such as Jekyll and Hyde or Sméagol and Gollum typically comprise a "good" side and a "bad" side, and they are portrayed as all the more sinister precisely because of that dichotomy. As we suggested in Chapter Two, mental health disorders that are popularly understood to be uncontrolled or uncontained are typically portrayed negatively in the media because they represent unbridled madness, unchecked divergence from the order and norms that typically govern human society.

For a poorly understood, seldom-portrayed disorder, it is perhaps no surprise that there is limited research available on depictions of DID in popular media. What little exists is chiefly comprised of academic theses concerned with cinematic representations and sometimes further narrowed in focus to specific films. A brief journal article published by Peter Byrne in 2001 examined DID in film and listed films such as *Fight Club* and *Sybil* (Byrne, "The Butler[s]"). Byrne notes that "DID films are a popular and enduring genre" with mixed representations because the films tend to confuse DID and schizophrenia while also typically featuring violence, thus both doing "much harm to people with schizophrenia" while doing "psychiatry a favour" with faithful representations of DID (Byrne, "The Butler[s]").

The following sections discuss how DID is handled in two television programs, *Criminal Minds* and *United States of Tara*. As noted before, they are worth closer examination because of their differences—one is a crime show; one is a comedy—as well as their similarities. Although *Criminal Minds* offers a range of portrayals of DID, including some which follow in the traditional way of violence and danger, among that range is a more sympathetic depiction, and this is the approach also taken in *United States of Tara*.

"I couldn't do that. Please tell me I didn't do that": DID in *Criminal Minds*

To a casual viewer, crime series *Criminal Minds* embodies the classic mode of mental health representation to an almost ludicrously simple extent: anyone with a mental health condition appears to be a dangerous serial killer. The very premise of the show hardly allows otherwise: here we have the Behavioral Analysis Unit (BAU) of the FBI, comprised of "an elite team of FBI profilers who analyze the country's most twisted criminal minds, anticipating their next moves before they strike again" (CBS), as the network's promotional material reads on the program's website. Who are these "most twisted criminal minds," the viewer might ask? To which we are given an answer in the very first episode, as one of the BAU team members explains, "you think all we do is serial killers? Trust me, we cover the whole spectrum of psychos"—a psycho batch that does indeed include serial killers, including those with DID.

Indeed, DID is the "disorder of the day" on several episodes across the seasons. For example, serial killers with DID appear in Seasons 2 and 4, offering viewers the classic DID type: childhood abuse, alternate personalities, almost entirely unsympathetic villains designed only to inspire fear and loathing among viewers. DID also becomes a focal point across Season 12 when a serial killer from a previous season, named Peter Lewis but better known as Mr. Scratch or Scratch, escapes from prison and targets people with DID to brainwash them into new identities for murderous or other purposes. These characters experienced childhood abuse and developed DID and alternate personalities as coping mechanisms, which aligns with the DSM and theories of the trauma model, as noted earlier.

Given the wealth of material within this one series and its hundreds of episodes, it is not possible to fully cover in this part of the chapter all DID representations on *Criminal Minds* let alone the "whole spectrum" of mental health disorders. And, given the sometimes rather simple link between DID and danger in *Criminal Minds*, there seems little point in even attempting to do so. As such, the following discussion is inevitably truncated and represents only a snapshot of one moment within the series; much more could be added; many alternative episodes or story arcs may have been chosen for mental health disorder representations on the program. Yet for the purposes of this book, we are limiting it to one case study of DID in *Criminal Minds*, chosen because it offers some deviation from the usual scope of uncontrolled murderous violence more typically linked to DID in the rest of the series. That episode is Season 8's "All That Remains," which screened in 2013.

The episode opens with a home video of an apparently happy family gathering to admire the older daughter Sera as she gets ready for homecoming, with a loving mother, protective father, and excited younger sister Katie—the "little one" of the family, as her mother puts it—gathered around her. The screen then cuts to "Two years later" and the members of the BAU listen to a 911 call as the father, Bruce Morrison, reports his daughters missing. Suspicion is soon cast on the father as it emerges that not only has he no recollection of the last day or more, but, more tellingly, this call was placed on the same day as one year ago when he called 911 to report his wife missing—she has never been found, and again Bruce reported no memory of the time his wife went missing. Viewers learn Bruce was the suspect at the time but could not be charged because of lack of evidence. The BAU team travels to the scene, theorizing about possible scenarios and motives and suspects, but conclude the father is indeed the only viable suspect on the basis of the known facts.

Over the course of the episode, the younger daughter's body is found and Bruce is interrogated as the main suspect in her murder. During an interrogation, the BAU members witness a second personality emerge from Bruce: a violent, assertive man named Johnny, who castigates Bruce's daughters as selfish and ungrateful children "who walk all over him any chance they get [...] [Bruce] is hiding, of course. See, when he can't handle it, I save his ass. Bruce's problem is, he can't handle anything." Bruce is unaware of Johnny, waking from his transitions with no memory, and here viewers find familiar ground for the "gentle/mental" trope. Bruce is quiet, anxious for his family's wellbeing, an English professor and writer on a forced sabbatical from college after his wife went missing and he was unable to work because of grief. Johnny is confident, violent and confrontational with the daughters (as shown in flashbacks) and neighbors. He also acts on Bruce's behalf to exert some kind of power or control when Bruce feels unable to do so—perhaps a kind of attempt to regain order in a chaotic mental state. Bruce admits he feels like "I'm losing my mind" and cannot believe he would be able to murder his family, saying "I couldn't do that. Please tell me I didn't do that," dialogue that both insists he could not have done such a thing while also opening the door to the possibility that he just might have, albeit as someone else—thus wanting reassurance because he no longer trusts himself or feels confident of his own identity.

In an attempt to solve the murder, the BAU team then triggers his identity shift by producing a mock threat to his daughter by implying that the man who had an affair with Bruce's wife is now involved with Sera. They successfully provoke Bruce's transition and an enraged Johnny reveals that he did, after all, take Bruce's daughters away from their house because he was attempting to scare them to teach them respect. Although Johnny insists he did not kill the girls, such an alternate identity is hardly construed in the episode as trustworthy and so the situation seems fairly clear to viewers: Bruce/Johnny murdered his wife and then his daughters. Indeed, Johnny reveals enough information for the BAU team to locate the older daughter, who is injured but alive; viewers then watch a scene in which Sera confronts her father and urges him to get help. Thus it appears the crime has been solved and murderer, the man with DID, has been successfully captured.

Given the contested nature of DID itself, it seems appropriate that the BAU team also exhibit uncertainty about DID, although they never dispute the validity of DID itself, just the diagnosis of it: they refer to Bruce having DID but also note that they cannot confirm his diagnosis "yet." However, viewers are never encouraged to doubt that Bruce has DID, other than in the local detective's dismissive remark implying the DID is convenient, if not faked: "this is an easy way to cop an insanity plea"—returning us back to the *Murder, She Wrote* idea mentioned earlier. Moreover, when the BAU members review Bruce's medications, he has never apparently taken any medication for DID. Indeed, the sum total of information provided for viewers on what comprises DID is brief in this episode: it involves two personalities and memory loss, is usually caused by sexual abuse, is linked to chronic alcoholism, and its triggers for transitions can be alcohol and/or stress. This fits with Bruce for the most part. Bruce has had blackouts since graduate school when he began drinking because of the "pressure," and these coincide with Johnny's appearances. Although sexual abuse is never mentioned, Bruce did have abandonment issues or trauma when his mother died early and he was left with an alcoholic father. Bruce also has chronic alcoholism which triggers his transitions—in fact, he was sober until he learned his wife was having an affair, which led to him drinking again before her death; and he also is found to have been drinking at the time of the girls' disappearance. That the murderer is Bruce/Johnny seems a foregone conclusion when we learn that Bruce is no longer taking his anti-alcohol medication disulfarim because the prescription was recently stopped and that his drinking at the time of his wife's and daughter's murders was the likely trigger for Johnny's emergence and murder of the family.

So far, so simple, and the episode has played in line with probably most viewers' expectations that the murderer is the "gentle/mental" man with DID, the man with the unstable, violent, alternate identity Johnny. It would not be able to play on this, of course, unless there was already a precedent and thus public perception that DID is (often or always) linked to violence, which obviously prior episodes of *Criminal Minds* have not dispelled. Yet it is at this point that the episode takes a turn. When JJ, a member of the BAU team, takes Sera home, they realize that all is not as it seems: Sera is behaving oddly, the team discovers it was she who cancelled her father's prescription—triggering the problems—and JJ discovers the mother's missing items in a box of quilts for Katie. They rapidly theorize that Sera has psychopathic tendencies and planned her mother's and sister's murders and framing of her father meticulously—all because of jealousy relating to her belief that her younger sister was taking attention away from her. The real danger, then, is Sera, not the man with multiple personalities. It must be said that an observant viewer might have played an armchair detective far better than the BAU experts given that Sera had earlier revealed to JJ that her mother used to wrap her in the quilt made "for her little girl" before she was born; yet Katie, not Sera, was the one their mother referred to as "little one" on the home video, and JJ herself had seen the box of quilts made for Katie in the family's basement in an earlier search. Moreover, the home video shown at the start of the episode had ended on a frozen image when all members of the family were smiling at the camera, except for Sera who was, rather oddly, staring at Katie.

Such are the clues on which armchair detectives thrive, and, as always, we cannot forget that television programs typically operate within certain genres: in this case, crime. As noted in Chapter Two, the essence of the crime narrative is that the order of society is disturbed by a crime. In that context, the OCD disorder was in some ways an attempt to re-assert order. We can consider the same concepts in the context of our current discussion of *Criminal Minds*. In almost all cases, the crime—the disruption to societal order, literally the disorder—is perpetrated by someone with a mental health disorder and commonly *because* of their disorder, or more accurately, because their disorder has not been adequately treated by the medical and/or psychiatric professions. This disorder is now double fronted: it is societal (a crime disrupts the way things should be in a normal functioning society), and it is also personal (a mental illness disrupts the way things should be in a normal functioning human). In almost all cases, the crime—the societal disorder—is resolved by episode's end (or season's end, depending on the length of the story arc), but the mental illness (the personal disorder) is not. This is seen in this episode of *Criminal Minds* too: Bruce Morrison is left in an apparent void at the conclusion of the episode, apparently receiving neither therapy nor anti-psychotic medication, left walking into his now empty home after learning his wife and younger daughter have been murdered by his older daughter, who framed him. Societal order has been restored by the arrest of Sera, but there appears to be little hope for Bruce. This is true of *Criminal Minds* more broadly as a series (and probably most crime shows): even in its most sympathetic portrayals of criminal characters with mental health disorders, *Criminal Minds* rarely provides viewers with any mention of what lies in store for the perpetrator following the revelation of the crime's solution; we might presume most are sent to prison hospitals and receive treatment but we do not know, and as such the true cause of the disruption to societal disorder—that society has failed to adequately treat those with mental health disorders, and protect others from the negative outcomes of that undertreatment—remains unresolved.

We cannot end this admittedly brief treatment of mental illness in *Criminal Minds* without noting two final points. Based on the program's premise and opening episode—the "whole spectrum of psychos"—it is tempting for viewers to immediately assume that the show adopts a simplistic demarcation

between the heroes of the BAU and the villains of the mentally ill, but as they quickly learn from the first episode, the BAU team itself is not exempt from mental health disorders: the team members regularly suffer psychological trauma and other ill effects of their work. Indeed, the BAU lead at the time of the series opener, Jason Gideon (Mandy Patinkin), had experienced a "nervous breakdown" as one character puts it (or a "major depressive episode," as another character corrects him).

In this context it is particularly telling to recall public comments made by the original series lead, Mandy Patinkin, published in 2012, five years after leaving the program. In what we can read as a case of blurring lines between representation and reality, Patinkin was quoted saying he found the experience of acting on the program "very destructive to my soul and my personality" (Paskin). According to Patinkin, "The biggest public mistake I ever made was that I chose to do *Criminal Minds* in the first place […] I thought it was something very different. I never thought they were going to kill and rape all these women every night, every day, week after week, year after year" (Paskin). Patinkin's unease with the content of the program also extends to the viewers, as he questions what effect such representations have on reality: "I'm concerned about the effect it has. Audiences all over the world use this programming as their bedtime story. This isn't what you need to be dreaming about" (Paskin). The determinedly serious *Criminal Minds*—beginning and ending each episode with a portentous quote voiced by one of the characters—offers a dark picture of the world and apparently little hope of restoration for anyone in it, whether those dangerous people with mental health disorders or those who hunt them. Order is always restored at a societal level, but never maintained; and order appears to be never restored at a psychological level. Ultimately, Bruce/Johnny becomes less of a dangerous character to fear than a tragic one to pity for what he has lost.

"Why can't Mom just be manic depressive like all the other moms?" *United States of Tara*

If *Criminal Minds* takes viewers on a familiar journey of the "gentle/mental" dual personality trope before then subverting that very same trope, *United States of Tara* attempts to forge a new path. First airing in 2009 and running for three reasons, *Tara* is a comedy-drama that tells the story of Tara Gregson, living in suburban Overland Park, Kansas with her husband Max and children Kate and Marshall, and several of her alternate identities.

Like *Criminal Minds*, the first episode of *Tara* begins with a home video, although unlike *Criminal Minds* this video is not a happy prelude to tragedy but casts viewers immediately into chaos. Tara uses a home video to explain that she feels unable to cope with the "pressure" (we are reminded of the same phrase used by Bruce in *Criminal Minds* to signal his onset of DID), which arises from her work (mural painting for wealthy women) and even more so from her feelings of failure as a parent, after she discovers her teenage daughter has a prescription for a morning-after pill. As the video ends with Tara visibly distressed and in tears, she transitions into one of her alters: T, a provocatively dressed teen with a rather one-note fixation on sex who then tells Kate that "your mom is in a bad place mentally" and viewers discover that it was actually T who aided Kate to get the "kill pills," which is somewhat ironic given Tara's comments on the video. T is gently humored by Tara's son and husband as they return home and seem unfazed by her appearance, providing a stark contrast to the reaction of Tara's sister, Charmaine, who is upset and dismissive when she realizes "my sister isn't home tonight." Charmaine is positioned as the skeptic, asking Max "why can't she just stop? I mean, it's not even a real disease." This skepticism is countered by the family's supportive, protective reactions, seen in a variety of responses: Max responds to Charmaine that is a real disease and that "we're all angry at the crazy" even despite living with it for seventeen years. Later, when T attempts to seduce Max, he refuses because Tara does not want sex with him during one of her transitions; Marshall attempts to hide the sounds of T's violent outburst from their neighbors to protect her from being judged; Kate is cast as a typically angst-filled, defiant teenager angry at the world (and particularly her mother) yet nonetheless defends Tara to her boyfriend and confesses she is happy her mother is no longer on medication. When Tara emerges again, she cannot remember what has happened during her time as T and attempts to make amends with her family. In a later scene she attempts to stop Kate's boyfriend who is behaving violently to Kate, but is unsuccessful, retreating to her car and crying; again she transitions but this time to Buck, a redneck male who smokes, shoots guns, and takes the opportunity to attack Kate's boyfriend when next Buck sees him.

These scenes of the opening episode offer five of the main themes that recur in the three seasons that follow: Tara transitions into her alters in moments of stress; her alters all attempt to perform mothering or protective roles when she cannot, albeit often in imperfect ways; her relationship with her family can be strained but is more usually characterized by a remarkably supportive husband and children; there are moments of skepticism about the legitimacy of the disorder that are variously articulated and then quashed; and on the whole Tara struggles to manage her condition but demonstrates agency in her commitment to do so, whether choosing to take medication or not, while consistently seeking counseling. Although a book could perhaps be written about the series' treatment of DID, here we take each of these themes in turn to examine how they work together to construct DID on screen.

From the very first scene of Tara's distress leading to her transition to T, viewers quickly understand that stress is a trigger for DID, which prompts Kate to say, "Everything is a trigger lately. Why can't mom just be manic depressive like all the other moms? You can't expect me to be the perfect child all the time just because mom acts like a bunch of different people when she's stressed out." As we saw in those early scenes, however, it is not simply feeling "stressed out" that triggers the transitions but Tara's feeling that she cannot cope and cannot fulfill the roles she has in her world. She then becomes someone who can. As much as these transitions involve a sense of the ridiculous and comical, then, they are, in fact, quite logical and rational in that they are almost always for the purposes of performing maternal and self-protective roles that Tara cannot take on herself. For instance, after Kate rejects Tara's attempts to talk about sex, and Marshall rejects Tara's help to solve a problem with his teacher, and fellow mothers from the children's school treat Tara condescendingly and imply she cannot be relied on for the bake sale, a third alter Alice appears, cast somewhat in the classic Stepford Wife mold: perfectly groomed, impeccably mannered, and an expert in all things baking. Alice both restores familial relationships—resolving Marshall's teacher difficulties, helping Kate connect with Tara by creating a photo album of family photographs—and social relationships, handing an elaborately decorated cake to the bake sale, to the surprise of the women. Similarly, Buck, as we saw earlier, stepped in to protect Kate when Tara could not, while T attempts to relate to Kate in ways Tara cannot. Even when T apparently acts against Marshall's interests by kissing a boy Marshall was attracted to, Kate explains that Tara/T did this to protect Marshall from someone who would do him harm. Thus, in these ways and others, all three identities perform helpful roles in Tara's place.

By far the most important role of these alters is to help uncover Tara's past so that she can understand and overcome her disorder, thus serving not only the needs of her family but also herself. As Max puts it, "we knew when you were off the meds the whole gang would resurface […] We can't begin to understand why you need them unless we let them show themselves." Tara has begun experiencing her three main alters since stopping her medication, and these help protect her children, but three others also emerge to provide a self-protective benefit to Tara herself. Gimme expresses the rage Tara represses; Shoshana is a therapist Tara becomes (and whom Tara believes she is seeing as her patient) when Tara is seeking more help and exploring her past; and Chicken is Tara's five-year-old self emerging as their quest to uncover her past trauma progresses (Buck also actively investigates Tara's past to help find the truth). All these alters are then construed in their variously flawed ways as helpful to Tara and those she loves; at one point, Tara even describes them as "friends."

Although these seem positive roles of the alters, it is also clear from the start of the program that DID has a significant impact on Tara's social and family relationships. Tara has no friends to speak of, dropped out of college because of a suicide attempt, finds her employment jeopardized when one of her alters sabotages a mural and gets her fired, has a difficult relationship with her sister for much of the series, and an even more negative relationship with her parents. On the whole, Tara's husband and children are supportive yet they are also variously at odds with Tara: Kate is openly hostile and angry in earlier episodes, although mellowing over the three seasons; Marshall begins as fully supportive but has several pivotal scenes where he turns against Tara; even Max, who is the most remarkably supportive husband, has moments of anger and rage, including some memorable scenes in the final episode of the series in which he rages against the world for allowing his wife to suffer as she has. Some cases of family conflict are caused by Tara's alters, such as when T kissed the boy Marshall liked, or Buck has an affair with a waitress, Pammy, who previously flirted with Max (and with whom Max later has an affair too). Yet by series end the family bonds have been restored, and even Tara's relationship with her sister is significantly more positive.

To this extent the series entirely avoids the "gentle/mental" trope mentioned earlier. However, this changes in the third season when a new alter appears, one who causes the most serious damage to Tara's familial relationships, her treatment progression, and her attempts to complete her college degree. Prior to the emergence of this seventh alter, Tara and her husband had been seeking therapy and attempting to understand what happened in the past that caused Tara's DID, because Tara has no memory of her childhood and her mother is unwilling to discuss it with her. Initially Tara and Max believe the cause of DID to be a rape when she was a teenager, but it emerges that the rape was a re-traumatization of a much earlier time of sexual abuse; her abuser was her step-brother Bryce Craine, who also abused Charmaine, and after some time their mother sent them into foster care until she could arrange for her husband's son to be removed and the girls to return home. They learn that the alter Alice is based on the foster mother of that earlier time.

It is against this backdrop of childhood trauma that the seventh alter makes an appearance. The alter is Tara's abuser (and now deceased) Bryce Craine, a menacing and violent personality who slowly decimates Tara's world. Bryce punches Tara's son Marshall and is only stopped from doing worse by the intervention of Max. Bryce cuts Tara and also poisons Tara's therapist at the time, Dr. Hattaras, in an attempt to kill him. Yet even this alter is performing a protective role, in a particularly twisted sense. As one of Tara's therapists puts it, the Bryce Craine personality is "a paradox, the self turning against itself" in an effort to protect Tara against the abuser. Bryce then proceeds to "murder" all of Tara's alters and tells Hattaras that Tara is next, and Tara's family discuss whether or not she might need to be committed; "locked up" in a "rubber-room country club," a prospect none of them relishes. However, the series ends with Tara herself "murdering" Bryce by jumping off a bridge in an apparent suicide attempt, during which viewers watch Tara torturing Bryce in water to kill him. In the final scene as Tara leaves for a new attempt at treatment in a specialist clinic in Boston, not only has Bryce apparently vanished for good but her original three alters from the first few episodes have reappeared: Alice, T, and Buck, signaling a relative return to normality for Tara.

It is clear that these aspects of the series reflect the major aspects of DID outlined earlier: a history of sexual trauma, multiple personalities, memory loss, and significant distress and impaired functioning (although the impaired functioning is debatable—Tara suffers in social and employment and academic settings but is remarkably functional in her familial environment, even insisting to Hattaras that "mostly I live a very functional life"). If this is reasonably aligned with the DSM-5 summary, it is also perhaps fitting that *Tara* directly addresses the confusion and skepticism about the condition. Initially the voice of doubt is Charmaine, who also blithely refers to Tara having a "schizophrenic situation," to which Tara replies—although ironically contributing to misinformation herself about mental health—that "schizophrenia is when you hear voices [...] I don't hear voices" (to which Charmaine dryly responds, "Right, you do the whole character"). Kate also echoes this skepticism at one point but does on the whole fall in line with the family acceptance; Charmaine later bonds with Tara via her alters and ceases to be skeptical. More skepticism is evident in scenes with the waitress Pammy. When Tara attempts to explain to Pammy that she has a disorder, using *Sybil* as an example, Pammy is angry and says, "It's always the disease's fault, isn't it? Never someone just being an asshole." The strongest voice of doubt comes in the character of Dr. Hattaras, who first appears in season three when Tara returns to college and takes his Abnormal Psychology course. Tara transitions in her first class and lectures to the class as her alter Shoshana; although she later apologizes and explains her situation to Hattaras, he is given a number of skeptical lines that encompass the main thrust of the arguments of the anti–DID camp:

> Psychology's most intriguing diagnosis, DID. [...] What if DID—which incidentally is rarely diagnosed outside North America—didn't really exist? Perhaps DID is nothing more than an excuse, a crutch that severely damaged people use to hide behind to avoid facing the reality of the pain they are feeling? Or is it a performance they put on merely to get attention? And you did get our attention. Now, if you have read my work and, please, don't patronize me, you will know which side of the debate I sleep on. But

perhaps I'm wrong. [...] It's junk psychology. It's just a way for victimized people to rationalize behaviors they'd rather not take responsibility for.

Hattaras eventually admits to Tara that he has changed him mind about the validity of DID, but this is at a high cost after he has been poisoned (by Tara as Bryce) and forbidden to see Tara again for counseling or any other reason.

Dealing with skepticism or rejection of the disease's very existence is not the only struggle Tara has to manage when it comes to DID. Others are articulated throughout the series, whether it is financial, with references to the expenses of Tara's treatment, or geographical in nature, with difficulties locating any local therapist who specializes in DID and resulting in Tara seeking treatment in Chicago and Boston. At one point, Max notes angrily that "the Overland Park mental health system hasn't exactly worked wonders for us in the past." Tara is devastated when her season one therapist Dr. Ocean tells her she needs to seek treatment elsewhere with someone else more experienced in DID; the concept of therapist inexperience with DID is reiterated later when Dr. Hattaras is castigated by his senior colleague for attempting to treat Tara and risking a lawsuit. Tara's experiences with medications seem equally unsuccessful, with the various medications either turning her into "drooling in the corner like a vegetable," or shown to stop working, such as when she finds her alters emerging despite the medication. During a stay at a DID clinic, Tara meets a fellow patient with DID who tells her that she has been successfully "integrated," although some doubt is cast over this when the woman then explains that a previous integration did not in fact last. Tara does, however, make progress in her therapy. She achieves "co-consciousness" with her alters and is able to communicate with them and even control them—in a pivotal scene Tara holds a summit with the alters and orders them to sign a contract because "I am dissolving the United States of Tara and declaring myself king." Across the series it is clear to viewers that there is no simple treatment or medication or solution to DID: whatever medication Tara tries, or therapist she meets, or however much she learns about her traumatic past, none of this can fully resolve her DID.

Ultimately, as with Bruce/Johnny in *Criminal Minds*, Tara is somewhat of a tragic figure, portrayed sympathetically as the victim of trauma that has left her unable to cope without splitting into various personalities to perform the roles in life she feels unable to manage. Unlike Bruce/Johnny, however, Tara retains a great deal of sense of agency: she is actively seeking help and has the (mostly unfailing) support of her family as she attempts to regain some sense of control and order in her life. The semi-comic tone of the series also naturally counteracts the sense of tragedy that might otherwise be inevitable, offering instead a more nuanced version of DID than the rather simplistic "gentle/mental" dualities seen more commonly. Most positively, the series ends on a note of hope as Tara pursues another course of treatment, again supported by her husband, and in this case the hope seems justified in that she has been referred to people who are considered experts in treating DID. She remains committed to wanting more from life; as she puts it, "I don't want to spend my entire life being the woman who has DID." The final scene shows her in a car with Max as they drive to the new clinic, with the lyrics of the song repeating, "Tell me who I am," underlining Tara's determined pursuit of regaining her identity and sense of self.

Conclusions

Often confused with each other, and both usually associated with unbridled and murderous violence, DID and schizophrenia do not typically fare well in terms of televisual representations being particularly nuanced or what one might consider accurate. Yet this appears to be changing to more sympathetic portrayals as seen in the episodes discussed here, with far more nuanced depictions than have been seen in previous decades. Allowing Buffy to be associated with schizophrenia offers the potential for a somewhat sympathetic rendering of the mental health disorder, despite the episode's more troubling aspects. And although both Bruce and Tara exhibit the "gentle/mental" stereotype of DID (with Johnny and Bryce respectively), both programs also position the characters sympathetically. Moreover, both *Criminal Minds* and *Tara* (perhaps unwittingly in the case of *Criminal Minds*), reinforce the failure of a society that has not adequately treated either person. The main differences lie in the final scenes for each character: Bruce is a tragic figure left without hope or family; while Tara is a loved mother and wife and sister, who is actively seeking help and attempting to regain her self and thus control over her life. In the next chapter, we turn to another disorder historically associated with uncontrolled violence: bipolar disorder.

FOUR

"The inspirational, the enthusiastic, the unusual"

Bipolar Disorder

The psychotic mood disorder bipolar disorder (sometimes still known by its previous common usage name of manic depression) is one which has often been represented on television. Where once it was used primarily as a device to explain the psychotic behavior of murderous criminals as with schizophrenia and DID, bipolar disorder has undergone something of a metamorphosis in recent years. This chapter surveys recent screen depictions to see how realistic they might be, how the illness is conceptualized, and how bipolar episodes are treated by the other characters. It particularly focuses on *90210* and *Homeland*, both of which won Voice Awards for showing leadership in raising awareness of mental health conditions, and *Shameless*, which has also opted for a more informed approach than used to be typical. In all three of these programs, at least one character with the disorder has a lead role, and the show's writing and production teams have expressed a sense of responsibility in their depictions, citing research and/or family experience as informing their story and character development choices.

Background: What Is Bipolar Disorder?

Bipolar disorder is a mood affective disorder. It is thought that bipolar disorder only affects about 2 or 3 percent of the population overall (Armstrong). Its most extreme form was once known as "manic depression," signifying the manic highs and depressive lows which can be characteristic of the illness. There are several variations of the ways in which the illness manifests, and these have typically not coalesced with popular conceptions. As

Fast and Preston argue, bipolar disorder should more properly be known as the "bipolar spectrum of disorders" or "multi-polar disorder" (Fast and Preston 18). These variants include Bipolar I, Bipolar II, cyclothymia, and rapid cycling bipolar.

According to the DSM-IV, a patient with Bipolar I experiences one or more manic or mixed episodes. Patients with Bipolar II, which is reported to be more prevalent (Belmaker), experience at least one hypomanic episode as well as major depressive episodes. Cyclothymia is diagnosed when the patient experiences hypomanic episodes but the periods of depression do not meet the criteria for major depressive episodes. Rapid cycling bipolar is properly defined as being experienced by those individuals who have four or more episodes per year and represents only between 5 and 15 percent of all people with the condition (Sadock and Sadock). This cohort is predominantly female and has typically had both depressive and hypomanic episodes. It is estimated that between 10 and 20 percent of all patients with bipolar are unipolar manic; that is, they do not experience periods of clinical depression (Sadock and Sadock).

Symptoms include:

- rapidity of speech
- an overuse of metaphor and alliteration
- hypersexuality
- irritability
- grandiosity
- wildly creative thoughts
- sleeplessness
- anxiety
- loss of judgment and impulse control
- paranoia
- problems maintaining focus, attention and concentration
- in some cases, hallucinations and/or episodes of violence may also occur

Psychosis (a severe break with reality) is the typical end result of an unmediated episode (Fast and Preston). Some patients may have a single episode; others may be seasonally affected; some are only diagnosed post-partum; others may enter into long periods of remission.

The key criterion for diagnosing bipolar disorder is the occurrence of manic episodes (Belmaker). Full mania is an elevated, expansive or irritable mood (Sadock and Sadock), moving into psychosis (an absence of judgment). A bipolar episode is considered to be a medical emergency because psychosis may be associated with mania, and suicidal ideation with depression (Belmaker). Clinicians are encouraged to seek collateral information from relatives, friends and co-workers as patients may appear to have moments of rationality even while in this state (Belmaker). Individuals who respond well to treatment, however, may go years without major incidents or hospitalization.

Unchecked hypomania may develop into mania but is less severe; although still characterized by sleeplessness, racing thoughts and hyperactivity, it lacks psychosis and symptoms which would suggest the individual may cause self-harm or harm to others (Belmaker 476). Although hypomania may lead to large scale mania, as is often depicted in popular television series, early intervention can prevent this. Ironically, the stigma that is in part created and continued by popular culture representations can prevent individuals from seeking assistance (*Mindframe*) and it is when symptoms are ill managed that psychosis is likely to develop.

Bipolar in the Media

Given the variety of types of bipolar, it would be understandable if there were a variety of on-screen representations, just as there are variations in the ways in which patients with the disorder present. Instead, most representations until relatively recently have kept to a clearly negative and under-nuanced stereotype: a less-than-functional person whose moods change radically several times a day, and who displays aggression, seductive behavior, eccentricity and self-obsession in their interactions with other characters (*Mindframe*). These characters are often violent criminals, despite the wealth of research which clearly demonstrates that people with mental health disorders are more likely to be victims than perpetrators of violence (*Mindframe*; SANE Australia).

Perhaps the biggest misconception around bipolar disorder is the notion that all patients will rapid cycle from extreme highs to extreme lows on a daily basis. Indeed, this presentation, known as Ultradian cycling (Tillman and Geller), is so rare that it is suspected to be a different illness altogether. Nevertheless, it appears to be the most common mass media representation of individuals with bipolar disorder and is often used for on-screen dramatic effect.

Bothersome Brothers, Mad Mothers and Delinquent Daughters

As noted earlier in Chapter Three, the mentally ill as erratic criminal is a trope that has long been used in dramatic television. A 2005 study of representations of mental illness within long-running police procedural *Law and Order*, for example, found that the incidence of perpetrators pleading "Not Guilty by Reason of Mental Defect" was some four to five times higher than the real-life prevalence (Gans-Boriskin and Wardle). So common have these been that a series of psychiatrist characters—Drs. Olivet, Skoda and Huang—have been added to the cast of the franchise in order to assess the criminally insane. In Season 7 of *Law and Order: SVU*, a teenager, Jamie Hoskine, makes false rape accusations against classmates before running down nine pedestrians and killing one as the direct result of failing to take her medication for bipolar disorder. Closer to home, Detective Elliot Stabler, then one of the two leads in the series, in Season 10 finally faces his estranged and unmedicated bipolar mother, Bernadette in order to help his second daughter, Kathleen, newly diagnosed with the illness and facing drug and theft charges.

In HBO's *Six Feet Under*, Billy Chenowith, the younger brother of Brenda, is given a significant amount of screen time over the series' six seasons. Billy's behavior is often troubling and sometimes sinister, ranging from incestuous jealousy to psychotic stalking. These excesses are blamed on his bipolar diagnosis. On Showtime's *The Big C*, main character and terminal melanoma patient Cathy Jamison is often shown worrying about her eccentric, anti-establishment and sometimes homeless brother, Sean. Sean clearly does not adhere to society's guidelines and is vocal in his rejection of consumerism, preferring to spend time at Cathy's home re-sorting her recyclables, and feeding himself by dumpster diving. It is not until the second season that Cathy mentions that Sean has a diagnosis of bipolar disorder, asking a psychologist for advice on how to break to him the news of her cancer. The counselor is singularly unhelpful, suggesting that she "call 911" if Sean takes the news badly.

Elsewhere, the character with bipolar who is unreliable and causes problems for family members can be found in a range of iterations, usually in a short term role: as Waverly Grady, the teenage daughter of a local pastor who takes her boyfriend for a sexy midnight swim after ceasing her medication in *Friday Night Lights*; Maggie Wyczenski, the mother of *ER*'s Dr. Abby Lockhart, whose very existence Abby denies and whose bipolar condition prompts Abby to have an abortion rather than risk passing on the disorder; in *Shameless*, first Marty, the brother of the Gallaghers' neighbor Veronica and then Monica, the estranged Gallagher matriarch, are introduced as characters whose bipolar disorder creates havoc. Marty is an alcoholic prison escapee with Tourette's Syndrome and bipolar disorder, whom Veronica describes as a "shrink's wet dream." Monica Gallagher returns periodically to the family she repeatedly abandons—notably leading to the conceptions of younger children (Debs, Carl and Liam), and her on-screen return to the family in Season 2 coincides with a bipolar episode and a suicide attempt during Thanksgiving dinner. In all of these representations, there is a suggestion that bipolar disorder is a destructive force that ruins lives and families.

Shameless does examine the disorder in a rather more nuanced way when it is later applied to one of the ensemble leads, middle child Ian, played by Cameron Monaghan. The series returns to the topic of bipolar disorder in the Season 4 finale, when it becomes evident that Ian has inherited the disorder from his mother. Despite this, viewers see Ian making sensible choices in his career and personal life as he—unlike his mother—commits to taking responsibility for managing his illness. Two other recent and more nuanced depictions of bipolar disorder are those of Erin Silver in *90210* and Carrie Mathison in *Homeland,* who also have lead roles within the respective televisual narratives. Both are sympathetic characters and are shown to be capable of completing studies and managing careers. Each lives independently from her family, requiring their support only when in a rare psychotic episode, or its immediate aftermath. In the space of a decade or so, bipolar disorder has moved from being televisual shorthand for erratic, violent and criminal behavior towards some more balanced and positive representations in recent series.

"I don't want my whole life to be about that": Bipolar Disorder in *90210*

Erin Silver is one of the six characters who led the ensemble cast at the heart of the 2008 reboot of the late Aaron Spelling's *Beverly Hills 90210* franchise. Generally known only by her surname, the half-sister of original characters Kelly Taylor and David Silver, Silver, seen as a baby and toddler in the original series, provides the crossover point between the two iterations. Throughout the first season she is shown to be a free spirit with unusual dress sense, obscure taste in music and a predilection for horror films. Towards the end of the season, however, Silver has her first manic episode. Silver later appears to be in remission for entire seasons, with one other notable manic episode in Season 3, but otherwise behaving much as the other characters do.

Early characterization and language demonstrate that the prevailing attitude within the series is that mental ill health or "madness" is undesirable, and slang terms to describe it are casually invoked. Within the text, Silver is described as being "out of her mind" by one of her peers in the very first episode of the series. Silver is characterized from the outset as being different from her peers at West Beverly High. Her tumultuous family situation—early in the season she moves into a women's shelter where she had previously volunteered—is in stark contrast with the stable home environment of small-town Kansas imports, the Wilson family. Silver's sense of not-quite-belonging within one's family is explored through her romance with Dixon Wilson. Silver confides to him that her mother drinks, but the language once again echoes commonly used descriptions of the mentally ill: "When she's like this, she's a completely different person. ... sometimes it scares me." Dixon bonds with her over their shared outsider status, for he is an African American teenager growing up within an Anglo-American family. He also obliquely mentions his birth mother for the first time, noting, "I know what it's like to be around someone who's wasted out of their mind. I know what that stuff does to people. I swore I'd never do it myself." This foreshadows the addictive tendencies he and his mother will be shown to share in the future as well as linking himself and Silver as adolescent children of addicts.

The greatest parallel in story arcs, however, is between the characters of Dixon's biological mother and Silver, when they are revealed to share a diagnosis of bipolar disorder. When Dixon first speaks about his mother's mental illness and how it led to his being adopted by the Wilsons, he uses common vernacular in his recount: "Unfortunately, she was crazy. Not so big on taking medication, so long story short: Social Services came. Took me away." Similarly, his reactions to Silver's behaviors are also somewhat unreconstructed. As he confides to a friend mid-season, he regrets that Silver is "a little much sometimes, with the whole negativity and moodiness." Somewhat problematically, her "negativity and moodiness" had not really been evident on screen up until that point. Indeed, it is immediately after this comment that the viewer sees the first signs of mania in Silver. Dixon interrupts her discourse on sandcastle architecture to tell her that he loves her, which startles her. Dixon is hurt that she does not respond in kind and Silver's emotional and verbose reaction is also surprising: "And now you're mad at me. That's fantastic. One minute you love me and the next you're mad at me? What is that? ... That's not fair. I didn't do anything. Why are you mad at me? Because I didn't say exactly what you said to me? Is that why you're mad? Because if that's what you want me to do, we'll do it. Or you could just write me cue cards. Then I could read what you want me to say." Dixon compounds matters by asking her to "stop acting like a freak," which prompts her to destroy the sandcastle and storm off. Throughout this scene, Silver's speech is faster than usual, and her emotions appear heightened, as is characteristic of a bipolar individual during a hypomanic phase.

Silver demonstrates a notable loss of empathy when hypomanic, and her sense of stability is further threatened when her favorite teacher, Mr. Matthews, returns to the school after a suspension and requests that she be transferred out of his class because of commentary she had placed on her vlog at the time of his departure. Silver appears to be truly baffled by this turn of events, unable to understand why her vilification of the teacher might lead to his not wanting to teach her. Silver comes up with a grandiose plan to "win Mr. Matthews back" by writing "the best paper on *Heart of Darkness* that has ever been written in the history of English papers anywhere. Ever." When her sister finds her the next morning, she asks if Silver was up all night, and the signs of mania (sleeplessness, intensity, lack of empathy, grandiosity and fast speech) are present as Silver exclaims, "Genius doesn't sleep." This hyperintense focus on an academic assignment is also explored in *Homeland*, as it was a similar incident in college which led to Carrie's diagnosis. It is a symptom of psychosis which is common among patients; indeed, hyperintensity and an increased interest in creative endeavors were mentioned by all of our interviewees with bipolar disorder (see Chapter Six).

Silver continues to demonstrate impulsivity, rapidity of speech, hypersexuality and hyper-enthusiasm, all signs of a manic episode. When we next see Silver and Dixon, Silver is excitedly ranking the places in which they've had sex: "So, media room: much better than under the bleachers but not as good as the cafeteria. Where do you want to try next? Some place really freaky!" When Dixon suggests a bed, she goes off on a tangent of associated words and ideas: "Bed in a furniture store? Tanning bed? Bed of flowers?" The connection of words is something which is characteristic of a manic episode, and which is also displayed as a significant symptom in *Homeland* and *Shameless*. Her behavior is similarly overenthusiastic when she discusses her English assignment with Mr. Matthews, declaring how much she loves poetry. Matthews is thrilled to see her "inspired" but goes on to say, "I also believe you could lay off the coffee a bit." Silver asks to be allowed to film her poetry response, a request to which Mr. Matthews agrees.

It is during this manic episode that she makes a decision that she wants to go into filmmaking as a career. During the filming process, Silver is shown to be unusually intense and driven. She claims that from the moment she decided to analyze the poem through film, she knew what each shot and each scene should be. It is important to note that the mania Silver is experiencing here is still somewhat true to her personality. Although she is in a manic state when she realizes that she wants to be a filmmaker, this is the career which she eventually pursues, long after the mania has passed. Even her arguments behind her career choice are cogent, despite her elevation (shown chiefly through the rapidity of her speech): "It totally makes sense. I've always been a visual person, but I'm crap at painting and drawing. So film is the perfect medium. I don't have to make the image, I just have to capture it and connect them." Mr. Matthews is encouraging, but when Silver announces that she needs 45 minutes to do her presentation, he is rather more dismissive: "Are you out of your mind? Aim for ten. We have other students in the class."

Not all of Silver's manic behaviors are true to her personality, however. Silver demonstrates symptoms of anxiety when the movie theater she has hired for the premiere of her movie, *Love, Love, Love,* is not full. She is also uncharacteristically devoid of empathy, when Dixon tries to reassure her about the size of the audience, Silver is rude and dismissive: "I put a big invite on my blog ... the people who read it are losers, what could they possibly have going on tonight?" When Mr. Matthews introduces her film, he refers to her as the "inspirational, the enthusiastic, the unusual Erin Silver."

Silver's enthusiasm quickly becomes problematic, however, when it becomes apparent that Silver has included a sexual tryst with Dixon in the film. Silver is oblivious as to why this makes her audience—not to mention Dixon—uncomfortable. Dixon asks what is wrong with her, pathologizing her behavior, and accuses her of having no boundaries. He is adamant that he does not want to see her again, and echoes Mr. Matthews' question: "Are you out of your mind?"

Silver's heightened emotional state, manic behavior and the repetition of this particular phrase combine to trigger full psychosis. When Mr. Matthews returns to his apartment, he discovers a smashed window and a furious Silver, who is talking rapidly and making paranoid accusations: "You never got over it, did you? You pretended to. You pretended to forgive me. ... You did this to turn Dixon against me.... You wanna know how I figured it out? Last night, in the media lab, you said to me: are you out of your mind? And then tonight Dixon said to me: are you out of your mind?" The episode ends with Silver erratic, violent and glaring. The suggestion that she may be dangerous while in this state is heightened by the use of discordant music over the final image of Silver in a chair, like a cornered animal.

At the start of the next episode, Mr. Matthews easily outsmarts and disarms a frightened and confused Silver, who then hides from him. The rest of the episode centers around the efforts of her friends, family and the police to find Silver before she harms herself or someone else. Dixon is forced to tell his parents about Silver's increasingly obsessive behavior; meanwhile, Mr. Matthews tries to convince Silver's sister Kelly that there is "something going on with her."

Silver is revealed to be at a railway station, seeking a train to Kansas— the state where Dixon and the Wilsons lived prior to moving to Beverly Hills. A stranger notices her erratic behavior and engages her in a conversation, which quickly becomes another fast-paced monologue on Silver's part, using a complicated analogy in which she and Dixon are baking soda and vinegar reacting chemically—somewhat ironically, given that her behavior at the time is the result of atypical brain chemistry. Her rapid-fire word association and absence of clear logic are common real-world behaviors associated with bipolar disorder and are also seen in *Homeland* and *Shameless.* When we asked interviewees which behaviors were accurately shown in these television portrayals, this aspect featured prominently (see Chapter Six).

The man from the railway station follows Silver, and he is later seen going through her wallet and taking her phone while she sleeps fitfully in a chair. The dramatic twist, here, is that although the people closest to her have remained oblivious to her disorder, the stranger identifies and understands what is going on, having witnessed a family member's psychotic episode. Silver is very vulnerable at this point and at risk of harm, but not from the apparently sinister stranger, who checks her identification and uses the phone to make contact with her loved ones and alert them to her whereabouts. Silver is still paranoid, however, and panics and runs for the tracks when she wakes and see him watching over her.

It is only when Silver races towards an oncoming train that Dixon recognizes an echo of his mother's behaviors. He then offers to assist Silver with finding help, to which she agrees. Dixon explains to his parents, "She's manic depressive. … Silver has bipolar disorder. Just like my birth Mom. It has to be." Again, the language used is noteworthy, as he first uses an outdated term for the disorder. His adoptive parents later excuse his responses to Silver's condition, saying that it "must have been like lightning striking twice" for him to have both a parent and a girlfriend with the same condition. Silver's uncharacteristic behavior is a symptom of an undiagnosed mental health disorder yet is treated rather less sympathetically than that of her boyfriend, whose unsympathetic behavior is due only to stubbornness.

Dixon admits that although he had recognized Silver's moods and found her conversations to be manipulative, as his did his mother's, he did not put it all together until he "saw how she shifted from so happy to so despondent. It all made sense." Unfortunately, this commentary of Dixon's makes little sense within the context of the program. Silver did not appear to be happy at the railway station; she was confused, paranoid and obsessive. Despite the generally very accurate depiction of bipolar disorder in the character of Erin Silver as played by Stroup, the lines given to other characters unfortunately align with earlier and arguably harmful stereotypes about rapid cycling from euphoria to depression.

The series *90210* is unusual in that it gives air time to Silver's care after her discharge from the hospital. Further, the character is given scope to voice her frustrations with others' responses to her after her diagnosis, including her sister's zealous attempts to minimize "excitement" in order to keep Silver's moods stable; the infantilizing effects of this; and the tendency of others to question the validity of Silver's moods and emotional responses, viewing them instead as potential symptoms of a medical crisis related her disorder.

Silver's diagnosis and all its heightened drama come two-thirds of the way through the season. A number of the episodes which follow examine the tensions which can arise between a person with bipolar recovering from hospitalization, and family members tasked with caregiving. Outpatient care recommendations include recreating the routine of hospital, limiting stimulation and encouraging medication compliance (bpHope). Silver finds this regime boring and is perfectly capable of articulating her frustrations, but her sister does not appear to hear her concerns. When asked to rate her level of irritation, Silver retorts, "I was a 4, but you asking me that question bumped me up to 6." When asked if she would like to journal before bed, Silver replies in the negative, and adds, "Nor would I like to use the word 'journal' as a verb." When Kelly bans Silver from attending a movie premiere, Silver uses the language of the mood chart strategy against her carer: "Mood: Angry. Level 10." Later in the episode she admits that the movie premiere would have been too much, but insists that she still needs some spontaneity, arguing cogently that she has a personality beyond her bipolar disorder: "I don't want my whole life to be about that." Silver neatly encapsulates the frustrations of adult bipolar patients who find the care regime to be somewhat infantilizing.

Following Silver's diagnosis and recovery, Dixon reassesses his perceptions about mental health and mental health disorders, confiding to Annie that he feels enormous guilt around his adoption, because he was "so mad at [his] mom for being crazy, you know? So I chose adoption. I left her. Ever since all this happened with Silver, I see things differently. She had a disease. It wasn't her fault. So I just want to see how she's doing. Tell her I'm sorry."

Dixon's new understanding of his mother's condition is particularly interesting since throughout the series he remains the character who uses the most unreconstructed language with regard to mental illness; from his repeated references to his mother being "crazy" and not compliant with her medication regimes, to the use of the discredited phrase "manic depressive" when he recognizes Silver's manic episode for what it is, to his jovial reminder that she is "a little crazy" when she is in early recovery, apparently meant as a term of endearment.

Silver's bipolar disorder is only seen on screen again late in Season 3, after a romantic rival, Adrianna, switches her anti-psychotic medication, Olanzapine, for placebos. The effect is seen almost immediately, causing a manic episode that thwarts Silver's ambition to be accepted into film school. When she receives a rejection letter from her college of choice, her new boyfriend Navid discovers her lying in bed in a darkened room. He recognizes the depth of her despair and asks about her medication, which causes Silver to ask him angrily why he "would even go there."

Silver is portrayed as a person who is responsible with her medication, and she rejects the possibility of this episode being anything other than a normal response to disappointment to missing out on film school. When her blood tests reveal that she has no medication in her system, it is naturally assumed that Silver has been non-compliant with her medication regime. Silver wonders aloud whether Navid's ex-girlfriend Adrianna swapped the tablets, but this is dismissed by the other characters as delusional paranoia brought on by the reintroduction of medication to her system. Adrianna attempts to capitalize on the situation, warning Navid that he will always have to deal with problems if he continues in a relationship with Silver: "Silver's always going to be this way. She's mentally ill. You don't just get better from something like that." The on-screen depiction of Silver, however, is in stark contrast to this assertion, for she is shown to spend months and even years in full remission while she is on her medication, which is in line with reality. People with well-managed bipolar enjoy normal, stabilized moods and are capable of experiencing fully functional family, school, and professional lives when they are well (Massachusetts General Hospital; *Mindframe*).

The depiction of Silver in *90210* is a valiant attempt to discuss the serious implications of the disorder, grounded though it is in the soapiest of teen dramas. Actress Jessica Stroup is generally convincing when depicting manic episodes. Through adherence to her medication regime and significant reflection and insight into her own personality and illness, Silver avoids bipolar episodes in the face of many melodramatic incidents, including the death of her mother, ill-judged romances, a kidnapping, pregnancy and legal arguments over the custody of her future child.

Silver is her high-functioning, likeable self for the bulk of her screen time, yet there are some subliminal messages that remain troubling. Unlike most of her peers, Silver never makes it to college; nor does she find a happy ending in romantic terms. Indeed, in the series finale she is diagnosed with cancer (Bently; Swift). Thus, the only character with a diagnosed mental illness (unlike some of her undiagnosed but manipulative and/or homicidal classmates from West Beverly High) is handed a death sentence. The mad woman in the world's most famous zip code, like Charlotte Brontë's Bertha Mason in the attic, cannot be allowed to live.

"I just came this way": Bipolar Disorder in *Homeland*

Like Silver, *Homeland*'s Carrie Mathison (played by Claire Danes) is a lead character in a popular television program who is shown to be an independent and functioning member of society, with occasional lapses into illness. Although they share the same diagnosis, the characters are extremely different, which is to be expected given that *Homeland* is a multiple award-winning prime time geopolitical thriller whereas *90210* is a melodrama aimed at a teenage audience. *Homeland* is an American adaptation of an Israeli series *Hatufim* (*Prisoners of War*), which airs on the U.S. cable channel Showtime. It centers around homeland security and terrorism, and the unlikely romance between a bipolar CIA agent and a suspected Al Qaeda terrorist. It has consistently broken ratings records and won Emmy, Golden Globe, Satellite and American Film Institute Awards.

Carrie Mathison is a CIA field agent, and evidently one of some renown; Deputy Director David Estes comments that she is "something of a folk hero" to the analysts. She has finely honed instincts and is introduced as having a prodigious knowledge of alleged terrorist Abu Nazir. She intuitively pieces together pieces of information that other agents miss and is shown to be of high intelligence and to have a strong memory. From the first episode of the first season, she is also seen to be taking the anti-psychotic drug Clozapine, which she hides in an aspirin bottle in her bathroom. When confronted about this, she admits that she has a mood disorder, but she does not, at this stage, name it as bipolar disorder. She also insists that it is not affecting the job she is currently doing; unauthorized surveillance of a recently released American prisoner of war, Marine Sergeant Nicholas Brody whom she alone believes may have been "turned" by Abu Nazir.

Viewers learn that Carrie is not under official medical care, but rather takes sample pills from her psychiatrist sister, occasionally supplementing these by taking some from her father, who shares the diagnosis. This is to avoid the stigma attached to having a mental illness, which Carrie believes would jeopardize her security clearance and her career; concerns which are later echoed by her CIA mentor, Saul, and ultimately proven when her boss, David Estes, fires her for her erratic behavior with regard to Sergeant Brody. Yet Carrie tells Saul that she has been "handling" her bipolar disorder since she was in college, meaning that her entire successful career has been built while she had the illness; yet her employer still believes that the illness makes her unsuitable for that career.

Carrie's disorder is one which is present from the series' outset, and as in *90210*, the language used to describe her behavior is significant. In the very first episode, Deputy Director David Estes tells Saul he has a problem with Carrie's temperament, not her resume; in the same episode, her colleague discovers Clozapine. He then questions her judgment given that they are embroiled in an illegal surveillance operation: "Just tell me I am not out here risking my freedom on behalf of a crazy person." Carrie responds by saying, "I am crazy," before clarifying, "I got a mood disorder, OK?... I've been dealing with it since I was 22."

Carrie's clouded judgment is shown when she has an argument with Saul and tries to fix it by making a sexual advance to him. Saul, who is married and sees himself as a father-figure and mentor to Carrie, is appalled. Carrie responds with a pattern of behavior which will become emblematic of her individual response to heightened levels of anxiety and distress: she plays jazz on her iPod, tries on numerous outfits, puts on a faux engagement ring and goes out in search of male company for the evening. When leaving the jazz club with a suitor, she notices the patterns of the finger movements employed by the musicians, and links these to Brody's repetitive fidgeting that he does whenever he is on camera. Thus the viewer is initially unclear whether Carrie is hypomanic and going into a related hypersexual phase, as implied by her inappropriate advance to Saul; an independent woman in charge of her own sexuality who is well and still subconsciously piecing together information even when she is off duty; or whether her hypomanic state actually aids her in gaining insight into the case at hand. This last view is arguably the most interesting: while studies have suggested a higher level of creativity in individuals with bipolar disorder (Andreasen, "Creativity and Mental Illness"; Santosa et al.; Jamison, "Mood Disorders"; Andreasen, "Creativity and Mood Disorders"), clarity of thinking may be impeded when the disorder is not well controlled. While some patients see their diagnosed condition as a gift that offers rare insights (reminding us of the themes in *Monk* discussed in Chapter Two), and other patients see it as a problem which makes daily life more complex, it would seem that the suggestion that bipolar disorder is something of a crime-fighting superpower is at least a little problematic.

The link between drive and hypomania is further explored in episode 2, when Saul surveys Carrie's apartment and then advises her to sleep, eat some real food, and clean up her house. This is advice which her psychiatrist sister Maggie will repeat at various points throughout the series. Significantly, Maggie only appears when Carrie is unwell or in need of medication or consolation. Unlike the empathetic bond between Carrie and her father, Maggie and Carrie share a relationship which sometimes appears more that of a doctor and patient than affectionate sisters.

A common perception is that those with mood disorders cannot work in high stress situations, a notion which is belied by Carrie's job. As a CIA agent, she has to keep her cover, think quickly, come up with plausible lies, deal with the deaths of informants and colleagues, piece together critical information and conduct major risk assessments. She is also well placed, when observing Brody through surveillance, to identify when he is having paranoid delusions and to assess his mental state.

In the middle of Season 1, Carrie begins an affair with her target. The following morning Brody undergoes a polygraph test, as the CIA are trying (at Carrie's suggestion) to identify a suspected mole who may have passed a razor blade to a prisoner, pre-empting his suicide. Brody denies involvement and passes the test. Carrie demands that he be asked if he has been unfaithful to his wife as a test question—which he also successfully denies, thus proving to Carrie that he is capable of beating the polygraph. Carrie's inability to judge whether she believes Brody or not and her confused emotions with regard to him ultimately lead to her being dismissed from the CIA.

When Carrie is hospitalized following a bomb blast late in Season 1, her covert medication regime is not maintained, and she has a manic episode. Claire Danes' depiction of a person with bipolar disorder is commendably accurate, aided by the writing of Meredith Steihm—who has a family member with bipolar disorder (*Under Surveillance*—DVD Extras)—and the YouTube research of Danes herself. Danes "found there [were] a lot of people who are manic and are up in the middle of the night and probably feeling a little desperate with the need to talk. And so they do. They film themselves" (*Under Surveillance*—DVD Extras). Carrie is first shown to viewers post-bomb blast as being distressed and fixated, demanding a green pen from a nurse and becoming increasingly frustrated when the nurse does not understand the import of her request. She slips into the rapid-fire word associations characteristic of a manic episode:

> Green is important. Green is necessary. It doesn't make sense if it isn't green and it's really not an unreasonable request…. Saul, thank God! My green pen is dry. I've asked four, five, six times for a new one, but there's no understanding; they offered me blue, they offered me black, I mean is green so hard? Is green elusive? I mean, my kingdom for a fucking green pen! … I am laser-focused on the green. But there's more. There's many many many more. The thing is, Saul, Abu Nazir has methods, and patterns and priorities. A single sniper? No, no, Abu Nazir doesn't do that. He never has. He goes big, he explodes, he maims *en masse*, we know that.

Here we again see the rapidity of thought, fixations and word associations which are characteristic of a manic episode.

As with Silver, there is some logic to be found in Carrie's ramblings, but it is thoroughly masked in the first instance. Saul realizes that something is wrong and asks Carrie to slow down. She continues to speak rapidly, fixating on language features like synonyms and alliteration: "There's a bigger, pernicious, Abu Nazir-worthy plot out there and we have little time. We have to code it, collide it, collapse it, contain it." She reacts with a childish squeal of delight when he offers her a green pen, which she identifies as the first priority in facing the terrorist threat. A baffled Saul tries to explain how listeners are receiving Carrie's messages, inadvertently listing the symptoms of a manic episode: "I can't follow you. You're talking very fast. Your thoughts are running together. All these ideas—I can't understand." When the doctor asks if there is someone they should call, Carrie immediately becomes compliant: "My sister." She later reassures Saul that "Maggie will come, Maggie's reliable, you can count on Maggie every time," again demonstrating the rapidity and repetition which are symptomatic of speech during a manic episode.

Saul, for his part, seems to feel a variation of survivor guilt. He seeks confirmation from Maggie that "this"—her disorder—is not "new." Maggie confirms that Carrie has bipolar and is stable on her medication but surmises that the explosion was a trigger for her current mania. She suggests Lithium and an anti-psychotic and asks Saul to help her supervise Carrie's return to normality. During his evening supervisory shift, Saul apologizes to a drowsy Carrie, saying that he knew she was "damaged" after Baghdad and saying that he "should have asked" if she were really all right. Despite Carrie's rather erratic behavior during this period, Saul still listens to her, and even goes to their Deputy Director to point out the sense of Carrie's argument that the sniper attacks seem out of character with Abu Nazir's usual Modus Operandi.

Saul decides to trust Carrie's judgment, despite her mania. Saul's deep friendship and long-term working relationship with Carrie are utilized when he begins to sort her color-coded documents, beginning with the "high purple" documents, which Carrie says are urgent. He then begins to organize the documents to her pin board, which covers an entire wall of her living room. When Carrie wakes in the morning, Saul has sorted and pinned all Carrie's collated data on Nazir's activities into a timeline and cracked her color code: the "fallow yellow," was when Nazir went dormant for a few months; the subsequent green shoots phase represented revenge and planning, and the urgent purple phase is one of imminent danger as he prepares to see through his plan.

Carrie appears delighted that Saul has understood the workings of her mind, and tells him more about her illness and diagnosis: "I've had this since college. I wrote a 45-page manifesto declaring I'd reinvented music. The Professor I handed it to escorted me to student health. I wasn't even in his class. You didn't do anything, Saul. I just came this way." The idea that bipolar disorder is linked with increased creative output is one with a long history (Jamison, "Mood Disorders"; Jamison, *Touched with Fire*; Horton; Ludwig; Andreasen). These studies have found, however, that the creative phase is linked with hypomania; full-blown mania, on the other hand, is an impediment to completing the tasks as the thoughts, while still racing, are no longer coherent or grounded in reality (Figueroa). Carrie's insight into unraveling Nazir's plot, therefore, is only plausible if she had been making the connections before the bomb blast. The trauma of psychosis would not be enough to trigger her making such leaps in logic, since the litmus test of psychosis is an absence of judgment; judgment is surely a prerequisite for taking down an international terrorist.

Although Carrie appears to be stabilizing well, she is still somewhat erratic and impulsive, which is consistent with a manic episode. Despite Maggie banning her from calling anyone, she decides to call Brody who was imprisoned by Nazir during the "fallow yellow" period of mourning and might therefore have insight into his thinking. Brody hears the rapidity and repetition in her speech as she asserts, "You can identify the impetus, the incident, the injury," and asks what is wrong; when he offers to come over to discuss things, she is delighted and anxiously prepares for him as though it were a date. Instead, Brody tells David Estes that they had had an affair, and Estes arrives with two officers to remove confidential information from her apartment and inform her that her office is being cleared. Carrie is understandably distraught, and this turn of events triggers a depressive episode which, as Maggie notes, is "much harder to treat" than the mania.

Saul advises Maggie that despite her talents, her diagnosis means that Carrie will never set foot in Langley again. The deputy director dismisses her timeline as a "wall of garbage … classified information … improperly removed from this office, assembled by a crazy woman into a crazy collage." This repetition of the word "crazy" effectively dismisses her entire career. Soon after, Carrie and her colleague Virgil witness a sniper attack on a political lobbyist, but only Carrie realizes that it is a distraction, with the real attack to come when the dignitaries are sequestered after the assassination attempt. Despite her romantic feelings for Brody, she still believes that he is a terrorist and correctly surmises that he is wearing a suicide vest and intends to take revenge on the vice president, who had ordered the drone attack which killed Nazir's ten-year-old son, Issa. This was the event that prompted Nazir's period of dormancy as well as triggering Brody's allegiance to Nazir because of his affection for the young boy. Saul, however, does not support Carrie in this instance, but tells an officer that she is unstable and needs to be "contained." Carrie pleads with Brody's daughter, Dana, to speak with him and convince him to abort his mission. Although Dana is dismissive, asking Carrie what is "wrong" with her and calling 911 to alert them that there is a "crazy" woman in their house, she does indeed call her father and make him promise that he will come home. Unfortunately, Carrie's ideas are read as delusional paranoia by the other characters, despite the audience being aware that she has read Brody's intentions correctly. This causes her to doubt herself and ultimately, her ability to successfully manage her condition.

Carrie's bipolar disorder is the focus of many of the characters in this pivotal episode, with Brody's wife Jessica characterizing her as "sick" and having something "seriously wrong" with her. Brody calls Carrie "crazy" and advises her to "get some help." This prompts Carrie to ask Maggie to take her to the hospital where she undergoes electro-convulsive therapy, despite protests from Saul that it will damage her memory, that he "loves [her] brain," and that she is strong enough to get through her current period of difficulty. She reassures him using an older popular culture reference, saying, "it's not *Cuckoo's Nest*, Saul." The Australian Mindframe document refers to the televisual focus on ECT as "a skewed picture of mental health treatment" (*Mindframe* 4); others have lamented the lack of nuance in the depiction of Carrie's treatment (Whitehead). Certainly, in this instance the depiction is designed to be confronting to the viewer, with the handheld camera operator straddling the actress on a bed, in order to get the full impact of Carrie's bodily reaction to the electric shocks from an overhead angle (*Under Surveillance*—DVD Extras).

Season 2 shows Carrie establishing her post–CIA life; teaching English to immigrants, pottering in her sister's vegetable garden, and taking her turn in cooking for the extended family. When one of her former "assets" resurfaces in Beirut with information about Nazir and insists that she will only speak to Carrie, she reluctantly agrees to return to Beirut to assist the CIA in making contact. She is shown to be having problems with memorizing her cover story and the address of the safe house, leading viewers to wonder alongside Saul whether she is still capable of this kind of work. There is much debate among the team over whether the informant can be trusted, and indeed, whether Carrie's assessment of her trustworthiness is itself reliable. Carrie overhears Saul telling their supervisor that he did not want her there in the first place, precipitating a major bout of anxiety. When Saul goes looking for her, she articulates her frustration: "It's not lost on me why people don't trust my judgement. ... I have never been so sure, and so wrong. And it's that fact that I still can't get my head around. It makes me unable to trust my own thoughts.... Look, the way I am now, I wouldn't trust me, either. But the Carrie who recruited her? That one I believe." Viewers can see a noticeable contrast between this reflective and insightful speech and those given during her manic phases. She is speaking in full sentences and able to construct a cogent argument which is free of alliteration and not dependent on metaphor.

Carrie's moods are apparently less stable than they had been when she returns from Beirut; her father finds her writing a report at 3.20 in the morning, and is not persuaded by her argument that she feels "pretty great," telling her that she is "[w]ired ... there's a difference." Estes compliments her on the unusual but excellent level of detail in her report, and checks that she was not hoping to be reinstated, a motive that Carrie denies. With her career apparently over, she attempts suicide, overdosing on her medications and washing it down with wine, before making herself vomit. She is still clearly depressed when she opens the door to an insistent Saul, who has found Brody's recorded confession on a camera disk, sewn into the lining of the bag which she took from an apartment in Beirut. Carrie begins crying when she sees that her assertions that Brody was a terrorist working with Abu Nazir were not the paranoid delusions that everyone had believed, sobbing as she asks, "I was right?"

Carrie is brought back into the investigation, and again becomes emotionally involved with Brody. Because of this, Carrie's judgment is consistently questioned by not only her on-screen colleagues, but also her real-world viewers. According to writer Gideon Raff (who wrote the Israeli series and also works as a principal writer on the U.S. version) this was deliberate and an advantage of the addition of bipolar disorder to the American version of the character; an adaptation which he called "genius," describing Carrie's disorder as a "big flaw, and then you don't know if you are supposed to believe her or not" (*Under Surveillance*—DVD Extras).

During the second season, Brody is kidnapped and assumed to be operationally and/or physically dead; Carrie is kidnapped by Nazir; Brody is embroiled in a successful plot to kill the Vice President; colleague Peter Quinn is employed to assassinate Brody to stop his political rise; and Brody decides to leave his wife and family, turning up on Carrie's doorstep and telling her it was her "all along." Throughout all of this, Carrie shows no signs of hypomania, mania or psychosis, even though she is rarely seen taking her medication. In the Season 2 finale they discuss their possible future together; however, Carrie warns Brody that her illness is an issue which should not be taken lightly, describing it as "hard. It's ugly."

Carrie's mental illness and her career continue to be intertwined in problematic ways. Quinn refuses to go through with assassinating Brody, citing Carrie's mental health as his main concern. Saul arranges for Carrie to be reinstated and promoted, which means she must choose between her career and her relationship with Brody, as she could not hold a position with the CIA while dating a confessed terrorist. She hesitates over the position and reminds Saul of her illness, which he dismisses, saying it is well under control, but she is tempted by the idea of a "more balanced life" with Brody.

In the Season 2 finale, however, a car bomb destroys part of the CIA, killing some 200 people who were attending a Memorial Service for the Vice President. Brody's car was used and his previous confession tape released by Al Qaeda as though it applies to the current incident. Carrie and Brody flee to the Canadian border, where she decides she will return to the CIA and attempt to clear his name. Again, throughout all of these extraordinarily stressful circumstances, Carrie appears to be making cogent decisions and be unaffected by her disorder, suggesting that Saul's assertion that it is well managed is correct.

This sets up the story for continuation in the third season, wherein Carrie and Brody are largely separated. In this season, Carrie is questioned before a Senate Select Committee, and information about her affair is leaked to the press. Saul makes public Carrie's diagnosis, and she leaks to a journalist in apparent retaliation. Saul then has her committed. This is later revealed to be a "play"; the very public breakdown of her loyal friendship with Saul is used to gain the trust of a target, Majid Javadi.

In the third season Carrie decides to self-medicate against depression by using copious amounts of alcohol, not stopping even when she becomes aware that she is pregnant with Brody's child. After being briefly reunited towards the end of the season, Carrie witnesses Brody being hanged, but even this does not trigger another bipolar episode. Instead, she is seen to be operating well on her own, without either Saul or Brody, ultimately and somewhat surprisingly being offered an overseas bureau chief position in Istanbul—the youngest person to ever achieve this status—when eight months pregnant.

Only at this point does she wonder aloud to Quinn how she could possibly be a mother, suggesting that her obsessions and ruthlessness are fitting to a station chief but are not particularly maternal in nature.

Season 4 sees these predictions come true, with Carrie a station chief in Afghanistan and her daughter, Frannie, being raised by Maggie. Carrie returns home following her father's death and struggles with suburban life and life as a single mother—at one point, alarmingly, almost drowning Frannie in the bath. Season 5 sees her working in the private sector in Berlin, happily partnered with a German colleague and raising Frannie together. As she attempts to help Saul discover which European CIA operative is a double-agent, she opts to bring on a manic episode in an attempt to get to a resolution "faster," asking her boyfriend to supervise proceedings and only then telling him that she has already ceased taking her medication once she had secured his reluctant agreement. Unsurprisingly, their relationship does not survive.

The pre-season publicity for Season 6 of *Homeland* was emphatic that Carrie would continue her "battle" with bipolar disorder (Arbonida). After allowing a traumatized Quinn to move into her home, Carrie finds that Frannie and her babysitter have become embroiled in an apparent hostage situation with Quinn at the center. Carrie is also discovered to have fallen asleep with a gun in her hands while protecting a sleeping Frannie. A Child Protective Services agent receives a tip regarding Carrie's diagnosis. This combination of events leads to her temporarily losing custody of Frannie, who is deemed to be at imminent risk of harm. Carrie's bipolar thus makes her doubly vulnerable, since it is used to build a case against her (even when she is non-symptomatic), and since the subsequent removal of Frannie then leads to poor impulse control, the immediate loss of her hard-won sobriety and a loss of professional standing.

As with *90210*, there are many positives to the representation of Carrie and her management of her illness. The portrayal is largely accurate and sympathetic; however, some of the subliminal messages are rather more problematic. A lead character with bipolar disorder who is gifted at her job is undoubtedly a positive iteration. Yet Carrie is also labeled a poor mother before she even gives birth; she struggles with addiction and other self-harming behaviors; and she seems determined to sabotage a number of her relationships, romantic or otherwise. Given producer Alex Ganza's insistence that "the fact [Carrie] is bipolar is central to her character [and] speaks volumes about how she chooses to live her life" (Arbonida), the question surely must become: to what extent should we read Carrie's rather tumultuous life as a function of being a character in a spy drama, and to what extent is it a function of her being a character with bipolar?

"You can't fix me, because I'm not broken": Bipolar Disorder in *Shameless*

Showtime's *Shameless* depicts characters dealing with a number of mental health challenges, including addiction and alcoholism, OCD, agoraphobia and bipolar disorder. Producers and writers often discuss "the *Shameless* way of doing things," which typically means being confronting, unapologetic and politically incorrect. Very little in the world of the Gallagher family is stigmatized—not underage drinking, arrests, juvenile detention, teen pregnancy, theft, homosexuality, drug use, drug dealing, or dropping out of school. The only thing the children really fear is becoming like their parents: narcissistic, drunken addict Frank, or promiscuous, drug addled Monica, who has a diagnosis of bipolar disorder that she refuses to acknowledge in any meaningful way. Indeed, for much of the early seasons, the six Gallagher children joke about their genetic lottery, running commentary on which child is most likely to be an alcoholic like father Frank, and who is most likely to inherit Monica's bipolar disorder.

As previously mentioned in the Introduction, *Shameless* at first appeared to be heading down the well-worn narrative path of introducing troublesome relatives with bipolar disorder, whose presence was designed to create drama within the lot. Veronica's brother Marty, for example, appears for only one episode, and sets fire to Veronica's wedding dress when he learns that she does not want him to attend her wedding. He is drugged and chained to a toilet to stop him from attending the wedding, but breaks the toilet to pieces, floods the house, and crashes the ceremony regardless. Curiously, he is never seen or even mentioned again, despite Veronica's mother Carol becoming a significant character in future episodes.

In Season 2 viewers learn that the estranged Gallagher matriarch, Monica, also has this diagnosis and that the children were traumatized by her untreated behaviors at various points in their childhoods. At some point, five of the six known Gallagher children—Fiona, Lip, Ian, Debs and Carl—express their concerns about how their mother had behaved, about inheriting the disorder, or both. Only the youngest, Liam, who initially appears to be developmentally delayed and barely speaks for the first several seasons, does not articulate these concerns.

Monica's on-screen reunion with her family in Season 2 is anything but what a viewer might expect from such an episode—upon finding her mother in the kitchen one morning, Fiona's only reaction is to greet her with "We don't have any money." The other Gallagher offspring are similarly unenthusiastic about his reunion, with Ian asking, "What the hell is she doing here?" His father, Frank, replies that he had asked their mother to come home. Ian rightfully retorts, "Oh, do you live here now, too?" These unemotional responses are explained in terms of the show's backstory: Monica first abandoned the children to foster care when Fiona and Lip were preschoolers. Ian was conceived during a brief drug-induced fling with one of Frank's brothers, although the family does not discover this until they have DNA testing years later—and each of the subsequent children is the result of a reconciliation between their parents. Monica and Frank are depicted as highly irresponsible characters, who openly discuss which child was conceived on which illegal drug.

During this visit, Monica is full of energy and full of plans, trying to clean the house and offering to paint Debbie's room. When Frank takes Monica to his local pub, she is greeted enthusiastically by the bartender, who notes that Monica looks well and asks, "you back on your meds?" Monica's reply is swift: "Oh, hell no. That gets me foggy and makes me fat. Besides, I am *not* bipolar." This is the first moment where her illness is mentioned; previously, the children have only spoken about her drinking, drugging and absence. While her denial of her condition and refusal to take meds is irresponsible, it is not necessarily an inaccurate or even unlikely depiction of some patients' relationships with that condition. Yet the character of Monica is somewhat more nuanced than other hapless, bothersome relatives like Marty—the suggestion is that Monica is a poor parent who just happens to have bipolar which has added an extra level of impetuousness to her parenting; rather than the more simplistic idea that her poor parenting is a symptom or result of the disorder.

In this first on-screen visit, Monica attempts to reconnect with her middle children, Ian and Debs, in particular. Unfortunately, she does not do well with either. She finds the family's emergency fund and spends it on a car and hundreds of dollars' worth of American Girl dolls that demonstrate how little she knows Debs, who is not only too old for dolls, but who runs an illegal daycare center over the Summer and has therefore no little to no interest in playing at feeding or changing young children. Monica, who has walked out on her lesbian lover to return to Frank and the children, tells Ian, who is gay, that he should never feel ashamed of who he is; somewhat misguidedly since Ian is most definitely not closeted or ashamed—before taking him to a LGBTI+ bar but paradoxically warning him never to come out at school. When Ian gets a C- in a midterm exam, rather than encouraging him to continue with his studies, she insists that he is wasting his time in school and drags him to a military recruitment office. Here he is told that he still needs to complete his high school diploma before he can enlist. Monica immediately goes into an elevated, ignorant and racist rant, screaming, "Since when do you need to know trigonometry to get killed for your country?" and finishing with "Army too chicken shit? Fuck you. We're going to the Navy."

The Navy recruiter is present and has, of course, witnessed the whole thing. There are several indicators in this speech that Monica is well on her way to a manic episode. Despite her woeful parenting, it does always seem as though she genuinely likes her children, but here she is aware but apparently unconcerned that Ian is likely to "get killed" for his country. Still her only emotion is directed at the recruiter who will not go outside policy in order to speed up that process. She also shows a lack of awareness of what is going on around her or the impact of her actions; apparently oblivious that the Navy recruiter is not only likely to be bound by the same rules as his Army counterpart, but also that he is unlikely to be convinced that Ian is mature enough to cope with the military if he presents with his apparently unstable mother as his champion. Her behavior up until now—such as the unregulated spending—can either be read as symptomatic, or merely as Monica being irresponsible. With this character, it is unclear which behavior is related to the disorder, which is related to her personality and character, and to what extent the former has impacted on the latter.

Monica's behavior intensifies, leading the older siblings having to explain the condition to the younger ones. Ian tells his sister very matter-of-factly—"Mom's bipolar, Debs." Debs asks, "What, like the North and South Pole?" The youngsters' lack of connection with their mother means that they have varying degrees of memories and awareness of the condition. Eleven-year-old Debs googles the condition, discovers that depression is hereditary, and then misinterprets her own adolescent angst as depression. When she discovers that there is a one in five chance that one of the children will have inherited bipolar, she deduces that it must be her. Older siblings Fiona and Lip joke that their money is on juvenile delinquent Carl. Fiona reminds Debs that one in five "are pretty good odds" and Debs later decides that it will be Lip, because he's "already halfway there as it is," having moved out of the house over a disagreement with Fiona.

Eventually Monica becomes so unresponsive that even Frank, the ultimate narcissist, can see that it is in Monica's best interests to go back onto her medication. He and Fiona coerce Monica from her cubbyhole under the stairs and ask her to participate in Thanksgiving dinner. Monica excuses herself to wash her hands, and then attempts suicide in the kitchen. In the chaos that follows, Frank is once again absent and disengaged, even as others leap into action.

Shameless returns to the topic of bipolar disorder in Season 4, when it becomes evident that middle child Ian has inherited the disorder from his mother. Clinicians sometimes judge particular behaviors to be the equivalent of a depressive episode, with Sadock and Sadock offering as an example of equivalence a formerly well-behaved adolescent who moves into a "triad of truancy, alcohol abuse and sexual promiscuity" (Sadock and Sadock). With Ian, who has been drinking since he was 10 and sleeping with married men since he was 14, it can be hard to judge against such an example, but it does seem true that he was gone from "formerly well behaved" in terms of how hard he was working towards his goal of entering Westpoint—a difficult goal, given his life circumstances—to being more erratic and impetuous. Having suddenly dropped out of school and enacted his mother's abortive enlistment plan by claiming to be Lip, who had just become the only Gallagher to graduate from high school, Ian then deserts after trying—and failing—to hotwire a helicopter.

Throughout this season, Ian's behavior changes noticeably, with sleeplessness, high energy and high enthusiasm becoming hallmarks of his behavior. He becomes frustrated by his relationship with the still-closeted Mickey Malkovich, saying that he has no interest in "being a mistress anymore," but then not embracing the newfound freedom in their relationship once Mickey comes out to the neighborhood. Instead, he takes to his bed for two days. Eventually Mickey alerts the Gallagher siblings, who recognize that Ian's behavior is symptomatic of bipolar. Mickey refuses to believe their suspicions, saying that Ian was happy while he was up all night, and suggesting that they just "hide the knives until he perks up."

Fiona and Lip are once more pushed into a situation of being *ersatz* parents, albeit with the significant impediment of having essentially been parentless themselves. Fiona admits that she was always worried that she would be the one to be given a mental illness diagnosis, musing that they were all facing "[m]ental illness Russian roulette, with Monica's DNA as the bullet." When she later uses this analogy with Ian, however, he rejects it out of hand. He insists that he is well; explaining away his behavior as a result of taking too much cocaine at the nightclub where he was working and telling her that he's still "betting it'll be Carl." Yet viewers can see more of Ian's symptomatic behavior than his family members can, with scenes of Ian sneaking away from family dinners for trysts with strangers in restaurant bathrooms. Mickey is also blissfully unaware of the full range of Ian's behaviors, noting cheerfully that Ian does not seem to be sick anymore, and pointing out to Ian's siblings the inherent difficulty of their lives on the Southside of Chicago: "Let's say Ian gets like depressed or manic or whatever, how the fuck do we know it's not from living in this shithole ghetto?"

Mickey's hopes are dashed, however, as Ian's behavior becomes increasingly unpredictable. Mickey's wife Svetlana observes, "Your boyfriend's losing his shit," prompting Mickey to ask the family for advice about "shrink stuff." When the unconventional family is short on cash, Ian comes home with $600 and blithely tells Mickey, "I did a porno. ... Don't worry. The guy I did a scene with said he was clean." Mickey—a criminal who is living with his Russian prostitute wife, their son, and his gay lover—has never been one to be conventional about morality in or out of relationships, but even he is concerned about the unprotected sex and recognizes it as risk-taking behavior. He gently tells Ian that they need to go to the hospital. Ian initially appears to comply but instead take Mickey and Svetlana's infant son, Yevgeny, on an impromptu road trip, heading for Florida. This psychotic break ultimately leads to police intervention and scheduling, yet Ian still refuse to recognize it for what it is, telling his treating doctor that he is not like Monica: "I didn't slash my wrists over Thanksgiving Dinner. I went for a drive. … I guess it was a really long drive and I didn't plan ahead. But I did not hurt that baby."

For quite some time, Ian refuses to participate in his own treatment or take medication, which he says stops him from feeling anything. After he has paranoid delusions and takes a swipe at his younger sister Debs with a baseball bat (believing her to be the military police), he is convinced to take the medication again, but then places his hand on the hot plate in the diner where he works, just to feel something. After a newly discovered older half-sister does indeed turn him in to the military police in a fit of spite, Ian sits quietly as his family members speak to the military tribunal about his illness and its effects. The use of over-exposure, sterile white rooms and the look of impotent fury on Ian's face depict his frustration at his apparent voicelessness in this situation. This feeling of being disempowered may go some way to explaining why he makes contact with Monica, who insists without a trace of irony that he needs to be with people who accept him as he is—effectively discounting the unwavering support of his family and Mickey. When Ian is released, he asks for it to be into her care. They hitchhike away, with her euphoric and shouting joyfully to the sky, and Ian sullen and silent; a tableau representing mania and depression. The relationship between Monica and Ian has always been dangerous, but here, where Ian is desperate to feel normal and accepted, he is receiving his acceptance from a mother who is irresponsible, erratic, and whose attempts at parenting have continually been misguided. Ian needs help in accepting himself as a person who also happens to have bipolar disorder, but Monica wants him to deny that any of his behavior is disordered, or even that he has an illness.

In subsequent seasons, Ian becomes more responsible with his medication and with the support of new partner Caleb, successfully undergoes training to be an emergency services worker. With Caleb's encouragement, Ian lies on the application form when asked about prior hospitalizations for mental illness; later, when his position is terminated over it, Caleb encourages him to confront his new employer, Rita. When Rita tiredly asks Ian if she should call the police to have him removed from the premises, he retorts that that is what "most people do when they see someone with a mental illness" and points out that he had had no real choice: "Check the box, you don't get the job. Lie? Maybe they won't find out. What would you do? You'd lie." Ian points out that it is illegal to discriminate against him: "I am handicapped. It's not my fault; I didn't do anything to bring this on myself. I have a disease." Part of the renewed employment agreement is later shown to include a plan for times when Ian becomes symptomatic, including recording a video wherein Ian reminds himself that he has agreed to go home, without argument, if ever Rita advises him to do so. This is actioned when one of Ian's judgment calls puts a mentally ill patient at risk. Ian at first refuses to believe that he could be symptomatic, because he is taking his medication; it is up to Fiona to point out that stress can also be a contributing factor and that Ian, who has just broken up with Caleb, is emotionally vulnerable.

Despite all of this Ian is, for the most part, a functional character with significant family responsibilities that he is meeting; his own relative youth and significant socio-economic disadvantage notwithstanding. Ian is a sympathetic, multi-dimensional character whose mental health challenges are given no more airtime than his sexuality, substance use, lack of education, or problematic parentage.

Conclusions

Historically, television characters with bipolar disorder have been either criminally insane or caused unimaginable grief to family members. These representations have been problematic because popular television is a prime source of information about mental illness for the general population and indeed, those who share the condition. As such, *90210*, *Homeland*, and *Shameless*, while still imperfect, are nevertheless groundbreaking representations in that they are well researched and depict the disorder as being largely a well-managed part of the individuals' lives, rather than as something that changes them irrevocably.

FIVE

"Maybe I don't have the right genetic make up"

Depression, Anxiety and Post-Traumatic Stress Disorder

Representations of mental health disorders on television have traditionally been in the form of short-term characters whose unpredictable and sometimes homicidal behavior is introduced as a means of pushing the dramatic story arc. Perhaps unsurprisingly, depressive episodes on screen have been scarce, relatively recent, and are often contextual—a brief episode after losing a job or relationship, for example. Similarly, anxiety is often contextualized as merely catastrophizing by an individual. Trauma-related disorders such as post-traumatic stress disorder, which are more directly linked to events and therefore are theoretically easier to include in narratives, have also been relatively under-represented in screen until recent years. Despite efforts from organization such as Mindframe to offer guidelines on how to more accurately represent characters with mental health disorders, anxiety and depression remain grossly underrepresented on television screens, as compared with the prevalence of diagnosis in society.

Anxiety and depression have been included in the same chapter because of the relatively small number of depictions as well as their high incidence of comorbidity. Selective mutism, a particular kind of anxiety disorder, is included here. We have also opted to include in this chapter post-traumatic stress disorder (PTSD), which was previously considered to be a subset of anxiety disorders (American Psychiatric Association), but which is now under the separate section for trauma and stressor-related disorders. This also allows us to explore in a single chapter the complexities of a multi-diagnosis household in *You're the Worst*.

In all of these disorders, the incidence of characters that are diagnosed within the narrative is much smaller than the numbers who are read that way by viewers; and the vast majority is seen as having less agency or their opinions and thoughts as having less validity by the neurotypical characters around them. This chapter will focus on *The Big Bang Theory* (2007–2019), which continues the tradition of not labeling their on-screen characters (as discussed in Chapter One), but which nevertheless represents them sympathetically; Australian drama *Offspring* (2010–2017), where the lead character's anxiety symptoms are recognized by all within the narrative, but which stops short of a clinical diagnosis, and *You're the Worst* (2015–2019) which does diagnose anxiety and PTSD in its lead characters, but in keeping with the overall feel of that program, puts the characters in situations where their likeability for audiences remains unusually low.

Background: What Is Depression?

The common features of all depressive mood disorders are the presence of sad, empty or irritable moods, manifesting in somatic and cognitive changes that impact an individual's quality of life and capacity to function (American Psychiatric Association 155). It includes disruptive mood dysregulation disorder, major depressive disorder, premenstrual dysphoric disorder as well as unspecified depressive disorders and those originating from a medication or another medical condition. Prevalence rates vary according to subtype, but major depressive disorder is estimated to affect 7 percent of the population. This figure increases in particular cohorts, including those over 65, and adolescent females (American Psychiatric Association). The manual also notes that the "disorder is a recurrent one in the majority of cases" (American Psychiatric Association 155).

Depression in the Media

Depression and depressive episodes have not traditionally received a lot of airtime in popular television, largely because it is a mental illness that leads to people withdrawing from the world, which does little to move narratives forward. Lists of characters with depression on popular television (Virzi) typically include those with very contested diagnoses (such as *House's* Dr. Gregory House—who is variously "diagnosed" by viewers as being depressive, having OCD, or being on the autism spectrum), or a rather alarming number of animated characters (Eeyore from *Winnie-the-Pooh*, Arnold from *Hey Arnold*, Jane Lane from *Daria*, Spinelli from *Recess*, Squidward from *SpongeBob SquarePants*). Academic searches that include the terms "depression" and "popular television" do not bring up results about representations on screen; but rather, seemingly endless studies on how watching the news is bad for your mental health It is only in very recent years that we have seen depression displayed on screen—Ian Gallagher's Season 5 depressive episode as part of his bipolar, wherein he lay on the bed, unresponsive, for example (see Chapter Four). This storyline aired in Season 5 of *Shameless*, or 2015; the same year that Gretchen's depressive illness was introduced in Season 2 of *You're the Worst*.

"I can't tell him my brain is broken": Depression in *You're the Worst*

The FX/FXX series *You're the Worst* which aired between 2014 and 2019 is one of very few series that openly diagnoses two of its four lead characters with clinical mental illness; depression in the case of Gretchen Cutler, and post-traumatic stress disorder (PTSD) in her housemate, Edgar Quintero. In neither case is the diagnosis used as a short-term narrative device in order to progress the narrative; instead the characters' diagnoses are part—but crucially not the whole—of the characters' stories.

You're the Worst is consistently realistic in its depiction of the mental illness of Gretchen and Edgar, both of whom live with the curmudgeonly and self-centered Jimmy Shive-Overly. Interestingly, neither moves in with Jimmy of their own free will, but each seems to fall into a long-term domestic arrangement rather accidentally; Edgar, after a chance reunion in the street when he is homeless, and Gretchen after she also finds herself homeless after a house fire, not long after her initial one-night stand with Jimmy morphs into something more closely resembling an exclusive relationship.

Jimmy may be the link between these two characters and have provided a home for each of them, but he is not a sympathetic or even necessarily a likeable character. Indeed, the title of the show comes from all that Gretchen and Jimmy know of each other when they meet: each has been told by mutual friends that the other is "the worst." At the risk of over-pathologizing fictional characters, all four of the main characters in *You're the Worst* are deeply flawed; Jimmy is an insufferable narcissist, excruciatingly lacking in self-awareness; his roommate Edgar is his former drug dealer, now a veteran with PTSD; Gretchen's friend Lindsay has strong nymphomaniac tendencies, little self-insight and even less empathy for others; and Gretchen has diagnosed clinical depression. With the exception of Edgar, whose family of origin never appears on screen and whose illness is clearly and consistently linked with his military service in Iraq, all have complex and dysfunctional relationships with their parents, to which viewers can, to greater or lesser degrees, attribute the characters' current levels of emotional immaturity.

To understand what is unusual or interesting about the depiction of

Gretchen's depression, we must first understand what depression is, and how it has been represented—or more accurately, largely ignored—on screen historically. The depiction of Gretchen's symptoms seems to particularly correlate with the features of Major Depressive Disorder, given that she demonstrates a depressed mood, diminished interest or pleasure in usual activities, hypersomnia, indecisiveness, and feelings of worthlessness, sometimes coupled with suicidal ideation; and that these symptoms cause clinically significant impairment in her social and occupational areas of functioning. Depression is also highly comorbid with self-medication, and there is significant research to suggest that maladaptive behaviors and depression can arise from hostile or poorly attaching parenting (Gluschkoff et al.; Agerup et al.; Davies et al.). Gretchen is shown to have some very unhealthy attitudes towards alcohol and drugs, at times openly using them as a form of self-medication to combat her illness. When she finally begins to engage with therapy, she also understands that her parents' attitudes and expectations have some causal links to her mental illness.

It should also be noted, however, that while individuals may meet these clinical criteria, the illness is episodic and the diagnosed may have times when they are functional and asymptomatic. Jimmy's typical failure to notice problems until some time after they arise is therefore arguably more nuanced than being merely self-serving; with little experience of depression, let alone how Gretchen's presents, he displays a tendency to compare symptomatic behaviors and if they are not identical to a previous experience, dismiss them. Crucially, viewers do not see Gretchen's illness until the second season, and there are long periods where it is not central to the storyline.

Mid-way through the second season, Jimmy asks Edgar if he's noticed that "something's up" with Gretchen. Edgar, who is well attuned to both mental illness and insomnia replies, "you mean how she's been sneaking out in the middle of the night?" This prompts Jimmy to follow Gretchen on her nocturnal adventures, discovering her sitting alone in her car, crying, and playing Snake on her phone. Rather than being concerned about this behavior, Jimmy only expresses relief that she is not cheating, and remarks cheerily that it is indeed a "classic game."

Jimmy misses an important clue here, for, as Jindal and Thase argue, "[p]oor sleep is such a fundamental aspect of depression that one needs to be careful in making a diagnosis in the absence of sleep complaints" (Jindal and Thase 19). These sleep disturbances may take the form of insomnia or hypersomnia, and throughout the course of the series, Gretchen experiences both. In this instance, she demonstrates problems with falling or staying asleep; later, when abandoned by Jimmy, she first refuses to leave her bed for some time (and indeed, develops agoraphobia and becomes unable to leave Lindsay's apartment for three months). The comorbidity of sleep disturbance and depression is extremely prevalent because sleep disturbances may either be a symptom of a depressive episode, or an antecedent to one (Jindal and Thase; Staner). This contributes to the high prevalence of depression, which Gluschkoff et al. have described as "one of the leading causes of disability worldwide" arguing that it affects 350 million people globally, affecting all communities and demographics. This makes its relative lack of on-screen depiction all the more unusual.

Throughout the series, Jimmy's responses to Gretchen's mental illness, and to her decisions around medication or otherwise, could best be described as bemusement. With strong narcissistic tendencies, Jimmy struggles to be a supportive partner in the face of clinical depression. Immediately after Gretchen tells him of her diagnosis, he attempts to jolly her out of her depression through distraction and fun activities; telling Edgar that "there's no way she'll be able to remain sad after a day like this." Gretchen understands the tactic and tries to pretend that her depressive episode is over, in order to stop the continuation of Jimmy's "help." Predictably, this strategy fails. She moves out of Jimmy's luxurious home and onto Lindsay's couch, beginning to take a variety of recreational drugs in an attempt to spark some interest or emotion. She is also very blunt with Jimmy, when he confronts her, telling him that she feels nothing: "About anything. Dogs, candy, old Blondie records, you, us. Nothing. So for the last time, please go." Jimmy responds with an intervention, inviting her friends and clients over, who regale her with tales of famous people with depression, before realizing that all of those cited have taken their own lives. Frustrated, Jimmy exhorts her to "snap out of it," characterizing her depression as "dramatic, and self-pitying, and frankly ... unbecoming." Despite her distance and the apparent demise of their relationship, Jimmy continues to try his awkward best to be supportive, turning down a weekend away with a new love interest to instead build a blanket fort around Gretchen, who is lying prone on the floor. Gretchen begins to feel "a little human" after this effort, and Jimmy again blunders in, suggesting that "the next time [she] feel[s] it coming on" she "could try switching [her] meds." Gretchen replies glibly that she does not take medication in order to not lose her edge, and brightly reminds Jimmy that he has just proven that she does not need medication: "you actually can fix me!"

Unlike Jimmy, Lindsay, as a long-term friend, is at least able to recognize what is happening for Gretchen and is the person who first encourages her to stop hiding her depression from Jimmy. Following an episode wherein Gretchen's irritability hits new highs, and she screams at Edgar to "get over the war," and at Jimmy that their shared home is "an emotional black hole," Lindsay gently asks, "it's back, isn't it?" before following up with "It's going to be like sophomore year, when you wore the same Hoobastank T shirt three weeks in a row, and only ate Special K red berries?" This suggests that in a depressive state, Gretchen is unable to function at even a basic level, like making simple decisions about food or clothing. Throughout this particular conversation, Gretchen only responds by nodding and or crying, until Lindsay prompts, "Are you going to tell Jimmy?" Gretchen's response is raw and swift: "No. I can't tell him my brain is broken." Lindsay reminds Gretchen that she has never been this much "her disgusting self around anyone" and encourages her: "Wear your stains on the outsides of your clothes, Gretch. Tell him." Beyond this compassionate advice, however, Lindsay does little to accommodate Gretchen's illness, even going along with Jimmy's aforementioned misguided attempt to jolly Gretchen out of her state.

Gretchen has not only been resistant to medication, but also counseling and other behavioral therapies. After Jimmy has a drunken meltdown of his own and insists that it is "his turn" to have an emotional crisis, Gretchen offers to "talk to someone about it. A doctor someone. Maybe see about some medication." She goes on to identify that previously, her depressive episodes have only impacted her, but now Jimmy, as her partner, is also affected. Despite these good intentions, Gretchen struggles to engage properly with the process. At her first counseling session, she installs Jimmy in the chair to speak for her, while she sits on the floor, distracted, fidgeting, and disengaged. When asked if she knows why she is there, she retorts that she thought the counselor would, and demands to know why the "happy pills" have not yet fixed her. She becomes enraged at the idea that she may bear some responsibility towards her illness, but rather than discussing it during scheduled sessions, she instead stalks her therapist, using social media check-ins as an invitation to turn up at various brunches, trivia nights and parties in order to air specific concerns as they occur to her. When her therapist moves away, Gretchen chooses to continue the professional relationship via Skype, but refuses to pay her bills and neglects to include important information about her relationships. This important clinical relationship, perhaps as much as any other, proves the truth of her repeated assertion to Jimmy that she "always has one foot out the door."

Gretchen's depression again becomes a significant part of the storyline when she and Jimmy consider marriage and parenthood. In Season 3, Gretchen begins to engage with the therapeutic process. One of her tasks is to try something she hates: opening mail. Emboldened when the first few contain nothing but bills, she then opens a missive from Jimmy's family in England, announcing that his verbally abusive and distant father is dead. Gretchen must then find a way to break the news to Jimmy that his father, the man who has caused his own complex psychological issues, has passed away—while simultaneously managing her own illness, and Jimmy's euphoria at signing a new book contract. Their competing issues make for a traumatic season, and Jimmy complains that this is not how things are supposed to be, and they cannot both be "broken," to quote Gretchen, at the same time—arguing that one person is supposed to be in the hospital bed, while the other sneaks home to shower. Despite this, neither chooses to leave. In the season finale, Jimmy proposes to Gretchen in a manner that is uniquely appealing to her—by staging a murder and taking her to the alleged crime site. Gretchen excitedly accepts, and remarks on the synchronicity—that Jimmy has just lost his father, but that they will now form a family of their own. Jimmy offers to go back to the car to get her a sweater, but instead reflects on her comment, and drives off. No one hears from him for the next three months. Gretchen's mental health again suffers, and she takes up residence on Lindsay's couch. She tells her clients that she is travelling in Europe, and proceeds to not set foot outside the one-bedroom apartment for the next three months.

Jimmy returns and apologizes for his behavior, and Gretchen reacts spitefully by moving back in and gaslighting an exhausted Lindsay and a puzzled Jimmy, insisting that she has always lived in his luxurious home. From this position she works hard to torpedo Jimmy's publicity for his new book, which was both inspired by and dedicated to her. As they both navigate complex emotional relationships elsewhere, they begin to have lengthy phone conversations. Despite being in another relationship at the time, Gretchen spends a night with Jimmy, only to panic and believe he has again abandoned her when he goes to get breakfast the next morning. Convinced that Gretchen no longer cares about him, Jimmy prepares to leave town, before making one last bid for her, leading to a loud but otherwise rather conventional love triangle resolution scene in the kitchen of Gretchen's boyfriend, as both men plead their cases. Gretchen declares that she is choosing herself over either suitor, and leaves. Soon after, however, she stops Jimmy's car, gets in, and instructs him to drive. In order to undercut the romantic comedy staples here, however, when Jimmy asks her why, she tells him, "You looked so sad when I left that I realized I now have the power to destroy you, and why would I give that up?"

Season 5 sees them planning not one, but two weddings. The first, an elopement in which Gretchen shows very little interest, fails when both are distracted and forget to turn up. Jimmy is distraught at having abandoned Gretchen again, this time inadvertently. Both bride and groom decide that they perhaps really want a wedding, but Gretchen is again distracted by work related anxiety, and does not really engage in the planning. This period coincides with Gretchen being offered new opportunities in her career. Having scammed her way into a bigger and better office, Gretchen now finds that she is expected to participate fully in strategy meetings, and has drawn the attention of her boss, who informs Gretchen that she has "accidentally" become good at her job, and encourages her to see what she can achieve when she tries.

Throughout the planning of the weddings, Gretchen and Jimmy are portrayed as having problems that might cause significant issues in the longer term. At their joint bachelor's/hen's party, they are interviewed about important life choices, and give opposite answers to everything. Chief among these is the issue of having children. Jimmy had previously told Gretchen that he could not imagine having children with her, and now reveals that he does not want them at all. Gretchen, on the other hand, has raised the idea of children with a number of people over the course of the series, and her reservations are not about whether or not she wants to have children, so much as whether or not she *should* have children, given her history of depression and own problematic relationship with her mother.

Against the backdrop of a surfeit of wedding planning, hints of domestic disaster pepper the fifth and final season, with flash forwards of their joint home for sale, of Gretchen's brand new "grown up car"—a gift from Jimmy—looking battered and old, images of Jimmy and their former wedding florist cheerily sharing a coffee and driving to a wedding together, as well as comments from Gretchen to Lindsay, saying that she is "OK about seeing him" and "isn't even mad at him anymore." These turn out to be narrative misdirections that reflect their unconventional life choices. The sale of their dream home is not because they have separated, but because it was not child friendly; Gretchen's and Jimmy's cars are both looking less than pristine because they are now family cars; the former florist, with whom Jimmy had a pre-wedding dalliance, is now completely uninterested in him, and has therefore been hired as a very "safe" nanny to assist with their daughter, the tellingly-named Felicity. Finally, it is Edgar, not Jimmy, with whom Gretchen was angry, and whom she has not seen in years.

Despite Gretchen's lack of interest in the wedding and Jimmy's pre-wedding wandering, he remains committed to marrying Gretchen, even in the face of some unexpected resistance. As best man, Edgar takes Jimmy to a number of activities, including a smash party where he is able to take out his leftover aggression to his now deceased father. Edgar—hitherto by far the most sympathetic and compassionate character—point blank tells Jimmy not to marry Gretchen, because they are not good for each other. Jimmy is furious and cold, insistent that he will marry Gretchen, but even this does not deter Edgar from waiting none-too-surreptitiously at the location of the nuptials, ready to speed Jimmy away. His complex motivations for this stance will be explored further, later in this chapter.

On the day of the wedding, Jimmy recognizes Gretchen's level of disengagement when he discovers that she has outsourced the writing of her vows. He also takes on board his future mother-in-law's advice that marriage is a commitment that Gretchen will eventually grow to resent. Edgar watches from his car, convinced—correctly, as it turns out—that the wedding will not go ahead, and ready to whisk Jimmy away. As he watches, however, Gretchen chases after Jimmy, and they explore the complexities of their relationship. Ultimately Jimmy and Gretchen both leave and go to order pancakes instead; opting not to marry yet stay together. Intercut with flash forward scenes and the chaos as their friends discover that both the bride and groom are missing from the wedding, the show's finale ends with a very dark joke about Gretchen's depression, when she warns Jimmy that "there's always a possibility that someday I might leave my phone and keys at home and step in front of a train. You know that, right?" Jimmy reassures her that he knows and promises to move on with record-breaking speed.

What is clear is that despite the chaos, Gretchen does better in her career and her life when she begins to take responsibility for her illness. The producers of the show are at pains to depict that acknowledging and do not lead to a loss of unconventionality, or diminish her personality. When she is ignoring her symptoms, however, there are bad outcomes for her professionally and personally. Ultimately, her clinical depression is depicted quite accurately and empathetically, and without her losing her edginess or becoming a pathetic character or victim. Nor is it trivialized or "fixed" by being in a stable relationship—even when Gretchen insists that Jimmy can fix her broken brain, circumstances make it quite evident that she needs to acknowledge when she is symptomatic and take responsibility herself. Jimmy and Gretchen continue to be highly imperfect characters, choosing to be imperfect together.

Background: What Is Anxiety?

Anxiety disorders are all disorders that share features of excessive fear and anxiety and related behavioral disturbances, including separation anxiety, selective mutism, specific phobias, social anxiety disorder, panic disorder, agoraphobia, medication-induced anxiety disorder and generalized anxiety disorder. The prevalence of the first two, which are generally diagnosed in young children, is small, coming in at 2 percent or under and varying according to age and circumstances. Panic disorder has a prevalence of around 2–3 percent, and the prevalence of panic attacks in European nations is similar but runs at around 11 percent in America. Specific phobias are estimated to affect between 7 and 9 percent of the population, and social anxiety around 7 percent. Generalized anxiety disorder is believed to impact around 9 percent of the population and is twice as common in women as men (all statistics are taken from the American Psychiatric Association's DSM-5).

Anxiety in the Media

Characters with anxiety are relatively uncommon on screen. Arguably supporting characters Cameron Frye and Allison Reynolds in 1980s teen movies *Ferris Bueller's Day Off* and *The Breakfast Club* demonstrated aspects of the disorder, but it is significant that Cameron was constantly pilloried for his concerns and that Allison, in the initial reductive stereotyping of the five main characters, was known as the "basket case" (although the original line remains in the movie, online trailers have renamed the character "a recluse"). It was not until *Amelie* in 2001 and *Eternal Sunshine of the Spotless Mind* in 2004 that viewers saw lead characters whose symptoms of social anxiety were portrayed sympathetically.

"A regular Nina-mental-case-anxiety attack": Anxiety in *Offspring*

The ability to manage mental health disorders, complex family relations and a meaningful career is central to the Australian television series, *Offspring*. From the opening moments of the original telemovie pilot, viewers become aware of the internal doubts of the main character, Dr. Nina Proudman (Asher Keddie) through a series of soliloquies in voiceover. This remained a key feature of the series throughout its original run (until 2014) and its return (2016–2017) after a hiatus and was the main means by which Nina's ongoing issues with anxiety were telegraphed to viewers.

Nina's anxiety is introduced in the very first episode. Even as the series' theme song plays over an opening montage of Nina swimming in the telemovie pilot, she kicks the wall and responds with an overdubbed interior monologue that is hyper-critical: "Oh, how embarrassing. I should keep practicing the turns. But what's the point? Maybe I just don't have the right genetic make-up to do tumble turns. Or run my life properly." This sort of self-criticism and catastrophizing becomes a hallmark of the character, who nevertheless successfully navigates some significant traumatic events over the course of the series.

From that first episode, Nina notes that she is very capable in her job as a hospital-based obstetrician, but that she struggles to keep her anxiety in check. In another monologue, she outlines the strategies that she uses to keep her cortisol levels low and her anxiety at bay: "Music, exercise, structure." She admits that her methods sometimes fail, and the scene changes from her serenely exercising in the present, to a moment when she is dressed in hospital scrubs, sitting on a toilet, breathing into a paper bag. She exhorts herself to keep life simple, but the episode's plotline indicates that her life is rather melodramatic, when she discovers that she and the baby that she is delivering share a father. As Nina navigates how to share the news with other family members, they begin to ask whether her concerns are real, or the product of anxiety. Her mother, Geraldine, sagely advises, "No matter how hard you work, you'll always be a bit anxious'" whereas her older sister, Billie, asks somewhat more bluntly, "was it a big crisis, or just a regular Nina-mental-case-anxiety attack?" Billie's attitude reflects the common, loaded nature of language used with regard to mental illness (Hinshaw). This is in stark contrast to that of her supervisor at work, Dr. Clegg, who encourages her to take a position at Johns Hopkins, and when she is successful, tells her that he wants to her to "fly to Baltimore with the knowledge that you are an excellent doctor and an admirable person."

The series establishes that Nina's anxiety began in childhood, with Geraldine noting that even then, Nina used to count emergency exits, and Nina stating that her first panic attack was at her eighth birthday party. Nina even wonders whether her anxiety is "genetic." Nina repeatedly characterizes her emotional engagement with her imagination and projections of what may happen as "exhausting." Yet it is also represented as a strategy that she is able to use in the face of real crises: family illness and loss, a fire, and the loss of her romantic partner while carrying his child. In a later episode, she becomes romantically involved with a crisis consultant, employed by the hospital, who characterizes her as "a major event." When Nina argues that she is not a walking crisis, he agrees, but points out that she is in a crisis pattern: that every decision she makes in response to these major life events seems to increase the pressure under which she finds herself, which in turn increases her anxiety.

Season 2 begins with Nina, again in voiceover, tallying her successes during her first five months in Baltimore, including 68 deliveries, three new friends, and no panic attacks. As she congratulates herself on being "centered, living in the moment," she receives a text from Billie to say that their father has had a heart attack, prompting her return to Australia. During this season, Nina begins a relationship with a fellow doctor, Patrick, which brings its own anxieties. During one conversation with him, she chides herself in voiceover: "You're babbling, when you need clear sentences." This kind of self-talk continues throughout the series, such as when she is preparing to appear on live television and reminds herself internally: "I am not in physical danger, and I am not going to panic." In Season 3, Nina begins to voice her concerns more directly. When Patrick tells her that he wants to know what goes on inside her head, she replies that she "imagined a bomb squelched me into a gelatinous mess." Unlike Nina's family, Patrick asks her why, and Nina voices her concerns that because her life appears to be going well, a disaster must be imminent. When her apartment catches alight later in the episode, she admits, "Part of me is relieved … disaster has struck. Balance is restored." This real disaster, however, prompts more anxiety, with Nina having panic attacks at night, waking, and trying to flee. Disorientated, she has to ask Patrick where she is.

In Season 4, Nina and Patrick are preparing for the arrival of a daughter and seek couples counseling. Nina explores why and how she uses her imagination to manage her anxiety symptoms, and Patrick discusses his former opioid addiction, prompted by the still birth of his son and subsequent breakdown of his first marriage. Patrick attempts to establish some boundaries with the Proudman clan, reasoning that Nina, well into her third trimester, needs rest, and will have ongoing changed priorities. The couple negotiates all this, along with a discussion about whether or not to get married, combine finances or to buy a house, with some success. On the way to their baby shower, however, Patrick sustains a serious head injury in a hit and run accident. He dies on the day of the baby shower, and his funeral is the day before their daughter's birth. In the period between his death and the funeral, Nina seeks out the counselor, concerned as to what her grief might be doing to her growing baby. She is encouraged to harness the power of her imagination and use it as a coping strategy. Moving into Season 5, therefore, viewers see the use of voiceover monologues replaced with conversations with the now-deceased Patrick. These scenes are then intercut with others reshot to show his absence; contrasting her preferred, imagined reality with the one experienced by everyone else. Over time, her sister comes to be able to recognize what she terms "Patrick moments," having previously described Nina's moments of being less-than-present as "psychotically calm and mystifying." Here again, Billie's language reflects common stigmatizing terms with regard to mental illness. As Hinshaw argues, clinical terms like "psychosis" and their lay counterparts such as "crazy" or "mad" are invoked whenever an unpopular idea or hint of rationality appears. As Wahl notes, these tendencies are not demonstrated only by those with no immediate experience with mental health disorders, but also by patients and their families (Wahl, "Mass Media Images").

Background: Selective Mutism

Selective mutism is an anxiety disorder that is rare, and which typically affects young children (Starke). It is an inability to speak in certain social situations, where the person is able to speak in others. The most typical presentation is a child that speaks at home and around family but becomes so socially anxious in other environments (such as school) that they do not speak in that environment (Starke; Capozzi et al., Diliberti and Kearney; Muris and Ol-lendick; American Psychiatric Association). Some individuals with selective mutism will not speak in the presence of adults, or strangers. It does affect a higher proportion of immigrant or bilingual children and is in these cases perhaps an extension of the confidence-based "silent period" in second language acquisition (Starke 46). It is also reported to be more common in girls than boys (Capozzi et al.). The key symptom usually dissipates or disappears within eight years, although those who were diagnosed may retain higher rates of psychiatric disorders into adulthood (Muris and Ollendick).

Selective Mutism in the Media

Selective mutism is rarely seen on screen; indeed, most searches bring up the case study we have examined below, that of Dr. Raj Koothrappali on *The Big Bang Theory*, and little else. The short film *Stuck in Mute* provides a rare exception, as does *Jumanji*, where the little boy, Peter, only speaks to his sister, and only when they are alone, after the death of their parents. Elsewhere, Australian young adult author John Marsden's first novel *So Much to Tell You* (1987) and its later stage adaptation (1998) also deal with this disorder.

"How can she take your order when you're too neurotic to talk to her?" Selective Mutism in *The Big Bang Theory*

The on-screen representation of Rajesh Koothrappali in *The Big Bang Theory* uses the ideas of selective mutism, but applies them to a well-educated, adult male who is incapable of speaking around women. Koothrappali's social anxiety and selective mutism are explicitly referenced on screen throughout the series' twelve-season run. In the early seasons, it is a cause of much amusement and arguably the distinguishing characteristic of the character. Late in Season 1, his neighbor Penny makes him a cocktail while training to be a bartender, and Raj discovers that he can speak to a woman when he drinks alcohol. This prompts him to characterize the grasshopper as a "sweet, green, miracle"; elsewhere he refers to beer as a "magic elixir that can turn this shy Indian boy into the life of the party." In the Season 6 finale, after his equally socially anxious girlfriend Emily breaks up with him, Raj debriefs to Penny about the relationship before they both realize that he is speaking to her while totally sober.

Raj's friends are able to observe the conditions in which mutism will occur. Leonard assures Penny that Raj will be able to participate in the Physics Bowl even though there are women in the audience, because "he only has a problem when they're one on one and smell nice." In Season 2 when he and Howard both vie for the attention of *Terminator: The Sarah Connor Chronicles* actress Summer Glau, Raj is able to speak with her until Howard points out that the "beer" Raj is drinking is non-alcoholic, thus destroying the placebo effect from which he was benefiting. In the same season, Leonard, in an attempt to redirect the critical attention of his psychiatrist mother, announces, "Howard lives with his mother and Raj can't speak to women unless he's drunk. Go." Dr. Beverly Hofstadter responds by declaring selective mutism to be "fascinating" and "quite rare."

Raj acknowledges that his inability to speak to women causes issues in both his personal and professional life. While drinking alcohol provides a temporary solution, his inappropriate behavior and comments when drinking lead to further problems. In Season 6 he drinks alcohol before meeting with the HR head, who is female and attractive. After his first unfiltered comments, he peers into his cup and comments: "This may have been a mistake." In both Seasons 1 and 4, Raj considers medication for his problem. In the latter instance, this development is played for humor, with his increased confidence as a result of the medication manifesting itself in bouts of public nudity.

In this character, then, we see the defining symptom of selective mutism, being played for laughs and in a character that is neither the most likely gender nor age to have this affliction. While Raj is bilingual, which does impact the likelihood of developing selective mutism, he also lived a life of great privilege and as an man in his twenties at the beginning of the series, who has studied at Cambridge, holds advanced degrees including a doctorate, and who only displays symptoms around those from his own peer group but opposite gender, he is far from the typical candidate to develop this disorder.

Background: Post-Traumatic Stress Disorder

Post-traumatic stress disorder is the development of fear-based re-experiencing and emotional and behavioral symptoms that relate to exposure to one or more traumatic events (American Psychiatric Association). Prevalence among adults in the United States is around 3.5 percent but is more than double in those over the age of 75, and much higher among veterans and those whose vocations increase the risk of traumatic exposure, such as Emergency Services. Between one third and one half of survivors of rape, military combat, military captivity, or ethnically or politically motivated internment or genocide will develop PTSD (American Psychiatric Association).

Trauma and stressor-related disorders are listed immediately after depressive and anxiety disorders in the DSM-5, with that missive noting accurately that many of the symptoms can "be understood within an anxiety- or fear-based context" (American Psychiatric Association 265). Crucially, however, people diagnosed with this kind of disorder might also externalize angry, aggressive, or dissociative symptoms (American Psychiatric Association). Of these disorders, PTSD is arguably the most well-known. The disorder develops after exposure to actual or threatened violence, and features recurrent and distressing memories, dissociative reactions (such as flashbacks), prolonged psychological distress to cues that resemble or symbolize those traumatic events, altered cognition or memory as a result of the events, diminished enjoyment, diminished interest in participating in significant activities, feelings of detachment or estrangement, hypervigilance, problems with concentration, problems with sleep, and an inability to experience positive emotions (American Psychiatric Association).

Post-Traumatic Stress Disorder in the Media

On-screen representations of PTSD include *Stranger Things*, *The Unbreakable Kimmy Schmidt*, and Marvel's *Jessica Jones*. Notably, these are all recent, and all Netflix productions. Other characters that viewers identify as having symptoms of PTSD include Rick Grimes from *The Walking Dead* (2010–2019) and Buffy Summers from *Buffy, the Vampire Slayer* (1997–2003) (Kalvesmaki). Some earlier movies, such as *Born on the Fourth of July* or *Forrest Gump*, include characters who are combat veterans having difficulty adjusting to injury and readjusting to civilian life, but these characters were not specifically diagnosed on screen.

"I'm screwed up because I watched my friends die": Post-Traumatic Stress Disorder in *You're the Worst*

Returning to *You're the Worst*, post-traumatic stress disorder causes Edgar significant issues in employment and relationships. Viewers do see some improvement in Edgar's mental health and independence over the course of the series, but equally the representation demonstrates the difficulties that may remain inherent in veterans finding appropriate assistance for this condition.

Edgar is, it seems, remarkably and uncomfortably representative. He is Latino, a veteran, formerly homeless and a criminal; all communities at higher risk of post-traumatic stress (Ramos et al.). Of the kinds of trauma that trigger PTSD as listed in the DSM-5, war trauma is first on the list (American Psychiatric Association). High comorbidity has been found between PTSD and alcohol and drug misuse, depression and anxiety (Ramos et al.), and a number of studies have found that Latino service members reported more re-experiencing of symptoms and more guilt than their Caucasian or Asian peers (Asnaani and Hall-Clark; Spoont et al.).

Edgar is diagnosed on screen in the pilot episode. The audience later learns via flashbacks that prior to his deployment, Edgar had been Jimmy's regular drug dealer. After Jimmy's book is published and he buys his rather impressive home, he has a chance reunion with Edgar in the street. At the time, Edgar is homeless, unemployed, and beating up a stranger who was wearing a T-shirt featuring an unpatriotic slogan. Edgar ignores Jimmy's suggestions that they keep in touch through the mediation of his publicist, and instead moves in "temporarily" to Jimmy's home.

There is certainly significant evidence that Edgar is initially unable to participate in society or the economy. At the beginning of the series he is financially dependent on Jimmy and seems to spend an extraordinary amount of time cooking elaborate breakfast dishes; a task for which he receives little appreciation from Jimmy. He tells Gretchen in the first episode that he does not drive and therefore cannot give her a lift to work because he has "PTSD and mild to medium battlefield-induced psychosis." Edgar continues to have other ongoing mental health conditions across all five seasons. It is perhaps worth noting, however, that he does make improvements with regard to societal and economic engagement. He is able to drive and owns a car in later seasons. He progressively attempts to live more independently from Jimmy, with varying degrees of success, and he does begin to once more engage in paid employment; first in menial jobs, but later as a comedy writer in television.

As Edgar begins to re-engage with the world, he even takes up a hobby, dabbling in improvisational comedy. He receives no support from Jimmy in this endeavor, who characterizes this development as even worse than Edgar's previous interest in heroin. Edgar eventually begins a relationship with his improv class tutor, and it soon becomes apparent that he has not been sexually active for some time. Faced with impotence because of a cocktail of prescribed medications, Edgar stops taking them altogether. He characterizes his medication regime as "one-size-fits-all-shut-up-pills," and says that he is not living, but merely turning down the volume on his life.

The sudden cessation of all medications, however, has an immediately and noticeable impact on his mental health, prompting Edgar's girlfriend, Dorothy, to note that he sometimes scares her. In an episode named "Twenty-Two," after the number of veterans with PTSD who commit suicide each day, Dorothy convinces Edgar to ask Veterans' Affairs for further assistance. The VA offers him a place in a new pilot program, only to immediately rescind the offer when they learn that he has stopped medication, arguing that they cannot allocate more resources to him while he is "hostile" to another prescribed treatment. Edgar thus finds himself seemingly being forced to choose between mental health and a relationship that might in itself have a positive impact on his recovery. Ultimately Edgar recognizes that he is not in a position to offer Dorothy the stability she seeks within her preferred timeframe, and they part ways.

It is when Edgar is trying to navigate whether impotence or insanity is the lesser of two evils that he attempts to confide in Jimmy. Edgar is making an elaborate dish in the kitchen when he broaches the topic, saying: "I'm more creative when I'm upset.... I have a problem." Jimmy seems unperturbed by this revelation, retorting that having a problem is Edgar's "defining characteristic." He further fails to consider the frequency with which Edgar creates gourmet breakfasts, or what this might mean in terms of Edgar's inner world.

Despite these very real issues, Edgar feels significant guilt for having only invisible injuries, at one point recycling cans in order to save enough money to buy Ambien on the black market. In Seasons 1 and 3, Edgar is resistant to the idea of seeking help from Veterans' Affairs and has to be talked into going by first Jimmy, and then Dorothy. In season 1, Edgar tells Jimmy that he does not want to use resources that could be "going to vets with real problems." It is inferred that physical injuries are "real" problems, while mental illness is something rather more elusive.

Edgar's only significant relationship for much of the first few seasons is the terribly dismissive Jimmy, and Edgar's attempts to be more of a friend than an unpaid butler and breakfast chef are consistently and immediately quashed. In a couple of episodes we also see Edgar in states of heightened agitation and hypervigilance; hiding behind cars and checking for snipers, or unable to sleep and filling his hours with exercise and calls to talkback radio. Later, after his disagreement with the VA staff, he finds his car being towed and the tow-truck driver asks if he is a fellow veteran, having seen paperwork left in the car. He then voices what Edgar has been experiencing, correctly guessing that in his state of heightened anxiety, Edgar will have been fearing that roadside garbage are unexploded IEDs, or that people on overpasses might be snipers. The tow-truck driver in a single episode displays more understanding and encouragement around Edgar's condition that the rest of the cast over the entirety of five seasons. He tells Edgar that a companion animal is what has reduced his own suicidality and encourages Edgar to find what works for him. In interview, actor Desmin Borges spoke of the intensive emotional and physical preparation he undertook with regard to this episode. He noted the import of its subject matter and of the decision to portray more completely, and from his character's point of view, events alluded to in passing by other characters in the preceding episode, saying: "Whenever you're dealing with any issue that is as prevalent and is as affecting as a mental health issue, your first goal is to tell the story as truthfully as possible.... We're getting the opportunity to give voice to the voiceless and to those who don't normally see themselves on TV" (Zuckerman).

Despite these ongoing and serious mental health issues, Edgar is the most aware and insightful character of the ensemble. Edgar's relationship with Gretchen is also of great interest, given that they become a dual-diagnosis household when she moves in. From the outset, Edgar recognizes that Jimmy's relationship with Gretchen must "mean" something because Gretchen stays over, which Jimmy never allows. Jimmy is dismissive of Edgar's insights because of his diagnosis: "Why would I even listen to you, eh? You're a mental case! You're on like a billion different medications that all say, 'take for batshit craziness.'" Nor is he at all moved by Edgar's response that he was defending his country. Jimmy, as a Brit expatriate, is not included in the phrase "our country," and shows no sign of this argument having resonated. Most of his actions and reactions throughout the series suggest that he believes himself to be superior to most, and certainly to Edgar, which only compounds his lack of compassion and understanding for Edgar's complex mental health conditions.

Edgar continues to demonstrate significant insight, however; he knows when Gretchen's birthday is, even though Jimmy does not; he tells her that as the girlfriend, she should now be the one to give Jimmy pep talks when required. As previously noted, he is aware that Gretchen is regularly sneaking out of the house at night long before her bed partner is, and when Gretchen moves in and the pair reacts by behaving in increasingly immature and dangerous ways, he tells them to pack in the drinking and drugs, stop masking their fear of commitment and get some sleep, because otherwise they are "gonna die." Later in Season 2, he is the one to recognize that a fleeing Gretchen is carrying her "best garbage bag" and ask if she is going somewhere. In Season 4, when Jimmy returns from solitude and makes contact with Gretchen and she tells him that she is fine, Jimmy chooses to believe her. Edgar is the one who suggests that there may be subtext, asking, "Did you notice *how* she said it? Weirdly flat?"

Edgar's understanding of human nature becomes of great value, somewhat ironically, when Jimmy, a paid professional writer, ultimately needs Edgar's assistance to co-write the screen adaptation of his own novel. As Edgar begins to re-engage with society and builds some self-confidence, this also impacts on his relationship with Jimmy. He regularly demonstrates insight where Jimmy has none, pointing out that Jimmy only likes him "when [he's] struggling" and articulating the changing power dynamic: "I no longer look up you.... I now see you as my equal." Further, he develops better coping strategies as the series progresses, to the point where he packs up his laptop and goes elsewhere to write, narrating his decision for Jimmy: "I didn't like the way you were talking to me, so I am calmly removing myself from the situation." This is a marked difference from the early seasons, where Edgar consistently stayed and listened to Jimmy's put-downs and verbal abuse.

Edgar is also the only one to become aware of the pressure that Gretchen is under in Season 5, when things appear to be going well in both her professional life and personal life, and yet the combined pressures of her promotion and upcoming wedding see her increasingly turning to self-medication. Jimmy dismisses Edgar's warnings, saying that Gretchen loves pills. Edgar insists that he does not "think it's for fun this time." When Jimmy refuses to act, Edgar takes matters into his own hands, clearing out his medicine cabinet so that Gretchen can no longer steal from it. He also learns that she has lost her job and confronts her about it. Echoing Lindsay's comments in Season 1 when she recognizes the signs of a depressive episode, Edgar encourages her to tell Jimmy the truth about her job loss and the state of her mental health. Despite his compassionate stance, Gretchen reacts at first with anger, telling him that she cut off her own parents for monitoring her actions, and "you're just *you*."

Gretchen does, however, take his advice and confess to Jimmy. Right before the wedding, Jimmy also develops some insight around Edgar's role in his life over the past several years, acknowledging how "thoughtful" a friend Edgar has been and that he has seen Jimmy at his worst yet always acknowledged his worth. Jimmy admits that while it has taken him years to see it, Edgar is both his best friend, and best man. It is at this juncture that we see Edgar display a new symptom of PTSD as listed in the DSM-5: self-destructive behavior (American Psychiatric Association). At precisely the moment that Jimmy gives Edgar the credit he deserves and the equality he has craved, Edgar willfully destroys the friendship, predicting marital disaster, advising Jimmy to jilt Gretchen, and refusing to back down in the face of Jimmy's cold anger. This depth of rift is what is required for Edgar to sever ties with Jimmy and begin to live independently, elsewhere.

On the morning of the wedding, Edgar's actions are progressively revealed to those around Jimmy. When Edgar tells Lindsay what he has said, she decides that they now have a definitive answer to the long-debated question as to which of the two of them is the dumb sidekick, telling him that he "killed the group." When Lindsay tells Gretchen what has happened, she too takes the opportunity to confront him, fuming as she insists that she liked but never respected him and that she only let him stay because of the humanizing effect he had on Jimmy.

While this is not immediately apparent in the events preceding the non-wedding of Jimmy and Gretchen, in flash forward we see that Edgar has worked through his motivations and come to understand that they were not altruistic, after all. It transpires that when he insists to Jimmy that just because Jimmy and Gretchen love each other does not mean that they are good for one another, this insight may be more a reflection of his own friendship with Jimmy. There is no doubt of his compassion and affection for his friend; nor that he has far more insight into Jimmy's emotional state at any given time than the man himself. His actions when he lobbies for Jimmy to leave Gretchen, which seem uncharacteristically heartless, are really an attempt to extricate himself from an often-abusive relationship that is seemingly about to be inherently and irrevocably changed. Similarly, Jimmy's early reactions to Gretchen's depression—that is, to ignore it until it inconveniences him—is understandable given that this is how he has routinely responded to Edgar's mental health symptoms.

Edgar is shown in the finale to be able to do better after he removes himself from his co-dependent relationship with Jimmy. In the intercut montage, we see that Edgar has moved to New York; he confesses to Jimmy that it took some time to get used to the noise and busyness, and to stop being triggered by the sounds of cars backfiring. But it took ending his existing relationships and moving to the other side of the country for Edgar to become truly independent, hold down a job and maintain an apartment without assistance.

Like Gretchen, Edgar's character is thoughtfully written; both individuals are depicted as being more than their symptoms, and not stereotyped. Their motivations and the antecedents for symptomatic episodes are nuanced, while remaining in line with behaviors outlined in the DSM-5. Jimmy, who appears to have significant mental health issues of his own (albeit ones that are not diagnosed on screen) is the pivotal connection between the two, and Edgar ultimately must destroy these connections in order to move on and deal with his trauma in a more independent manner. Gretchen also has to learn to take responsibility for her own illness and its treatment, and Jimmy learns to support her as best he can. Despite these different approaches, in the flash forward montage at the end of the series, we see that they have rebuilt their lives and careers; moreover, Edgar has adjusted to life in New York, and Gretchen has fulfilled her long-held dream of motherhood. Ultimately, this represents arguably the single most significant development in on-screen representations of anxiety and depression-related disorders in recent on-screen adaptations: rather than being a short-term plot device, mental illness is represented as a single, significant but ultimately not all-encompassing facet of the characters' personalities.

Conclusions

In this chapter we examined arguably the most commonly diagnosed mental health disorders: anxiety (including selective mutism), depression, and post-traumatic stress disorder. Despite their commonness, these disorders have been under-represented on screen until relatively recently. Anxiety has been relatively unseen on screen because of the difficulty in displaying a character's internal thoughts, a challenge that is overcome in *Offspring* via voiceover. Similarly, in *the Big Bang Theory* Raj's intermittent absence of speech is mediated by having his friend Howard relay his conversations for several seasons. Depression has been shown as situational and short-term, with the exception of Ian's bipolar depression in *Shameless*, and Gretchen's more nuanced and longer term clinical depression in *You're the Worst*. In the same program, we see a depiction of post-traumatic stress disorder that is also carefully crafted, played with great sensitivity by Desmin Borges and explicitly labeled within the narrative. It is encouraging to see such depictions, yet alarming that they have only made it to air so recently in televisual history, given that responsible representations of mental illness and treatment shift the public conversation from "'badness' to 'sickness'" (Payton and Thoits), which would assist in reducing misperception (Vogel and Kapalan) and stigma (Payton and Thoits).

Six

"The reality
is much murkier"
Reality and Representation

In our final chapter we turn to the other side of the television screen to examine how the televisual representations of mental health, as explored in the preceding chapters, are received in reality. For this we include here the perspectives of those with (or living with someone who has) a mental health disorder. This chapter presents interview data in the context of the textual analysis employed in the previous sections to contextualize and ground the overall analysis in reality. "Reality" is, of course, dependent on the lived experience of the particular person with a disorder, hence our inclusion of participant quotes.

In addition to the studies of mental illness on screen to which we alluded in the Introduction, there have been a number of biographical and autobiographical works that attempt to include the perspectives of those diagnosed with the disorders. These include television specials including *True Life: I'm Bipolar* and *Biography: Margot Kidder*; books by John Elder Robison, Margo Orum and Liane Holliday Willey; media reportage of anxiety (Johnston); and personal anecdotes within academic texts (E. Martin). Most recently, Australian television personality Osher Gunsberg has published a full-length memoir of his issues with anxiety, addiction, and OCD, supplementing his podcast discussions around mental health and recovery (Gunsberg, *Back*).

Each provides an insight into the personal and lived experience, with the autobiographical works providing unmediated responses. We wished to capture this immediacy with regard specifically to viewers' responses of their own diagnoses. Although we had hoped to include perspectives from people diagnosed with each of the disorders, only some disorders are represented in our participants, which is arguably indicative of the ongoing stigmatization of mental health diagnoses. The comments that were collected, however, were rich in insight and this chapter thus represents an opportunity to directly give voice to people with the mental health orders discussed elsewhere in this volume.

Interviews

Ethical Approval

The interviews were conducted with institutional ethics approval from the University of Wollongong human research ethics committee. Participants were provided with an information sheet and written consent form and were free to withdraw consent at any time and withdraw from the project if they wished. Where participants were known to the one of the authors, they were given the opportunity to correspond with the other author only, in order to protect their privacy, and a number of our interviewees did avail themselves of this opportunity.

To protect participants' confidentiality more generally, any interview data presented in this chapter have been anonymized. Random pseudonyms have been assigned alphabetically and accompany participant quotes in this chapter. Any identifying information has been removed.

Participants and Disorders

Seven people provided commentary and insights for this project. All participants were older than 18 years of age, with ages ranging from 20s to 50s. The group comprised four women and three men from urban and regional parts of Australia.

All but one participant identified as having (or having had) a mental health disorder; the exception was the partner of someone with a diagnosed mental health disorder. A formal diagnosis was not a criterion for participation, but most participants said they had a diagnosed condition. There are several reasons why an individual may recognize they have mental health disorder symptoms yet not seek medical help, including societal stigma, and very real concerns about the impact on future career choices or paths. Formal diagnoses of some conditions (such as ASD) are often sought in relation to support funding and early intervention; for adults with established coping strategies, then, there may be little or no incentive to seek a diagnosis, but perceived significant career or personal disincentives to do so. Still other conditions may be prone to misdiagnosis. One study suggested that people with bipolar disorder waited an average of thirteen years for an accurate diagnosis

(Campbell), with many individuals being given inappropriate treatment in the interim (Kvarnstrom).

Most participants identified as having bipolar disorder, and other disorders included ASD, anxiety/depression, agoraphobia, and panic disorder. Although participants particularly focused on these disorders in their responses, they also often discussed other disorders portrayed in television programs, including OCD, DID, schizophrenia, hoarding disorder, and kleptomania.

Angie	Diagnosis of bipolar disorder
Beth	Partner has diagnosis of bipolar disorder
Cate	Diagnosis of bipolar disorder, panic disorder, agoraphobia
Dan	Identified as being on the autism spectrum
Edward	Diagnosis of bipolar disorder
Flynn	Diagnosis of bipolar disorder
Grace	Identified as having anxiety/depression

Television Series

Television series discussed or mentioned by participants included *Homeland, 90210, Empire, Big Bang Theory, Law and Order: SVU, Buffy, the Vampire Slayer, Eastenders, Six Feet Under, Neighbours, Monk, Numb3rs, Doc Martin, Bones,* and *United States of Tara.* One also referred to the film *Rain Man.*

Data Collection

Participants' insights were collected via telephone interviews or via email. The interview format was very flexible and most were conducted in a semi-structured approach with several broad questions/topics rather than a strict set of questions (see below for the broad topics); these questions were used as starting points only and the full interviews developed from there based both on what the interviewer chose to ask and draw out from participant responses and also on what topics participants chose to discuss. Participants could discuss any television program they had watched. They were asked to provide any additional comments not covered in the questions if they wished and were also invited to follow up after their interviews with any additional comments they wished to make. Not all data collection took the form of interviews; participants could also choose to simply provide general comments rather than following the interview questions specifically.

Broad Interview Topics
1. Do you have a diagnosis of mental illness?
2. Are you the partner, parent or carer of a person with a mental illness?
3. Have you ever watched television shows which appear to depict characters with either a diagnosed or implied mental health disorder (e.g., schizophrenia, mood disorders [anxiety and depression; bipolar disorder], social disabilities [selective mutism], obsessive compulsive disorder, dissociative identity disorder [multiple personalities], autism spectrum disorder [including the disorder formerly known as Asperger's Syndrome])?
4. How accurate do you find these portrayals to be?
5. Is there anything that frustrates you about these portrayals?
6. Have you ever been able to use a character or a scene from a television program to explain an aspect of the real-life disorder to those who are unfamiliar with the diagnosis and its symptoms?
7. Do you enjoy watching these programs? Do you find the comedy/drama to be appropriate/realistic?
8. Are there any particular scenes or incidents within the program on which you would like to comment?
9. Is there anything else you would like to add?

Data Presentation

We have chosen to provide participant quotes in some length and detail with minimal interpretation, both to avoid the researchers' voices overtaking that of the participants and to give greater voice to the participants so that their impressions can be conveyed in richer detail. People with mental health disorders have often been a silenced, under-represented cohort whose representations have been dictated by others; accordingly, we have allowed space for their voices.

In the following sections, we have included the qualitative analysis in two main sections. In the first section, we discuss four key themes that arose from the interviews and that can be, broadly, applicable across disorders and across television series. The first two themes relate to the medium itself: television. Participants suggested that television has limitations for mental health representations for two main reasons: because its episodic format relies on dramatic imperatives that inevitably entail storytelling shortcuts, and also because certain genres (e.g., comedy) prove hostile to endeavors to provide more sensitive or complex depictions of disorders. As well as these two themes, the third theme centered on the positive elements of on-screen representations such as the utility—or otherwise—of television programs for participants to reflect on and conceptualize the disorder to themselves and their friends and family. The final key theme was of negative aspects of television portrayals, such as creating stereotypes or providing misinformation.

In the second part of the analysis, we move on from a discussion of general concepts that apply across programs and illness types to instead focus on specific mental health disorders and their representations in television, as discussed by participants. Here, we include lengthier, more detailed excerpts from interviews to give a fuller picture of participants' thoughts.

"We need to bring in a character who's going to go mad and kill everyone": Drama in Television Series

Television relies on drama and on shortcuts in storytelling, both broadly because televisual narrative demands conflict (something must happen, there must be a problem that needs an attempt to solve it) and also more specifically because the episodic nature of television requires rapid storytelling given the limited minutes available to convey story. These dramatic requirements of television transcend genre: regardless of whether a television series is categorized as "drama" or "comedy" or "reality" or anything else, every episode of every program relies on dramatic storytelling imperatives to propel story.

As several participants noted, this demand for drama inevitably curtails more complex explorations of the experience of a mental health disorder as well as opens up the opportunity for overly dramatic and unrealistic scenes.

> ANGIE (DIAGNOSED WITH BIPOLAR): As TV programs they are about drama so of course the emphasis in on communicating the spectrum of the disorder quickly and clearly for the audience. [...] In truth the condition has so many other dimensions, other symptoms that don't make it to television because they cannot be as easily converted into dramatic moments and just aren't as interesting.
>
> CATE (DIAGNOSED WITH BIPOLAR, PANIC DISORDER, AGORAPHOBIA): I think they've [producers of *Homeland*] just fallen into the trap that a lot of people do. I mean, it's not just bipolar. If you were a Marine watching this, you'd probably go "flawed, flawed, flawed" watching this [...] that's just the way it is. They've just had to work the bipolar into the show and I think they've had to make some shortcuts in there for the sake of production.
>
> BETH (PARTNER DIAGNOSED WITH BIPOLAR): Carrie [main character of *Homeland*] is the most accurate representation [of bipolar], but the show has well and truly jumped the shark. By the end of Season 3 she's supposedly watched her lover be hanged in front of her and she's eight months pregnant with his love child, and she's off to be bureau chief. Meanwhile, the child *in utero*'s been subjected to alcohol from when she couldn't cope with the pregnancy and was self-medicating, and presumably lithium etcetera once she took some responsibility. It's like, okay writers, where could this possibly be heading? What, she sailed through all this without an episode so you thought you'd send her overseas and away from her support, her family?

Beth also critiqued what she saw as poor storytelling in *90210* which meant that, in her eyes, the writers sacrificed character consistency for dra-

matic storylines: "I could have throttled her boyfriend [the boyfriend of Silver, who has bipolar] for his lack of empathy, and I couldn't believe it when
his parents just excused his complete lack of care for her during her first
manic episode. That just didn't seem to fit with their characters." This was
echoed by Angie in her discussion of *90210*, when she noted that sometimes
bipolar was "just exaggerated as a plot device, like someone switching her
meds to steal her boyfriend." For Grace (identified as having anxiety/depres-
sion), such shortcuts mean that television series can then become "a bit silly,
too dramatic" to adequately represent mental health; instead, they can play to
clichés of mental health, as in an episode Grace cited from *Buffy, the Vampire
Slayer* which, in her words, showed "the crazy lunatics in the asylum" rather
than what she felt was more realistic.

As well as taking shortcuts to convey story more quickly, television was
seen by participants as prone to stereotypical depictions of people with mental health disorders as villains, although participants felt that television representations have evolved over time and current depictions tend to be more
nuanced. As Edward (diagnosis of bipolar) said, "Some of the previous representations have been a bit 'we need to bring in a character who's going to
go mad and kill everyone.'" Yet Edward felt that this trope is being gradually
overtaken by more complex depictions in current programming. Edward also
felt that drama actually aided storytelling because it can be beneficial to creating more sensitive television depictions of mental health disorders, citing the
case of Carrie in *Homeland*:

> The fact that her condition actually brings her down to her knees, quite a few times,
> it's relevant. It's also showing her humanity and vulnerability, as well. So I haven't got
> a problem with it being used for dramatic effect. The only concern that I have about
> having a character like that was that she not be turned into a monster, or you know,
> some psycho who's going to shoot everyone. That was what I was afraid of, before I
> started watching the show. I'm happy to say I was comforted by the fact that she was
> made into a real person. With complex thoughts, and wants, and needs. So no, I don't
> have an issue with that being used for dramatic effect.

Beth echoed this point, saying that although there might be some problems with how current programming represents bipolar, overall representations have improved over time: "At least they [characters with a disorder]
aren't the homicidal cameos we used to see. [...] I worry about the back
catalogue of myths about bipolar out there. But at least these depictions [in
Homeland and *90210*] are a little more responsible than the very cynical, 'we
need to write a character out, let's make her boyfriend bipolar and he can run
her over' kind of storyline." Angie also agreed, concluding that whatever the
problems of previous representations, in general "the portrayals [of mental
health disorders on television] over the years have gotten better."

"There's nothing funny about it": The Use of Genre in Television Depictions of Mental Health Disorders

As well as the drama inherent in any television narrative, genre plays a role in how a mental health disorder is portrayed. Edward raised concerns about how there was a tendency in television to show the illness rather than the person and that this was exacerbated in the reality television genre. As he put it, reality programs about hoarding or OCD focus on disorders whereas fictional drama programs allow more time for character development:

> the really visually spectacular tough disorders, like germaphobia or someone who's collected about three tonnes of material into two rooms [...] I think shows like that are actually worse than the drama in some ways, because they really just show you the madness, the illness, and not much more of the person. Whereas I think something like *Homeland*, because you're seeing a lot more of them, has a better opportunity to get it straight. I think the dramas actually do it a lot better than reality TV. [...] In a way I'm glad that [there is no formal diagnosis of bipolar] in the show [*Homeland*]. I'm really glad it's not there. Because she's not a bipolar character, she's a character with bipolar.

Not just reality television but also fantasy, comedy, and soap opera genres came under question by participants who were concerned about the additional potential for misinformation. For instance, Grace felt that the fantasy framework of *Buffy, the Vampire Slayer* was problematic in depicting mental health disorders in *Buffy* because it ran the risk of trivializing the diseases: "So you have depression or anxiety or schizophrenia or kleptomania, you add in demons and actors running around in ridiculous looking makeup and costumes, and obviously you risk making the whole thing a bit of a joke, or so unreal that nobody can get the connection or take it seriously." Meanwhile, Flynn (diagnosis of bipolar), discussed the challenges of portraying bipolar in the soap opera/teen drama *90210*, which can result in "ridiculous" scenes of high drama, exacerbated by the use of an inherently melodramatic genre anyway.

Several participants were uncomfortable with using the comedy genre to portray mental health disorders. Angie described feeling unable to watch comical representations of bipolar, explaining she did not find them amusing. Cate, who has bipolar, felt that certain disorders were more suited to drama than comedy, and that although comedy might be possibly used respectfully for certain disorders, it could not possibly be a suitable vehicle for representing bipolar:

> Autism, OCD, all that sort of stuff, I think that the media, the entertainment industry can be quite disrespectful in the way they represent those things. I think that you could do [a respectful depiction of autism, OCD, using comedy], if you were going to do it and do it well, to work it into a comedy or whatever other kind of show that you

wanted to use [...] but I honestly can't think of a way that you could work bipolar into a comedy, because there's nothing funny about it. [...] I don't think you could work it sensitively into a comedy, without looking like you were being disrespectful. Without making a caricature of it.

Dan (who identifies as having Asperger's Syndrome) said that he had no objections to using comedy to portray Asperger's Syndrome, even though there were limitations to its accuracy: "To me, it's not laughing *at*. It's more laughing *with*. I don't see it as derogatory. [...] Sheldon is a comedy character. So you can't kind of take him all at face value. [...] You can't say it's being derogatory because yes, it's tongue-in-cheek but it's also providing a service. People are actually willing to look at it, listen to it and watch it, the whole lot, and in that sense it kind of helps us more." Genre, then, was noted by participants as a factor influencing depictions of mental disorders, beyond the basic demand for drama and storytelling shortcuts inherent in television. For some, it was a potentially problematic consideration while for others, any genre was appropriate provided it raised the profile of the disorder.

"It does serve as a good reference point": Positives of Television Representations of Mental Health Disorders

Some of the positive comments made by participants about television centered on television's ability to provide a framework or touchpoint for helping conceptualize the disorder, whether for the individuals themselves with the disorder, or for their friends or family. Participants noted that such examples were either helpful (in raising awareness about a disorder and explaining symptoms and behaviors for family or friends who otherwise would not know or experience the disorder) or unhelpful (in showing inaccurate depictions that needed correcting to avoid misinformation and misrepresentation). However, in this respect it did not matter if the representation was accurate or otherwise because the value was in visibility and creating a space for a disorder that may be otherwise silenced or hidden. This was a common theme for participants.

Dan felt that *The Big Bang Theory* offered a valuable platform for explaining to other people what Asperger's Syndrome is and to set people's expectations, even if the on-screen depictions were not necessarily accurate: "It does serve as a good reference point when people talk to me and they go, 'there's something different about you,' and I say, 'Think Sheldon Cooper, just not as nightmare-ish.' And they look at me and go, 'Okay. Fair enough.' [...] I use Sheldon Cooper because he's probably the most well-known. His popularity does help a lot more than people realize. However, I do make it clear that I'm not, you know, crazy."

As Angie put it,

Television isn't a diagnostic tool although it can help to put a face to issues and a positive feeling of not being alone. [...] I don't seek them [films showing bipolar] out, but I am always interested to watch it on film to see if anything they say strikes a chord and gives me an example I can show [my family] or use to explain myself. [...] In the midst of trying to get my medication on track I showed an episode of my favorite soap to [my family]. [...] What I did like [about *Empire*] was that we saw him [the character with bipolar] functioning as a successful exec while on his medication and it showed that [if bipolar is well] managed you can be a high functioning person.

In a similar way, Edward found *Homeland* useful in explaining symptoms of bipolar to his manager at work:

I actually talked to her about the *Homeland* show. And I said "look, there's this really interesting show"—she'd never watched it, I don't know if she has now—"but, there's a really interesting show that actually portrays, really well, certain things that go on with bipolar. You know, you'll be up for days and days and days and days, or it might last weeks, even, and then she's off, or has her active days when she's in sync, but it's not you know, daily volatility." [And my manager said:] "Oh yeah, all right."

Grace discussed how watching episodes on fear in *Buffy, the Vampire Slayer* helped to create a sense of community and reduce some of her feelings of isolation, which, in her eyes, was an important and positive effect: "That very small thing of feeling like what I was experiencing was something others had also experienced and overcome, was a big deal."

Several participants thought there was value in assigning certain disorders to popular characters in the potential to perhaps reduce stigma. Edward cited the example of Tara from *The United States of Tara*, saying, "I thought it was a bloody good show. It was entertaining, the character was extremely likable. You really felt for her. And you know, she was deeply flawed—even in her own personality, she was deeply flawed. And her multiple personalities were really fun, they were entertaining to be around. So I think it showed that, as a disorder, in a much better light [than reality programs]." Grace also described the portrayal of anxiety and depression on *Buffy, the Vampire Slayer* as "quite sensitively done. When you give these disorders to characters that viewers love, I think it helps—people might find it more sympathetic." Similarly, Flynn, who spoke of his experience with bipolar, found *90210* to have positive aspects because it was shedding light on a relatively misunderstood disorder and doing so in a "sympathetic" way: "It's a very good attempt at getting people to understand the illness. [...] It's a sympathetic portrayal. You can have a go at the detail [as being unrealistic], but it's realistic enough. How hard must they have fought to get that storyline?" Flynn also pointed out that raising the profile is important when it comes to mental health disorders: "I think it's good that there's bipolar episodes in mainstream [TV]. It's not that common an illness, and it's not very well known what it does to you."

"Any credibility she had has just gone out the window": The Role of Family and Friends on Television

There were mixed responses from participants about the role of family and friends on the television programs. No participant was asked about this topic specifically, but it arose in several interviews as participants reflected how television series plots reflected their own life and experiences. Dan found intervention and advice from other people in real life to be helpful for him personally in navigating social worlds in his experience of Asperger's Syndrome, which he linked to *The Big Bang Theory* and the role of Penny in Sheldon's life:

> For instance, I believe that the relationship with Amy Farrah Fowler wouldn't have happened if it were not for Penny. Well it wouldn't have lasted as long as it did if it weren't for Penny saying, "Sheldon, you need to do this. Sheldon, you need to do that." And that's actually a big one that happens every time. Reflecting into personal life, I still will heavily rely on the advice of friends at University, that if I do something wrong, and I don't know it, or it doesn't bother me *per se*, they have to go, "Listen, this is not right. You've got to do the right thing, here."

Beth, whose partner has a diagnosis of bipolar, felt that both *Law and Order SVU* and *Homeland* offered some positive aspects in their portrayals of different family dynamics in the context of mental health disorders.

> The *Law and Order* depiction was interesting, because it showed a range of family responses. Stabler was being all military/cop and actually handed over evidence that [his daughter] Kathleen had been stealing while manic. Cathy, as the mother [of Kathleen], was furious, because she thought their first responsibility was to their daughter. And I remember thinking that I didn't know whose side I was on. But then they kind of just dropped it, or maybe I stopped watching. I do remember that years later when Stabler and Cathy were separated it was Kathleen who was given the immortal line, "we're your family, Dad, not a booty call." So of their four kids, she was the one designated to have insight and social awareness of what was going on in the household.

Beth also mentioned that she could "really relate" to Carrie's father in *Homeland* because of his role in encouraging Carrie to be accountable for her disorder (he "calls her on her behavior and tells her when she's 'acting bipolar'"), which was similar to what she had experienced with her partner.

Edward spoke of experiencing a similar response to Carrie's father in *Homeland*, and felt that Carrie's father's own experience of having bipolar gives him increased capacity for empathy and insight:

He's bipolar as well. He's on the medication, but he still knows. He understands her. You see? I know he's got to be loving and caring because he's Dad, but he's the character who really understands her, and where she's at. Whereas the sister is sort of: "Ugh. You know you're manic?" Whereas the dad will say, "Have a look. Have you had a look at yourself? Have you seen what you're like?" It's a different message to convey to someone, where you're asking them to have a bit of insight, as opposed to sounding critical of them.

Although Edward found the portrayal sensitively done, Cate discussed the same theme in *Homeland* but found it troubling because it resonated with her own feelings of vulnerability and loss of credibility with family and friends. Cate explains that when Brody [Carrie's love interest] discovers Carrie has bipolar disorder it gives him "the upper hand" and "any credibility she had has just gone out the window":

> I thought she played that part really, really well, because that did actually happen to me. [...] You're this person and they [family/friends] find out you've got bipolar, and they start using phrases like, "I think you're letting yourself get a bit upset now. I think you really need to calm down. Do you think you need to talk to someone? Is there some medication you should be taking?"—and then your whole world, this world that you've created and you've worked so hard for, has just gone out the window.

There was recognition, then, among participants of some realistic televisual attempts to portray the experience of the disorder particularly in the context of familial and social relationships.

"All the old tired clichés of insane asylums and crazy inmates": Negatives of Television Representations of Mental Health Disorders

Participants identified a range of problematic depictions of mental health disorders which could have negative outcomes, and their responses covered several basic and more complex concerns. At its most basic, television can recycle unhelpful and untrue clichés, perpetuate myths, and propagate misinformation. As its worst, television can negatively impact participants' own self-image. For example, Cate described her difficulty in watching bipolar on television was simply due to the fact that it was a reminder of her own life. "I found it [*Homeland*] confronting, but that's only because of my own personal experience." This is supported by other published studies, such as the one by Fennell and Boyd, who wrote that some viewers with OCD found that representations of OCD increased their own symptoms, (Fennell and Boyd) as well as by our own anecdotal evidence. For instance, a friend on the spectrum wished to participate in this present study but shared that she found it difficult to watch *The Big Bang Theory.* Ultimately, she opted not to proceed with the interview as a consequence of her discomfort with the humorous depictions of symptomatic behavior. Indeed, it is possible that this effect may be found in many forms of television—comedies about aging parents such as *Mother and Son* (Australia), for example, were arguably less funny for viewers whose parents were not only aging but ailing.

Participants noted several concerns with how the programs treated mental health and the potential for misinformation. Grace reflected that schizophrenia, as represented in *Buffy, the Vampire Slayer,* had fallen victim to "all the old tired clichés of insane asylums and crazy inmates" because of its use of mental health institutions. Even positive clichés can be problematic, as Cate pointed out; for example, Cate felt that television series such as *Homeland* perpetuated myths that all people with bipolar disorder were geniuses or particularly creative, as seen in Carrie's uncovering of a terrorist plot while hospitalized with mania. This narrative is part of the longstanding tradition of Ronald Fieve's so-called "Midas effect" (Fieve), which linked bipolar with creativity. In subsequent years Kay Jamison (herself diagnosed with the disorder) retrospectively diagnosed two hundred creative minds including Walt Whitman, Vincent Van Gogh and Virginia Woolf in her 1980 publication, *Touched with Fire.*

Cate and Edward both raised the concern that television shows could give the wrong impression to viewers about the role and efficacy of medication. Cate described her skepticism of Carrie's recovery, describing Carrie as being "all over the shop, and it gets sorted really quickly? Yeah, no, that's completely—having been through it myself and having watched other people go through it—no way. It's days or weeks." As well as the unlikely speed of recovery as seen on television, Edward also pointed out the potential for viewers to think that treatment is only comprised of medication. In his discussion of *Homeland,* he described feeling frustrated with how the protagonist Carrie responds to treatment:

> At the beginning of the show she was actually like psychotic but her sister's a GP who was medicating her. The focus on medication is actually the focus on when she cracks. That, I kind of have a bit of a problem with, because whilst medication is good, it's not the be-all and end-all answer for everyone. It doesn't really work for every single person. [...] When she was put in the Psych ward, she was there for quite some time. And then she was an outpatient as well, with her sister, so I can see what they're getting at, but I had to look at the timeline in one of the episodes a couple of times before I got the fact that there was actually a lengthy time on the timeline of her being in hospital. Not just one or two days. There's a lot that goes on. [...] You don't get better after one pill, not by a long shot.

While cognitive behavioral therapies (CBT) are a common treatment and are routinely included in contemporary autobiographical accounts

(Gunsberg, *Back*; Johnston) few programs include CBT, although one of the exceptions to this is a minor character, Mrs. Tishell in *Doc Martin*, after a criminally psychotic break. As previously noted, Carrie in *Homeland* undergoes ECT, Silver from *90210* does mindfulness activities, as does *Offspring's* Nina, and we see characters in therapy sessions and/or taking medication in *Tara, Monk,* and *Glee*. Edward's critique is correct, however, in that most onscreen representations with an on-screen diagnosis involve a discussion about medication and that the recovery period is, for narrative purposes, vastly truncated when compared with a real-life convalescence after an episode of symptomatic mental illness.

"The meaning of life is hidden in their mania": Representations of Bipolar Disorder on Television

As well as general comments across genres, programs, and disorders, participants spoke in some detail about specific elements of disorders that they felt were portrayed well or not on certain programs. Bipolar was the most common disorder experienced by participants, and as such received the most attention in interviews. Most comments focused on *Homeland*, but other programs were also discussed by participants, such as *90210*.

Angie, Beth, and Flynn all nominated *90210* as a (somewhat) positive example of how to portray bipolar disorder. As Beth put it, "I thought the actress did a fabulous job of showing Silver's bipolar symptoms, and to their credit, the writers didn't trot it out all the time." Angie, too, mentioned *90210* as one of the more realistic depictions of bipolar disorder, saying, "OK, it's a teen show but they actually did a really good job of showing the extremes of the illness."

Several participants pointed out that certain parts of bipolar disorder can be helpfully explained by reference to a television character. Flynn reflected on several areas in which *90210* achieved—and did not achieve—a realistic portrayal of bipolar and its specific symptoms. For instance, he felt that the character with bipolar, Erin Silver, exhibited symptoms that were realistic for bipolar, such as rambling and mania, although this is in some ways limited by the soap opera/teen drama genre of the show, as mentioned in passing earlier.

> They're already getting it right in that they're saying that she [Erin Silver] doesn't accept what's real. Bipolars [in psychotic episodes] are either depressed or manic, and they're trying to find reality. So they've set this girl up as someone who doesn't really know reality. And they're trying to say that that's a characteristic of this.
> [...] But what's interesting is trying to portray a bipolar person in a soap opera. Everyone's having these massive mood swings, and that is a bit ridiculous in itself.

Almost every character, in order to create drama, has to be emotionally up and down or all around. I think they've done a good job with that mania.

[…] Apart from the bipolar story, I don't like any of the other stories [storylines in *90210*]. What I think has happened, I think they've got themselves an advisor on mental health, and they've done a pretty good job. But everything else, and how they talk to each other … [is not realistic].

Most participants felt *Homeland* offered a mostly realistic representation of bipolar disorder, despite some qualms, and they related much of the program to their own experiences. Cate, for instance, found several realistic elements in *Homeland*.

I think it's a well-made series. I think it's interesting. It's got a good storyline. […] I think the catalyst for her becoming manic was good. And realistic. Having a major physical injury like that. And it's interesting, too, that her father is bipolar as well. When they talk about it being genetic, and all. In my case, it came from my Aunt … so yeah, I think it's good to have the father in there. I think it's interesting that her sister's treating her, because her sister's probably crossing a whole pile of lines that she shouldn't be crossing as well. And also her realization that she's probably always going to be alone. I thought that was interesting as well. I think the writers have done a good job.

Edward found similar realism with Carrie's depiction in *Homeland* and explained that he could recognize some aspects from his own experience of bipolar:

I thought that was an accurate portrayal. I thought her manic mood was quite accurate. I thought the depressive mood was actually quite accurate, because it shows that full extent of how far away from your baseline normal mood you can be. Just, off your rocker. […] It's really hard to say because there are many parts of it, and everyone's bipolar is going to have its own nuances, right? […] When I look at the Carrie character, there are parts that I recognize, like the irritability for one, like when she went through a really manic, manic phase just brimming with energy and capable of doing a million and one things, not being able to stop; you know, your brain is just so charged that you can't keep up with it.

[…] When she got really depressed in the first season and just could not talk, could not get out of bed. It's a long, consistent mood as well, so the series shows how profound and crippling that depression can be. I think they did that really well, and I think—I hope—that people who have never come across anyone who's bipolar would look at that and see that what characterizes the illness is not the volatility so much as it is the distance and the depth, the depth of the emotion that's there. So I actually thought it was done really well, the way she doubted herself and her own sanity was done really well. I really related to it. I thought it portrayed the experience really well, just that absolute depth of despair. I have, you know when people watched that, seen them go, oh wow, geez, they're really going through a rough time, this is not just a little walk in the park or a bit of whimsy, this is really unwell. Really sick. When I used to get hypomanic I could be really irritable. I could go from 0 to 100 and just explode. It was a problem I had. But that's a very small part of it. And with the general public out there there's still this idea that if you're bipolar, you're going to be happy and sad about five thousand times a day. Now, how do you explain it to them? Like, seriously?

Other participants felt that programs could offer a good opportunity to explain the experience to other people. For example, Beth felt that *90210* and *Homeland* offered the opportunity to explain to people with no experience of bipolar how the disorder can look:

I think the rapid word associations were really accurate. My husband was like that when he was manic. And he's talkative at the best of times, so it was exhausting when he wanted to share every thought that came into his head. I remember sitting up in bed weeping as he was riffing on something, and he suddenly asked, "What's wrong?" I told him I was just tired, not sad. He smiled and said, "Oh, that's the mania." It was so all-consuming, he'd forgotten that the mania was his and not mine. I think either Silver's baking soda [on *90210*] or Carrie's green pen monologues [on *Homeland*] would be good to show someone: this is what it looks like. This is the point where you go to hospital.

Cate agreed, feeling that *Homeland* offered some utility in helping other people (without bipolar) to differentiate between behaviors due to bipolar and those that anyone can have. Using an example of her children, Cate said,

When I'm yelling at you [my kids] because your rooms are disgusting and we've got visitors coming? It's not because I'm bipolar, it's because it's messy. It [*Homeland*] would help in those ways. To explain to people what it is, and what it isn't. I think she's [Claire Danes] done a good job. I think it would be incredibly hard to do. What she's done. Without, there's a risk to her of going too far either way—not giving it enough? Or giving it too much and being completely unrealistic.

Participants also discussed the concept of disorder versus personality, with some noting the difficulty they have experienced with people attempting to attribute—and thereby dismiss—specific character traits to the disorder. Watching this on television could be challenging. As Edward put it, the complex depiction of Carrie in *Homeland* has its positive side, but also negatives.

I do think those aspects are very well scripted, and well acted and well directed, but I see other elements in the character, but you can't tell where the bipolar ends and her personality begins. She's very prickly, the moment her boss says anything to her or looks at her sideways, she gets really prickly about it. When he was saying she should stay on and choose career over love, she got really nasty with him, like "Saul, I'm not your daughter. What do you think you are doing?" It's too easy to dismiss people's behavior when they're bipolar, in terms of the bipolar. "Oh, so-and-so's acting this way because she must be going through a manic phase or she must be depressed." So in terms of accuracy, I think there's a lot of accuracy in there. I think there's a lot of grey area in terms of her character. And I actually quite like that, because it's not supposed to be this clear-cut, "she's a loony case," and therefore you can put things down to her either going through a manic or a depressive phase. I do like the greyness of it. There are other parts of it, like her prickliness that—well, I think she's a bit of a bitch, to be honest. I think she's actually quite nasty to the people who've helped her immensely just to keep her job. So I think it's a bit of a mixed bag with that character. But I don't think the parts of bipolar that they represent are bad. I actually think there's a lot of accuracy in there.

[...] Sometimes I look at the character and I go, are you just really manic when you're going ga-ga over him [the love interest, Brody], did you have this whole fantasy all in your head, or are you really that much in love with him? You know who he is, you know his faults, you know his limitations as a person, his major, major mistakes. I don't think the writers and producers meant for that character to be 100% sympathetic. She's complex and complicated.

Edward noted that these blurred lines could be problematic and potentially confusing for the audience because the behaviors might be erroneously attributed to bipolar when they are in fact a part of anyone's behavior, as we noted earlier in the chapter.

There's the portrayal of Carrie as an entire person, versus the portrayal of her illness. Her, as an entire person, yeah [...] like the defensiveness when she's questioned on anything. That, I get annoyed with, because I think she's quite unpleasant, and ungrateful. But I don't think that's the illness, you see; I think that's her personality, her way of coping with the world. And it might have come from feeling very vulnerable in the past, when her moods were running amok, but the point is, she's got that. And in some ways it's not a big deal if that's what she's done to protect herself, and a lot of people have that, with bipolar, but in another way, that part of her I have a bit of a problem with, because you lose a bit of sympathy for the character. She's really quite nasty. That's what I get annoyed with. [...] That's my major issue. Things like that, people will go, oh that's just manic, or she's just depressed, or she's just paranoid. You know, up her meds and she'll be fine. That's the part I find a bit disturbing.

These themes of blurred lines between personality and disorder were raised by other participants. Cate found this frustrating to watch in *Homeland* as it reflected her own experience in life: "Any emotion that you have, anything like that, is automatically twisted to become part of your mood disorder. It's not because it's a logical reaction." As Angie put it, "The painfully accurate part of the portrayal [in *Empire*] is that his accomplishments are always appended to or undercut by his condition: 'That was smart, when he's on his meds he is valuable.' His illness also makes a convenient excuse to discount his opinions and ideas when they don't want to listen to him."

Beth, too, discussed similar themes in *Homeland* and in another show, the Australian soap opera *Neighbours*:

I really like the way Carrie has a life and a job. Sometimes she's not in control and sometimes you can't tell if she's acting out because she's manic or just genuinely frustrated. And I like that it shows the characters in the supporting or caring roles: Maggie, her dad and Saul. I really relate to her Dad, who calls her on her behavior and tells her when she's "'acting bipolar.' I have to do that sometimes; say do you realize you said/did X, Y and Z? Does that sound right to you?" Of course, [Carrie's dad's] situation's a bit different because he's got bipolar too.

[...] I think *Neighbours* had a bipolar ex on it a few years back. I watched one episode when I heard about it, to see what she was like, and it was once again, trying to kill off the rival while hubby did the, "Oh, she's bipolar" thing. My husband doesn't get to use his bipolar as an excuse for his behavior. He's an adult. I promised I would never leave him because of behavior if it was related to that or any other illness, but I also told him that means he has a responsibility to take his medication and stay well. You can't play with these things and you can't use them as a get-out-of-jail-free card.

Beth was more critical about the representation of bipolar disorder on *Six Feet Under* as portrayed through the character of Billy Chenowith (Jeremy Sisto), feeling that it served only to perpetuate or in some cases create stereotypes that were untrue about bipolar:

> *Six Feet Under* I started watching because I heard there was a bipolar character in it (and then I heard he was played by Elton from *Clueless*, so...). And while I fell in love with the show, I hated what they did with that character. He stalked people, he self-harmed, he hit on his sister, he wept, he complained about his lack of sex drive and creativity while on meds, he was supposed to have burned the house down when he was a teen—it was just going back to every stereotype. And as much as his sister Brenda would correct all the people who were scared of him and say, "oh he's sick, he can't help it," in some ways that just made her seem like a bit of a patsy. And when he started talking about his feelings for Brenda and kissed her, I thought, oh no. People watching this are now going to think people with bipolar are into incest. Because some people watch TV like everything's a documentary. It's where they get their information, and they don't question it.

This concern about inaccurate depictions of bipolar on television was also shared by Cate and Angie. Cate criticized *Homeland*'s depiction of bipolar as succumbing to well-worn clichés linking bipolar and creative genius.

> The part where she's absolutely manic, and she's divided up all the paperwork, you know, "my kingdom for a green pen." And she's got all the colors going on, and then, Saul comes in and puts it all up on the wall and deciphers it, and everything like that. [...] When you are like that, you are not a freaking mad genius. You are completely off the show.
> [...] So that thing, it's kind of like, now people who have only ever seen an autistic person in the film *Rain Main* now believe that all people who are autistic are bloody geniuses who can count cards and all that sort of stuff. I think that anyone who's had no exposure to bipolar, for them to come across this part of the series and to see Carrie doing that and Saul working it out and all the rest of it, they would now believe that people who are bipolar, when they're manic, they can create absolute magic. Whatever they touch—it might look a little bit messy and you might have to sort it out—but all the answers are there, the meaning of life is hidden in their mania.
> [...] Up until that point, up until Saul starts going through and sorting it out, everything was completely believable. Her fixation with the green pen, the colors, her belief that she was solving something, that was all completely believable. But when he took her absolute rubbish and turned it into an answer? No.

Cate also spoke at length about other flaws she perceived in *Homeland*, specifically about the unrealistically quick time for Carrie's recovery—mentioned briefly earlier—and Carrie's very role in the intelligence and security sector, both of which she felt were far from reality for someone who has bipolar disorder.

The other minor thing, I would say, was that it was a little bit too quick to go from mania back onto a level playing field. And also, the depression came too quickly. From being up here to down, to normal, to into depression, that was too quick. I suppose they had to do it for the show, for the storyline, sort of thing, but that was way too quick. But it is fairly, the depiction is, I think, fairly realistic.

[…] She [Carrie] would be on administrative leave, and then you'd be terminated for not being fit to do that job [as a spy]. Because you're a security risk. Because you might become manic and say something wrong.

[…] The other one with regards to medication and condition that was a bit of out whack, is where she had decided to have the ECT. […] she then makes this decision to have ECT, but she's talking to Saul, like it's just a normal conversation. In that scene there's no evidence of her being depressed. There's nothing to relate that back to previous scenes where she's been depressed. […] But the physical signs of depression like we were saying would have still been there. I imagine her more likely to be curled up in the bed and saying "just get it over and done with" or something like that. But no, she engages him, just like the two of them with their normal sort of banter. I don't think that was realistic. But it could be a production issue, you know, time, trying to get everything in.

Angie similarly spoke about how some programs tended to rely heavily on storytelling shortcuts rather than more realistic depictions of the experience of bipolar.

Recently I was hooked on the show *Empire*—the first family of Hip Hop—and one of the sons has bipolar disorder. They captured perfectly the accelerated speech, the erratic nature and unpredictability of what will be said next. I feel like the problem with the portrayal is that it happens in an ad break but it's TV so you don't expect it to take the creeping, slow descent as it does in real life. They always portray ultra-rapid cycling which is very uncommon. […] I think it is the black and white, up and down portrayal of it for dramatic brevity. The reality is much murkier. It creeps. […]

[…] Jean Slater in *Eastenders* is bipolar, she is usually portrayed as dippy and "Just being Jean" but it showed her staring off into space, it showed her losing her train of thoughts. It showed others seeing these things and checking in with her to make sure she was taking her medication when she started to slip. It showed that even on the medication you can have break through episodes. She had some really powerful scenes explaining how it feels, it was so accurate and not glorified, it was not an extreme depiction. It showed her struggling, not just in full blown mania. The main thing it showed was how someone who isn't clearly off their tree can feel so desolate that they will do something silly. She was quiet and still and yet she was on the brink. That is bipolar to me, and it was so meaningful to me to see her go through it realistically.

[…] I can function, I get moving because I have to […] but I will believe that I can rebuild our back fence, start a vineyard in our backyard and that I can take the man in the carpark in a fight. Retold, these [examples] sound benign, a bit comical but the reality of how I feel in those moments isn't benign. These times bring lows after the invincibility that need to be endured and it is intensely private unlike a TV show and I just need to remember that sometimes.

Angie had a number of criticisms of how television portrays mental health, explaining that she felt only one series realistically portrayed the fuller experience of bipolar, and that in general television programs missed key parts of her experience of the disorder while at the same time emphasizing other parts that resulted in her feeling, in some ways, as if her experience of bipolar disorder was somehow illegitimate or in question because of the way it differed from television.

> I've yet to see anything that makes it truly understood and illuminating apart from *Eastenders* [...] The main thing, the single most important part that they all miss, bar one [*Eastenders*], is the fear. There is shame, confusion and being frightened. It is so frightening to have these things happen to you [...] They portray all of these characters as being unaware of what is happening to them, that they are entirely different people. I am excruciatingly aware of what is happening to me. [...] What worries me about the TV depictions is seeing the stereotypical version of bipolar, with the depression that leaves you bedridden and the manic highs of absolutely loss of control, is that people will think I'm not really sick, mine [my bipolar] isn't bad because I'm not doing what they see on TV [...] I feel invalidated because I don't compare with the dramatized version.

"You can be suffering in this kind of bleak neverland and nobody may even know": Representations of Anxiety/Depression on Television

Grace discussed her thoughts on how *Buffy, the Vampire Slayer* handled the disorders of anxiety and depression, feeling that the show had some positive aspects when it came to portraying the experience of the disorders:

> I remember an episode about fear, where people's fears were becoming literally true. Like, you fear that nobody really cares about you, and then you literally become invisible, like Xander. And then there was another episode where they kind of repeated it again, it was about nightmares coming to life, like spiders or being naked in front of other people, being buried alive, dying, failing your responsibilities, or whatever. I really was struck by a line in the episode where The Master [a demon, kind of an arch villain] said something like, "We are defined by the things we fear, if you face your fear, it cannot master you." Not exactly rocket science but somehow it struck a chord with me and I found it helpful in a time of life when I felt very, very alone, and like fears were crushing me.
>
> [...] That musical episode [in *Buffy, the Vampire Slayer*], it was about going through the motions, I remember Buffy singing about sleepwalking through life, going through the motions, faking it. Then in the last scene, Buffy reveals—accidentally, or maybe unwillingly—but she had no choice I think, it was a spell, she reveals the secret to her friends that instead of being rescued from hell, which they thought they did when they brought her back to life after she died, they had in fact taken her from heaven back to earth. Something which obviously shocks them and it's this killer moment in the program, very dramatic and really well done. Despite Whedon's sketchy and vague, nonsensical philosophies and trite lyrics, there is some truth in the idea that you can be suffering in this kind of bleak neverland and nobody may even know this, I thought

they got that concept right. [...] The episode ends with Buffy and Spike kind of getting together. It's the first real part of her descent into that deeply unhealthy relationship, where she simply wants to feel something, anything. And I thought that's also pretty true that people with serious depressive bouts can sometimes turn to self abusive behaviors just to try to feel something other than pain (or to stop feeling entirely), and it might be unhelpful behaviors around alcohol or drugs or sex.

"I'm doing homework on how to integrate with the rest of society": Representations of ASD on Television

Dan found much of use in on-screen depictions of *Bones* and *The Big Bang Theory*, although most of his discussion was of the latter. For Dan, the chief value of the programs was two-fold: in explaining himself to the world, and in explaining the world to him. There was value, he felt, not only in using the programs to explain to others what the experience of Asperger's Syndrome is like, but also in observing how someone else with the same disorder navigated the world.

[...] There was an episode of *Numb3rs* that involved an Aspergic [sic] person. *Big Bang Theory*, of course. I have seen a few episodes of *Doc Martin*, but I wasn't too interested in it; it isn't the type of thing that I'm interested in. I still understood the checkpoints, I understood like, his character. There's actually an interesting question around both *Doc Martin* and *The Big Bang Theory* in that they claim that the characters are not on the spectrum, and that's just how they are. Sheldon Cooper is obviously an over-exaggeration. He's a comedic character. But there are certain things that he states or says or does, it's very clear cut. It's all very law-based or to me, number-based. To me, law is a number-based thing, there is a clear response. Yes it is subject to certain interpretations but it is still at the end of the day, a clear cut response. The way he operates is that clear-cut response. If this doesn't happen, therefore that doesn't happen. If this happens, then I don't have to do this. His personality algorithm depicts that of someone with—I wouldn't say a disability, I prefer to see it as a condition rather than a disability, but they do have perks. Yes, they do have plus sides and they do have negative sides.

Some [depictions] are accurate, however, when I see it, it's clear and bright to me that he is an over-exaggeration of the epitome of, like a Level 10 kind of thing. It's like he's segmented into certain things, certain frames. On the issue of *Bones*, she's probably more real-life, in that sense that she's brilliant at what she does—she's focused and brilliant at what she does, however, at the same time she also has less social skills and always is asking for confirmation on how she should go about something. Especially when it comes to her relationships, she's always asking Angela, the worldly character, who's all about social skills, whereas Bones is all about academic skills.

[...] In a sense it has brought to light certain things but they [my friends] don't realize that, the way I see Asperger's, there is not just one clear-cut answer, there are different things about it, like, there's different symptoms of it. The portrayal on *Bones*, that's pretty good in the way that they've done the character, the way that they've done the research on said character. Certain things I can relate to and I can see in myself, from both characters. Like for instance, Sheldon Cooper's inability to form a romantic relationship until he meets somebody who's very similar to him, and is like: This is what I want. This is how I want it.

[...] But using Sheldon is probably the easiest method because everyone knows the character. They know he's not exactly crazy—well, he is a little bit crazy—but there is a method to his madness. And that's what a lot of people don't seem to twig to. There is a method to his madness, and that's him basically trying to understand the world around him as best he can.

Dan spoke of not only enjoying *Big Bang Theory* but also finding it useful for navigating his own world:

Despite the fact that it's over-portrayed, if an encounter or an incident happens, something that happens in there, I can go, "Hang on, this is what happened in there. Turn it down a few notches, make a few tweaks, I can then use this situation to an advantage." So in a sense, I'm doing homework on how to integrate with the rest of society. And because of that, a lot of people don't pick up Aspergic [sic] until a little later on. Now it's becoming more noticeable that people aren't picking up on it for about an hour or so.

[...] When people have asked me, I've been like, yes, I have this condition. It's what I've got but it's not what I am. And most of the time they're taken aback by that but then it's like, well listen. We'll compare me with, as I said, Sheldon, because I use him the most. I'll explain to them, "yes, I do like this, yes, I do like this, but no, I don't like any of that." And they go, "OK, fine." So because of that, these things that he does, I don't do. So I'm educating them that there is no clear cut diagnosis or clear cut one size fits all kind of thing for Asperger's Syndrome.

Dan also offers a useful insight into the individual nature of these disorders. In response to being asked about the accuracy of these screen representations, he replied: "[...] I can't really comment categorically if *The Big Bang Theory, Bones* or *Doc Martin* or any of those aren't misrepresenting Asperger's Syndrome, is because there is no clear cut case for Asperger's Syndrome. You can find certain symptoms that can be common."

Conclusions

In noting the usefulness of universal characters, we again see the need for these representations to be accurate and educational, rather than stereotypical and melodramatic. As we have long understood from the works of Wahl, Philo et al. and others, pervasive television images become the key source of information for many with regard to these complex conditions (Philo; Philo et al., *Making Drama*; Wahl, "Mass Media Images"; Wahl, *Media Madness*).

In this final observation, Dan explains the usefulness of these characters who display symptomatic behavior, in providing a universal touchpoint: "[...] I find a lot of people, when I use the Sheldon analogy, are more willing to accept it. Only because they go, hang on, he's not the unknown anymore. It's something they can actually relate to."

Conclusion

As we have seen, television programs that feature an implied or clear diagnosis of mental health disorders have become increasingly prevalent in recent years. As both diagnostic rates and awareness of mental health issues rise, this is perhaps to be expected. This increase in representations is accompanied by what appears to be a growing tendency for audiences to "diagnose" televisual characters even when no on-screen diagnosis is ever made, a trend that is not without its pitfalls. Indeed, as a recent Australian documentary discovered, even highly trained and experienced professionals struggle to identify mental health disorders purely by observation. Despite close observation of a number of cognitive and social tests, the experts were unable to correctly match any of the ten participants with their mental health diagnosis. As the documentary noted, the delineations between mental health and mental illness, between situational and clinical anxieties, and between personality traits and symptomatic behaviors, are different for every individual (*How "Mad"*). Yet, as we noted in the introduction, certain behaviors or injuries are understood by audiences to denote particular disorders and this is unlikely to change soon.

With this increasing prevalence of mental health disorders on screen, what can we conclude about these representations? It is clear that most disorders have been traditionally portrayed in rather negative, inaccurate ways, and this book argues that Mindframe, Shift and other organizations past and present have instead offered information and examples around how to most responsibly convey mental health disorders on television to avoid such negative representations. As we note throughout the book, some series have taken just such a responsible approach; others appear to have willfully ignored it. A more promising wider change is the shift away from short term psychotic "guest" and undiagnosed lead characters, towards open diagnosis of major characters who live with mental illness, rather than being defined by it. We are hopeful that this is a trend that will continue and strengthen.

What remains disappointing is the scarcity of programs that specifically diagnose the characters, show them engaging effectively with treatment, and having positive outcomes as a result. In the Australian documentary example cited earlier, the participants were asymptomatic and assessed as being well enough to be included. It is suggested that the reason the experts were unable to distinguish the past diagnoses was because the patients' treatment regimens were so effective. While there are a few fictional examples of characters successfully managing their illness, such Emma Pillsbury on *Glee* or Dr. Nina Proudman in *Offspring*, these are extremely recent. Although such depictions continue to be countered by simplistic, negative portrayals in other programs in which the disorder serves as drama and little to nothing is said of available therapeutic options, it is nonetheless our hope that the more nuanced, positive stories are the start of a significant shift in representation on our screens.

By far the prevalent and continuing stereotypes perpetuate stigma and stigmatizing language, with casual commentary about others being "crazy," "psycho" or "lunatics" for having an unusual or slightly irrational opinion still being the order of the day. Again, this is disappointing, given that concerns about this language have been raised in numerous studies over the years (Hinshaw; Link; Wahl, "Mass Media Images"). It is also interesting to note the degree to which our respondents in the previous chapter used older ("Asperger's," "manic depression") or pejorative ("crazy," "mad") language. The predominance of this language in our society has long been noted and is attributed by some as leading to self-stigmatization and a reluctance, in some cases, to seek appropriate professional help (Hinshaw). An alternative viewpoint is that our study participants used such words ironically or even as acts of linguistic reappropriation or reclamation, as a symbolic way to reclaim agency in the same manner as other stigmatized groups over time.

At first glance, it may be easy to dismiss television representations as fictional entertainment, and therefore unimportant. This view is overly simplistic and erroneous. As Hinshaw notes, people with a mental health disorder also tend to share the stereotypes and (mis)conceptions of the general public with regard to mental health disorders, reinforced as they are by representation in popular culture. Television, which is consumed in the safety and privacy of one's own home, regularly and sometimes for years on end, may appear deceptively innocuous, but self-stigmatization can lead to denial, withdrawal, and isolation. These in turn lead to poor outcomes from those whose symptoms are such that they should be actively seeking treatment at that time.

Our interviews with people who are themselves diagnosed with these disorders provide a unique and useful insight into the impacts of contemporary televisual representations. Their remarkably honest comments reflect both the positive and the negative of on-screen trends: that depictions can be used as a shorthand language to explain one's own diagnosis, its manifestations and its treatment; and equally, that those representations can become all-consuming and limiting when particular symptoms and behaviors become seen as the only "real" experience of a disorder (e.g., the popular belief that all people with OCD have a cleaning compulsion) and thus potentially de-legitimize the alternative symptoms and behaviors experienced by others. Adding a wider array of alternative symptoms or behaviors to the repository of our collective understanding by means of televisual depictions would not only solve this problem but also perform an educational role by informing the general public that the experiences of one disorder will vary depending on the individuals who have that disorder.

As we acknowledged in the Introduction, it is not possible to include an encyclopedic analysis of every television representation of mental illness in history. Indeed, given the historical propensity to not overtly name mental health disorders on screen, it would be nigh impossible to even build a list of such programs. Instead, we have chosen programs that are widely interpreted by audience as having a character with symptoms of mental ill heath, which in some cases have also been explicitly identified within the narrative. Our approach has been to discuss key means of representing these disorders, as compared with clinical literature including the DSM-5, and in comparison and contrast with first-person responses from our interviewees. Inevitably such an approach means that some that would be worthy of study are missed, as we focus our attention elsewhere. We nevertheless hope that this book encourages more scholarly attention and dialogue round mental health disorders and their depictions in popular culture and enriches already existing works in this field.

References

The A-Word. BBC. 2016–2017.

The A-Word, DVD Extras. BBC. 2017.

Adreon, D., and J. Durocher. "Evaluating the College Transition Needs of Individuals with High-Functioning Autism Spectrum Disorders." *Intervention in School and Clinic* (2007): 271–279.

Agerup, Tea, et al. "Associations Between Parental Attachment and Course to Depression Between Adolescence and Young Adulthood." *Child Psychiatry and Human Development* 46 (2015): 632–642.

Amelie. Dir. Jean-Pierre Jeunet. UGC-Fox, 2001.

American Psychiatric Association. *Diagnostic and Statistical Manual of Mental Disorders.* Fifth Edition. Washington: American Psychiatric Association, 2013.

_____. *Diagnostic and Statistical Manual of Mental Disorders.* Fourth Edition. Washington: American Psychiatric Association, 2000.

Anderton, Ethan. "Watch Trailers for ABC's New 2017–2018 Shows: *Roseanne* Returns, Zach Braff forms *Alex, Inc.* and More." 17 May 2017. *Slashfilm.* 6 June 2018. http://www.slashfilm.com/abc-2017-series-trailers/#more-416921.

Andreasen, Nancy C. "Creativity and Mental Illness: Prevalence Rates in Writers and their First-Degree Relatives." *American Journal of Psychiatry* 144 (1987): 1288–1292.

_____. "The Relationship Between Creativity and Mood Disorders." *Dialogues in Clinical Neuroscience* 10.2 (2008): 251–255.

Anxiety and Depression Association of America. "OCD PSA with *Monk* Star Tony Shalhoub." n.d. *Anxiety and Depression Association of America.* 28 June 2019. https://adaa.org/about-adaa/press-room/multimedia/ocd-psa-monk-star-tony-shalhoub.

Arbonida, Jilianne. "*Homeland* Season 6 Premiere Spoilers: Carrie Continues Battle with Bipolar Disorder." *Christian Today* (2016). https://www.christiantoday.com/article/homeland.season.6.spoilers.carrie.continues.battle.with.bipolar.disorder/79779.htm.

Armstrong, Thomas. *Neurodiversity: Discovering the Extraordinary Gifts of Autism, ADHD, Dyslexia and Other Brain Differences.* Cambridge, MA: Da Capo, 2010.

As Good as It Gets. Dir. James L. Brooks. Tri-Star, 1997.

Asnaani, Anu, and Brittany Hall-Clark. "Recent Developments in Understanding Ethnocultural and Race Differences in Trauma Exposure and PTSD." *Current Opinion in Psychology* 14 (2017): 96–101.

Aswell, Sarah. "Why *Atypical* Is Not the Show We Were Hoping For." 12 August 2017. *She Knows.* 9 September 2018. https://www.sheknows.com/entertainment/articles/1135562/netflix-atypical-review.

Attwood, Tony. *The Complete Guide to Asperger's Syndrome.* London: Jessica Kingsley, 2007.

_____. "The Pattern of Abilities and Development of Girls with Asperger's Syndrome." Attwood, Tony, and Temple Grandin (Eds). *Asperger's and Girls.* Arlington: Future Horizons, 2006. 1–7.

Atypical. Netflix. 2017–.

"Autism; Synaesthesia Is More Common in Autism." *Mental Health Weekly Digest* (2013): 50.

The Aviator. Dir. Martin Scorsese. Miramax, 2004.

Baron Cohen, Simon. "Book: Leo Kanner, Hans Asperger, and the Discovery of Autism." *The Lancet* 386 (2015): 132–30. 11 September 2019

_____. *Mindblindness: An Essay in Autism and Theory of Mind.* Cambridge: MIT Press, 1995.

Baron-Cohen, Simon, and Sally Wheelwright. "The Empathy Quotient: An Investigation of Adults with Asperger Syndrome or High Functioning Autism, and Normal Sex Differences." *Journal of Autism and Developmental Disorders* 34.2 (2004): 163–175.

Baron-Faust, Rita. "Me, Myself & Irene." *BMJ* 321.7263 (2000): 770.

Baudrillard, Jean. *Simulacra and Simulation.* (Trans. Sheila Faria Glaser. Simulacres et Simulation. 1981). Ann Arbor: University of Michigan Press, 1994.

BBC News Health. "TV Mental Health Portrayal Rapped." 22 November 2010. BBC News. 22 November 2012. http://www.bbc.co.uk/news/health-111800017?print=true.

A Beautiful Mind. Dir. Ron Howard. Universal Pictures, 2001.

Belling, Catherine. "Reading the Operation: Television, Realism, and the Possession of Medical Knowledge." *Literature and Medicine* 17.1 (1998): 1–23.

Belmaker, R. H. "Bipolar Disorder." *The New England Journal of Medicine* 351.5 (2004): 476–86.

Bently, Jean. "*90210* Series Finale: One Happy Ending, and a Bunch of Ambiguous Ones." Hollwyood.com (2013). www.hollywood.com/recaps/55013649/90210-series-finale-then-and-now.

Beverly Hills 90210. Fox. 1990–2000.

Bianculli, David. "Jim Parsons on the Science of Sheldon, *Big Bang*." NPR (2010). 30 September 2016. http://www.npr.org/templates/transcript/transcript.php?storyId=130156625.

The Big Bang Theory. CBS. 2007–.

The Big "C." Showtime, 2010–2013.

Big Brother. Endemol. 1999–.

Biography: Margot Kidder. 27 June 2001.

Bollard, Gavin. TV Series Review: *Doc Martin.* 7 December 2011. 28 June 2019. https://life-with-aspergers.blogspot.com/.

Bones. Fox. 2005–2017.

Bonner, Francis. "Looking Inside: Showing Medical Operations on Ordinary Television." King, Geoff (Ed.). *The Spectacle of the Real: From Hollywood to Reality TV and Beyond.* Bristol: Intellect, 2005. 105–115.

Born on the Fourth of July. Dir. Oliver Stone. Universal, 1989.

Bowen, M., P. Kinderman, and A. Cooke. "Stigma: A Linguistic Analysis of the UK Red-Top Tabloids Press' Representation of Schizophrenia." *Perspectives in Public Health* 3.1 (2019): 147–152.

Boysen, Guy A., and Alexandra VanBergen. "A Review of Dissociative Identity Disorder Research." *The Journal of Nervous and Mental Disease* 201.5 (2013): 440–443.

_____, and _____. "A Review of Published Research on Adult Dissociative Identity Disorder: 2000–2010." *The Journal of Nervous and Mental Disease* 201.1 (2013): 5–11.

bpHope. *bpHope:Hope and Harmony for People with Bipolar.* n.d. 29 June 2019. https://www.bphope.com/.

Bradshaw, Stephen. *Asperger's Syndrome—That Explains Everything: Strategies for Education, Life, and Just About Everything Else.* London: Jessica Kingsley, 2013.

Brand, Bethany, Christa Krüger, and Alfonso Martínez-Taboas. "Separating Fact from Fiction: An Empirical Examination of Six Myths About Dissociative Identity Disorder." *Harvard Review of Psychiatry* (2016): 257–70.

Brand, Bethany, Richard Loewenstein, and David Spiegel. "Disinformation About Dissociation." *The Journal of Nervous and Mental Disease* 201.4 (2013): 354–356.

Brand, Bethany L., et al., "A Survey of Practices and Recommended Treatment Interventions Among Expert Therapists Treating Patients with Dissociative Identity Disorder and Dissociative Disorder Not Otherwise Specified." *Psychological Trauma: Theory, Research, and Policy* 4.5 (2012): 490–500.

The Breakfast Club. Dir. John Hughes. Universal, 1985.

The Bridge. Sveriges; DVR. 2011.

Buffy, the Vampire Slayer. WB-UPN. 1997–2003.

Butler, Jeremy R., and Steven E. Hyler. "Hollywood Portrayals of Child and Adolescent Mental Health Treatment: Implications for Clinical Practice." *Child and Adolescent Psychiatric Clinics of North America* 14 (2005): 509–22.

Byrne, Peter. "The Butler(s) DID it—Dissociative Identity Disorder in Cinema." *Medical Humanities* 27.1 (2001): 26–29.

_____. "Stigma of Mental Illness and Ways of Diminishing It." *Advances in Psychiatric Treatment* 6 (2000): 65–72.

Camp, Mary E., et al. "*The Joker*: A Dark Night for Depictions of Mental Illness." *Academic Psychiatry* 34.2 (2010): 145–149.

Campbell, Denis. "People with Bipolar Disorder May Wait 13 Years for Diagnosis." *The Guardian* (2012): 1–3. 24 June 2019. https://www.theguardian.com/society/2012/jun/27/bipolar-disorder-diagnosis-survey.

Canadian Mental Health Association. "What's the Difference Between Dissociative Identity Disorder (Multiple Personality Disorder) and Schizophrenia?" 2015. *Canadian Mental Health Association, BC Division.* 3 August 2019. https://www.heretohelp.bc.ca/q-and-a/whats-the-difference-between-dissociative-identity-disorder-and-schizophrenia.

Capozzi, Flavia, et al. "Children's and Parents' Psychological Profiles in Selective Mutism and Generalized Anxiety Disorder: A Clinical Study." *European Children's Adolescent Psychiatry* (2018): 775–783.

Cefalu, Paul. "What's So Funny About Obsessive-Compulsive Disorder?" *PMLA* 124.1 (2009): 44–58.

Chapman, Simon. "Should the Spectacle of Surgery Be Sold to the Highest Bidder?" *BMJ* 342.d237 (2011): 283.

Clement, Sarah, and Nena Foster. "Newspaper Reporting on Schizophrenia: A Content Analysis of Five National Newspapers at Two Time Points." *Schizophrenia Research* 98.1–3 (2008): 178–183.

Collins, Paul. "Must-Geek TV: is the World Ready for an Asperger's Sitcom?" 6 February 2009. *Slate.* 29 September 2016. htpp://slate.com/articles/arts/television/2009/02/mjustgeek_tv.html.

Community. NBC-Yahoo. 2009–2015.

Corderoy, Amy. "Hey *Revenge* Writers: Be Careful How You Portray Mental Illness." 2 May 2012. *Daily Life.* 22 October 2012. http://www.dailylife.com.au/action/printArticle?id=3260822.

Corrigan, Patrick W. "How Clinical Diagnosis Might Exacerbate the Stigma of Mental Illness." *Social Work* 52.1 (2007): 31–39.

Criminal Minds. CBS. 2005–.

Daria. MTV. 1997–2002.

The Dark Knight. Dir. Christopher Nolan. Warner Bros., 2008.

Davies, Caroline. "TV Dramas Give Misleading View of Mental Illness, Claims Report." 22 November 2010. *The Guardian.* 22 October 2012. http://www.guardian.uk/society/2010/nov/22/tv-programmes-mental-illness/print.

Davies, Lorraine, William R. Anson, and Donna D. McAlpine. "Significant Life Experiences and Depression Among Single and Married Mothers." *Journal of Marriage and Family* 59.2 (1997): 294–308.

Davis, Robert A. "Buffy, the Vampire Slayer and the Pedagogy of Fear." *Slayage: The Online International Journal of Buffy Studies* 1.3 (2001). 4 February 2011.

Debord, Guy. *Society of the Spectacle* (Trans. La Société du Spectacle. 1967). Detroit: Black and Red, 1977.

Diament, Michelle. "Actors with Autism Join Netflix Series *Atypical*." 11 September 2018. *Disability Scoop.* 12 September 2018. https://www.disabilityscoop.com/2018/09/11/actors-autism-netflix-atypical/25474/.

Diefenbach, Donald L. "The Portrayal of Mental Illness on Prime-Time Television." *Journal of Community Psychology* 25.3 (1997): 289–302.

Diliberti, Rachele A., and Christopher A. Kearney. "Anxiety and Oppositional Behavior Profiles Among Youth with Selective Mutism." *Journal of Communication Disorders* (2016): 16–23.

Doc Martin. ITV. 2004–2019.

"Doc Martin an Aspie?" 30 October 2007. *Wrong Planet.* 28 June 2018. https://wrongplanet.net/forums/viewtopic.php?t=47315.

Dodd, Susan. *Understanding Autism.* Sydney: Elsevier, 2004.

Doll, C., T. F. McLaughlin and A. Barreto. "The Token Economy: A Recent Review and Evaluation." *International Journal of Basic and Applied Science* 2.1 (2013): 131–149. 19 September 2015. http://insikapub.com/Vol-02/No-01/121JBAS%282%29%271%29.pdf.

Dollhouse. Fox. 2009–2010.

Dosani, Sabina. "The House of Obsessive Compulsives." *British Medical Journal* 331.7513 (2005): 409.

Draaisma, Douwe. "Stereotypes of Autism."

Philosophical Transactions of the Royal Society B.364 (2009): 1475–1480.

Eastenders. BBC. 1985–.

Edwards, Nicola. "Representation of Mental Illness on TV." 12 January 2011. *Free Your Mind.* 22 October 2012. http://free-your-mind-campaign.blogspot.com.au/2011/01/representation-of-mental-illness-on-tv.

Eldred-Cohen, Colin. 1 October 2016. *The Art of Autism.* 11 November 2018. https://the-art-of-autism.com/6-creatives-on-the-autism-spectrum-actors-and-filmmakers/.

Empire. Fox. 2015–.

ER. NBC. 1994–2009.

Eternal Sunshine of the Spotless Mind. Dir. Michel Gondry. Focus, 2004.

Fast, Julie A., and John D. Preston. *Loving Someone with Bipolar Disorder: Understanding and Helping Your Partner.* Second Edition. Oakland: New Harbinger, 2012.

Fennell, D., and M. Boyd. "Obsessive-Compulsive Disorder in the Media." *Deviant Behavior* 35.9 (2014): 669–686.

Ferris Bueller's Day Off. Dir. John Hughes. Paramount, 1986.

Fienberg, Daniel. "ABC's New Shows: A Critic's Rating." 16 May 2017. *Hollywood Reporter.* 7 June 2018. https://www.hollywoodreporter.com/fien-print/abc-new-show-trailers-ranked-1004483.

Fieve, Ronald R. *Moodswing: The Third Revolution in Psychiatry.* New York: William Morrow, 1976.

Fight Club. Dir. David Fincher. 20th Century Fox, 1999.

Figueroa, C. G. "Virginia Woolf as an Example of a Mental Disorder and Artistic Creativity." *Revista Medica de Chile* 133 (2005): 1381–88.

Fiske, John. *Television Culture.* Second Edition. 1987. London: Routledge, 2011.

Floris, Jessica, and Susan McPherson. "Fighting the Whole System: Dissociative Identity Disorder, Labeling Theory, and Iatrogenic Doubting." *Journal of Trauma & Dissociation* 16.4 (2015): 476–493.

Forrest Gump. Dir. Robert Zemekis. Paramount, 1994.

Found in Translation. Dir. Anthony Sines. 2017. http://www.abc.net.au/austory/found-in-translation/8986178.

Friday Night Lights. NBC. 2006–2011.

Funk, Michelle, et al. "Mental Health and Development: Targeting People with Mental Health Conditions as a Vulnerable Group." 2010. *World Health Organization.* 4 February 2011.

Gans-Boriskin, R., and C. Wardle. "Mad or Bad? The Boundaries of Mental Illness on Law and Order." *Journal of Criminal Justice and Popular Culture* 12.1 (2005): 26–46.

Ginn, Sherry. "Memory, Mind, and Mayhem: Neurological Tampering and Manipulation in Dollhouse." *Slayage: The Journal of the Whedon Studies Association* 8.2–3 (2010). 4 February 2011.

Girls. HBO. 2012–2017.

Gleaves, D.H. "The Sociocognitive Model of Dissociative Identity Disorder: A Reexamination of the Evidence." *Psychology Bulletin* 120.1 (1996): 42–59.

Glee. Fox. 2009–2015.

Gluschkoff, Kia, et al. "Hostile Parenting, Parental Psychopathology, and Depressive Symptoms in the Offspring: a 32-year Follow-up in the Young Finns Study." *Journal of Affective Disorders* (2017): 436–442.

The Good Doctor. ABC. 2017–.

Graetz, Janet E. "Autism Grows Up: Opportunities for Adults with Autism." *Disability and Society* 25.1 (2010): 33–47.

Granello, Darcy H., and Pamela S. Pauley. "Television Viewing Habits and Their Relationship to Tolerance Toward People with Mental Illness." *Journal of Mental Health Counselling* 22 (2000): 162–175.

Greenstein, Laura. "The Best Movies About Mental Health." 20 December 2017. *National Alliance on Mental Illness.* 28 June 2019. https://www.nami.org/Blogs/NAMI-Blog/December-2017/The-Best-Movies-About-Mental-Health.

Gunsberg, Osher. *Back, After the Break.* Sydney: HarperCollins, 2018.

_____. *The Osher Gunsberg Podcast: Why Sharing Stories is So Important—A Life on Screen with Doris Younane.* Sydney, 3 June 2019.

Hatufim (Prisoners of War). 20th Century Fox. 2010–2012.

Henderson, Lesley. *Social Issues in Television Fiction.* Edinburgh: Edinburgh University Press, 2007.

Hey Arnold. Nickelodeon. 1996–2004.

Hinshaw, Stephen P. *The Mark of Shame: Stigma and Mental Illness and an Agenda for Change*. Oxford: Oxford University Press, 2007.

Hoffner, Cynthia A., and Elizabeth L. Cohen. "Responses to Obsessive Compulsive Disorder on *Monk* Among Series Fans: Parasocial Relations, Presumed Media Influence, and Behavioral Outcomes." *Journal of Broadcasting and Electronic Media* 56.4 (2012): 650–668.

Holton, Avery E. "What's Wrong with Max? *Parenthood* and the Portrayal of Autism Spectrum Disorders." *Journal of Communication Inquiry* 37.1 (2013): 45–63.

Homeland. Showtime. 2011–2018.

Homeland Season 1: Under Surveillance. DVD Extras. 2011.

Horton, Stephanie Stone. "'Their Lives a Storm Whereon They Ride': The Affective Disorders and College Composition." http://www.inter-disciplinary.net/wp-content/uploads/2010/08/hortonpaper.pdf, 2010.

House. Fox. 2004–2012.

The House of Obsessive-Compulsives. Channel 4, 2005.

How "Mad" Are You? SBS. 2018.

Hühn, Peter. "The Detective as Reader: Narrativity and Reading Concepts in Detective Fiction." *Modern Fiction Studies* 3.3 (1987): 451–466.

Hyler, Steven E., Glen O. Gabbard, and Irving Schneider. "Homicidal Maniacs and Narcissistic Parasites: Stigmatization of Mentally Ill Persons in the Movies." *Hospital and Community Psychiatry* 42.10 (1991): 1044–1048.

Hyler, Steven H. "Stigma Continues in Hollywood." *Psychiatric Times* 20.6 (2003): 1–4.

International OCD Foundation. "Exposure and Response Prevention (ERP)." 2019. *International OCD Foundation*. 28 June 2019. https://iocdf.org/about-ocd/treatment/erp/.

Jacobsen, K. "Asperger's." 6 February 2019. *Doc Martin Lovers—Blog*. 28 June 2019. http://docmartinlovers.com/2019/02/06/aspergers/.

Jamison, Kay Redfield. "Mood Disorders and Patterns of Creativity in British Writers and Artists." *Psychiatry* 52.2 (1989): 125–34.

_____. *Touched with Fire: Manic Depressive Illness and the Artistic Temperament*. New York: Free Press, 1993.

Jessica Jones. Netflix. 2015–2019.

Jindal, Ripu D., and Michael E. Thase.

"Treatment of Insomnia Associated with Clinical Depression." *Sleep Medicine Reviews* (2004): 19–30.

Johnson, Davi A. "Managing Mr. Monk: Control and the Politics of Madness." *Critical Studies in Media Communication* 25.1 (2008): 28–47.

Johnston, Kerryn. "The Moment Kerryn Johnston Had an Anxiety Attack on Live TV." 9 May 2016. *Mamamia*. 25 June 2019. https://www.mamamia.com.au/kerryn-johnston-talks-anxiety/.

Jordan, Rita. "Autism Spectrum Disorders in Current Educational Provision." Roth, Iloa, and Payam Rezaie (Eds.). *Researching the Autism Spectrum*. Cambridge: Cambridge University Press, 2011. 364–392.

Jorm, A. F. "Mental Health Literacy: Public Knowledge and Beliefs About Mental Disorders." *British Journal of Psychiatry* 177 (2000): 396–401.

Jumanji. Dir. Joe Johnson. Tristar, 1995.

Kalvesmaki, Felix. "10 Fictional Characters People with PTSD Relate To." 5 February 2019. *The Mighty*. 3 August 2019. https://themighty.com/2019/02/tv-movie-characters-ptsd/.

Khaleeli, Homa. "Law and Disorder." *The Sydney Morning Herald: The Guide* (2012): 5.

Kinder, Marsha. "Doc Martin." 2004. *Interacting with Autism*. 28 June 2019. http://www.interactingwithautism.com/section/understanding/media/representations/details/50#comment-2061478653.

Klimas, A., and T. McLaughlin. "The Effects of a Token Economy System to Improve Social and Academic Behavior with a Rural Primary Aged Child with Disabilities." *International Journal of Special Education* 22.3 (2007): 72–77. htpp://www.internationaljournalofspecialeducation.com/issues.cfm.

Kromer, Kelly. "Silence as Symptom: A Psychoanalytic Reading of 'Hush.'" *Slayage: The Online International Journal of Buffy Studies* 5.3 (2006). 4 February 2011.

Kulage, Kristine M., Arlene M. Smaldone, and Elizabeth G. Cohn. "How Will DSM-5 Affect Autism Diagnosis? A Systematic Literature Review and Meta-Analysis." *Journal of Autism and Developmental Disorders* 44 (2014): 1918–1932.

Kvarnstrom, Elisabet. "The Dangers of Mental Health Misdiagnosis: Why Accuracy Matters." 4 August 2017. *Bridges to Recovery.* 24 June 2019. https://www.bridgestorecovery.com/blog/the-dangers-of-mental-health-misdiagnosis-why-accuracy-matters/.

LA Times. ""Doc Martin" Star on the Making of the British Series." 12 April 2012. *LA Times.* 28 June 2019. https://latimesblogs.latimes.com/showtracker/2012/04/martin-clunes-talks-doc-martin.html.

Law and Order. NBC. 1990–2010.

Law and Order: SVU. NBC. 1999–.

Lilienfeld, Scott O., et al. "Dissociative Identity Disorder and the Sociocognitive Model: Recalling the Lessons of the Past." *Psychology Bulletin* 125.5 (1999): 507–23.

Link, Bruce G. "Understanding Labeling Effects in the Area of Mental Disorders: An Assessment of the Effects of Expectations of Rejection." *American Sociological Review* 52 (1987): 69–112.

Livingston, Kathy. "Viewing Popular Films about Mental Illness Through a Sociological Lens." *Teaching Sociology* (2004): 119–128.

Loewenstein, Richard J. "Dissociation Debates: Everything You Know is Wrong." *Dialogues in Clinical Neuroscience* 20.3 (2018): 229–242.

Ludwig, Arnold M. *The Price of Greatness: Resolving the Creativity and Madness Controversy.* New York: Guildford Press, 1996.

Luterman, Sara. "How Season 2 of *Atypical* Improves the Show's Depictions of Life as an Autistic Person." *The New York Times* (2018): 1–4. https://www.nytimes.com/2018/09/11/arts/atypical-season-2-autistic-depiction-improvements.html.

Lynn, Steven J., et al. "Dissociation and Dissociative Disorders: Challenging Conventional Wisdom." *Current Directions in Psychological Science* 21.1 (2012): 48–53.

Lyons, Margaret. "*Community*'s Dan Harmon Discovered He Had Asperger's While Writing Abed's Character." 23 September 2011. *Vulture.* 11 November 2018. https://www.vulture.com/2011/09/community-dan-harmon-wired-aspergers-abed.html.

Ma, Zexin. "How the Media Cover Mental Illnesses: A Review." *Health Education* 117.1 (2017): 90–109.

Mac Suibhne, Seamus, and Brendan D. Kelly. "Vampirism as Mental Illness: Myth, Madness and the Loss of Meaning in Psychiatry." *Social History of Medicine* (2010). 4 February 2011.

Marsden, John. *So Much to Tell You.* Canberra: Walter McVitty, 1987

_____*So Much to Tell You.* Sydney: Hatchette, 1998.

Martin, Emily. *Bipolar Expeditions: Mania and Depression in American Culture.* Princeton: Princeton University Press, 2007.

Martin, Sam. *Madness in the Media: Demystifying the Emergence of an OCD Trope in Television.* Clemson University, 2017. Dissertation. https://tigerprints.clemson.edu/all_theses/2724.

Massachusetts General Hospital. "Massachusetts General Hospital Psychiatry." 2012. *Understanding Bipolar.* 2014 May 23. www.massgeneral.org/pyschiatry/services/bipolar-understanding.aspx.

Matchstick Men. Dir. Ridley Scott. Warner Bros, 2003.

McMahon-Coleman, Kimberley. "Teaching Little Professors: Autism Spectrum on TV and in the Classroom." Janak, Edward, and Ludovic Sourdot (Eds.). *Educating Through Popular Culture: You're Not Cool Just Because You Teach with Comics.* Lanham: Lexington, 2017. 145–169.

_____. "Why Doc Martin Hates Being Called Doc Martin." *Peer Reviewed Proceedings: 6th Annual Conference.* Wellington: Popular Culture of Australia and New Zealand, 2015. 124–132. http://popcaanz.com/conference-proceedings-2015/.

McMahon-Coleman, Kimberley, and Kim Draisma. *Teaching University Students with Autism Spectrum Disorder: A Guide to Developing Academic Capacity and Proficiency.* London: Jessica Kingsley, 2016.

McMahon-Coleman, Kimberley, and Roslyn Weaver. *Werewolves and Other Shapeshifters in Popular Culture: A Thematic Analysis of Recent Depictions.* Jefferson, NC: McFarland, 2012.

McNally, K. "Schizophrenia as Split Personality/Jekyll and Hyde: the Origins of the Informal Usage in the English Language." *Journal of the History of Behavioral Sciences* 43.1 (2007): 69–79.

Me, Myself, and Irene. Dir. Peter Farrelly and Bobby Farrelly. 20th Century Fox, 2000.

Miller, Lindsay Mae, Brett J. Deacon, and David P. Valentiner. "The OCD Project: Educational or Sensational?" *Journal of Cognitive Psychotherapy: An International Quarterly* 29.2 (2015): 116–122.

Mindframe. Mental Illness and Suicide: A Guide for Stage and Screen (P3–2557). Canberra: Commonwealth of Australia, 2007.

Minghella, Dominic. "Doc Martin TV Series." 5 April 2012. *Dominic Minghella.* 28 June 2019. https://www.minghella.com/work/doc-martin-series/.

Monk. USA Network. 2002–2009.

Morgan, Blake. "What Is the Netflix Effect?" 19 February 2019. Forbes. 17 June 2019. https://www.forbes.com/sites/blakemorgan/2019/02/19/what-is-the-netflix-effect/#74374f605640.

Morris, Gary. *Mental Health Issues and the Media: An Introduction for Health Professionals.* London: Routledge, 2006.

Mother and Son. ABC. 1984–1994.

Mullen, Ann. "TV's Misinformation on Bipolar Disorder." *Ezine Article* (2012): http://ezinearticles.com/?TVs-Misinformation-on-Bipolar-Disorder&id=4374322.

Murder, She Wrote. CBS. 1984–1996.

Muris, Peter, and Thomas H. Ollendick. "Children Who Are Anxious in Silence: A Review on Selective Mutism, the New Anxiety Disorder in DSM-5." *Clinical Child and Family Psychology Review* (2018): 151–169.

Murray, Noel. "TV Club Interview: Jim Parsons." 1 May 2009. AV Club. 29 September 2016. http://www.slare.com/articles/arts/television/2009/02/mustgeek_tv.html.

Murray, Stuart. *Representing Autism: Culture, Narrative, Fascination.* Liverpool: Liverpool University Press, 2008.

National Alliance on Mental Illness. "Dissociative Disorders—Treatment." 2019. *NAMI.* https://www.nami.org/Learn-More/Mental-Health-Conditions/Dissociative-Disorders/Treatment.

Neighbours. Grundy-Fremantle. 1985.

The New Adventures of Winnie-the-Pooh. The Disney Channel. 1988–1991.

NHS. *Symptoms: Obsessive Compulsive Disorder (OCD).* 28 September 2016. 28 June 2019. https://www.nhs.uk/conditions/obsessive-compulsive-disorder-ocd/symptoms/.

NIMH. *Obsessive-Compulsive Disorder.* January 2016. 28 June 2019. https://www.nimh.nih.gov/health/topics/obsessive-compulsive-disorder-ocd/index.shtml.

_____. "Schizophrenia." n.d. *National Institute of Mental Health.* 2 August 2019. https://www.nimh.nih.gov/health/publications/schizophrenia/.

Nim's Island. Dir. Jennifer Flackett and Mark Levin. 20th Century Fox, 2008.

90210. CBS. 2008–2013.

90210 4Eva: DVD Extra. 2013.

North, Carol. "The Classification of Hysteria and Related Disorders: Historical and Phenomenological Considerations." *Behavioral Sciences* 5.4 (2015): 496–517.

North, Gary. "Orgs Praise *Monk's* Depiction of OCD." 4 September 2008. *Variety.* 28 June 2019. https://variety.com/2008/scene/features/orgs-praise-monk-s-depiction-of-ocd-1117991603/.

Numb3rs. CBS. 2005–2010.

NYU Steinhardt: Metropolitan Center for Urban Education. "Culturally Responsive Classroom Management." 2008. 19 September 2015. http://steinhardt.nyu.edu/scmsAdmin/uploads/005/121/Culturally%20Responsive%20Classroom%20Mgmt%20Strat2.pdf.

OCD UK. Types of OCD. 22 July 2018. 28 June 2019. https://www.ocduk.org/ocd/types/.

The OCD Project. VH1, 2010.

Offspring. Endemol. 2010–2017.

One Flew Over the Cuckoo's Nest. Dir. Milos Forman, 1975.

Orley, Emily. "How *Parenthood* Broke Down the Autism Awareness Barrier." 25 September 2014. 23 October 2018. https://www.buzzfeed.com/emilyorley/how-parenthood-broke-down-the-autism-awareness-barrier.

Orum, Margo. *Fairytales in Reality.* Sydney: Macmillan, 1996.

Owen, Patricia R. "Portrayals of Schizophrenia by Entertainment Media: A Content Analysis of Contemporary Movies." *Psychiatric Services* 63 (2012): 655–659.

Packer, Sharon (Ed.). *Mental Illness in Popular Culture.* Santa Barbara: Praegar, 2017.

Parenthood. Dir. Ron Howard. Universal Pictures, 1989.

_____. NBC. 2010–2015.

Paris, Joel. "The Rise and Fall of Dissociative Identity Disorder." *The Journal of Nervous and Mental Disease* 200.12 (2012): 1076–1079.

Paskin, Willa. "Secret Agent Mandy." *NY Mag* (2012). http://nymag.com/arts/tv/fall-2012/mandy-patinkin-2012-9/.

Pavelko, R.L., and J.G. Myrick. "That's So OCD: The Effects of Disease Trivialization via Social Media on User Perceptions and Impression Formation." *Computers in Human Behavior* 49 (2015): 251–258.

_____, and _____. "Tweeting and Trivializing: How the Trivialization of Obsessive-Compulsive Disorder via Social Media Impacts User Perceptions, Emotions, and Behaviors." *Imagination, Cognition and Personality: Consciousness in Theory, Research, and Clinical Practice* 36.1 (2016): 41–63.

Payton, Andrew R., and Peggy Thoits. "Medicalization, Direct-to-Consumer Advertising, and Mental Illness Stigma." *Society and Mental Health* 1.1 (2011): 55–70.

Peeling, Caitlin and Meaghan Scanlon. "'What's More Real? A Sick Girl in an Institution... or Some Kind of Supergirl...': The Question of Madness in 'Normal Again,' a Feminist Reading." *The Slayage Conference on Buffy, the Vampire Slayer.* Nashville: Slayage Conference on Buffy the Vampire Slayer Archive, 2004.

Philo, Greg. "Changing Media Representations of Mental Health." *The Psychiatrist* 21 (1997): 171–172.

Philo, Greg, Jenny Secker, Steve Platt, Lesley Henderson, Greg McLaughlin, and Jocelyn Burnside. "The Impact of the Mass Media on Public Images of Mental Illness: Media Content and Audience Belief." *Health Education Journal* 53.3 (1994): 271–281. www.10.1177/001789699405300305.

Philo, Greg, Lesley Henderson, and Katie. McCracken. *Making Drama Out of a Crisis: Authentic Portrayals of Mental Illness in TV Drama.* Glasgow: Glasgow University, University Media Group, 2010.

Pingani, Luca, et al. "How the Use of the Term "Schizo*" has Changed in an Italian Newspaper from 2001 to 2015: Findings from a Descriptive Analysis." *Psychiatry Research* 270 (2018): 792–800.

Pirkis, Jane, R., et al. "On-Screen Portrayals of Mental Illness: Extent, Nature, and Impacts." *Journal of Health Communication* 11.5 (2006): 523–541.

Priester, Paul E. "The Metaphorical Use of Vampire Films in Counseling." *Journal of Creativity in Mental Health* 3.1 (2008): 68–77.

Rain Man. Dir. Barry Levinson. MGM/UA, 1988.

Ramos, Zorangeli, et al. "Post-Traumatic Stress Symptoms and their Relationship to Drug and Alcohol Use in an International Sample of Latino Immigrants." *Journal of Immigration Minority Health* 19 (2017): 552–561.

Recess. Walt Disney Television. 1997–2001.

Reinders, A. A., T. Simone. "Cross-Examining Dissociative Identity Disorder: Neuroimaging and Etiology on Trial." *Neurocase* 14.1 (2008): 44–53.

Robison, John Elder. *Look Me in the Eye: My Life with Asperger's.* New York: Crown, 2007.

Rogers, Bill. *Cracking the Hard Class.* Lisarow: Scholastic Australia, 1997.

Rosen, Alan and Garry Walter. "Way Out of Tune: Lessons from Shine and its Exposé." *Australian and New Zealand Journal of Psychiatry* 34 .2 (2000): 2327–244.

Ross, Colin A. "Commentary: The Rise and Persistence of Dissociative Identity Disorder." *Journal of Trauma & Dissociation* 14.5 (2013): 584–588.

Rubin, Lawrence (Ed.). *Mental Illness in Popular Media: Essays on the Representation of Disorders.* Jefferson: McFarland, 2012.

Sadock, B. J., and V. A. Sadock. *Kaplan and Sadock's Synopsis of Psychiatry: Behavioural Sciences/Clinical Psychiatry.* Tenth Edition. Philadelphia: Wolters Klewer Health/Lippincott Williams and Wilkins, 2007.

SANE Australia. "Mental Health and Violence: Fact Sheet 5." 2012.

Santosa, C.M., et al. "Enhanced Creativity in Bipolar Patients: A Controlled Study." *Journal of Affective Disorders* 100.1–3 (2007): 31–39.

Şar, V., M.J. Dorahy, and C. Krüger. "Revisiting the Etiological Aspects of Dissociative Identity Disorder: A Biopsychosocial Perspective." *Psychology Research and Behavior Management* 10 (2017): 137–146.

Schlozman, Steven C. "Vampires and Those Who Slay Them: Using the Television Program *Buffy, the Vampire Slayer* in

References 169

Adolescent Therapy and Psychodynamic Education." *Academic Psychiatry* 24.1 (2000): 49–54.

Schomerus, G., et al. "Evolution of Public Attitudes About Mental Illness: A Systematic Review and Meta-Analysis." *Acta Psychiatrica Scandinavica* 125 (2012): 440–452.

Sepinwall, Alan. "Reader Mail: Does Sheldon from *The Big Bang Theory* have Asperger's?" 13 August 2009. *The Star-Ledger.*

Shameless. Showtime. 2011–.

Shepard, Dax. *Armchair Expert with Dax Shepard: Ashton Kutcher.* Los Angeles, 14 February 2018.

_____. *Armchair Expert with Dax Shepard: Joy Bryant.* Los Angeles, 14 February 2018.

Shine. Fine Line, 1996.

Siegel, D. E. *The Portrayal of Characters with Obsessive-Compulsive Disorder in American Films.* West Hartford: University of Hartford, 2014. Dissertation.

Silberman, Steve. *NeuroTribes: The Legacy of Autism and How to Think Smarter About People Who Think Differently.* Crows Nest: Allen & Unwin, 2015.

Simeone, J.C., et al. "An Evaluation of Variation in Published Estimates of Schizophrenia Prevalence from 1990–2013: A Systematic Literature Review." *BMC Psychiatry* 15 (2015): 193.

Simone, Rudy. *Aspergirls: Empowering Females with Asperger Syndrome.* London: Jessica Kingsley, 2010.

Six Feet Under. HBO. 2001–2005.

Spanos, Nicholas P. "Multiple Identity Enactments and Multiple Personality Disorder: A Sociocognitive Perspective." *Psychological Bulletin* 116.1 (1994): 143–165.

Spiegel, David, et al. "Dissociative Disorders in DSM-5." *Depression and Anxiety* 28 (2011): 824–852.

SpongeBob SquarePants. Nickelodeon, 1999.

Spoont, Michele, David Nelson, Michelle van Ryn, and Margarita Alegria. "Racial and Ethnic Variation in Perceptions of VA Mental Health Providers are Associated with Treatment Retention among Veterans with PTSD." *Medical Care* 55.9 (2017): S33–42.

Standley, Emily. "What I Want to Tell Tony Shalhoub from *Monk* as Someone with OCD." 1 August 2017. *The Mighty.* 28 June 2019. https://themighty.com/2017/07/

tony-shalhoub-monk-obsessive-compulsive-disorder/.

Staner, Luc. "Comorbidity of Insomnia and Depression." *Sleep Medicine Reviews* (2010): 35–46.

Starke, Anja. "Effects of Anxiety, Language Skills, and Cultural Adaptation on the Development of Selective Mutism." *Journal of Communication Disorders* (2018): 45–60.

Sterponot, Laura and Jennifer Shankey. "Rethinking Echolalia: Repetition as Interactional Resource in the Communication of a Child with Autism." *Journal of Child Language* 41 (2014): 275–304.

Stranger Things. Netflix. 2016–.

Stuart, Heather. "Media Portrayal of Mental Illness and Its Treatments: What Effect Does It Have on People with Mental Illness?" *CNS Drugs* 20.2 (2006): 99–106.

Stuck in Mute. Dir. Shane Mewissen. Paper Universe, 2015.

Suskind, Ron. "Why the Team Behind Sesame Street Created a Character with Autism." December 2017. *Smithsonian Magazine.* 13 November 2018. https://www.smithsonianmag.com/innovation/team-sesame-street-created-character-autism-180967218/.

Swift, Andy. "*90210* Series Finale: Silver didn't deserve her tragic ending." *Hollywood Life* (2013). http://www.hollywoodlife.com/2013/05/14/90210-silver-cancer-series-finale-ending.

Sybil. Lorimar, 1976.

Tartakovsky, Margarita. "Media's Damaging Depictions of Mental Illness." 2009. *PsychCentral.* 22 October 2012. http//:psychcentral.com/lib/2009/medias-damaging-depictions-of-mental-illness/all/1/.

Tillman, R., and B Geller. "Definitions of Rapid, Ultrarapid, and Ultradian Cycling and of Episode Duration in Pediatric and Adult Bipolar Disorders: a Proposal to Distinguish Episodes from Cycles." *Journal of Child and Adolescent Pharmacology* (2003): 267–71.

Touch. Fox, 2012–2013.

Travers, Ben, and Steve Greene. "Also on ABC's Upcoming Docket: a Breakup Dramedy, a Rapping Mayor and FBI Magicians." 16 May 2017. *IndieWire.* 7 June 2018. http://www.indiewire.com/2017/05/the-mayor-the-gospel-of-kevin-for-the-people-abc-fall-tv-trailers-ranked-1201818046/.

Treffert, Darold A. "The Savant Syndrome: An Extraordinary Condition. A Synopsis: Past, Present, Future." *Philosophical Transactions of the Royal Society* B.364 (2009): 1351–1357.

True Life: I'm Bipolar. 25 July 2002. Series 3, Episode 24.

The Unbreakable Kimmy Schmidt. Netflix, 2015–2019.

United Nations Educational, Scientific and Cultural Organisation (UNESCO). "Inclusion in Education: The Participation of Disabled Learners." 2001. 30 October 2018. http://unesdoc.unesco.org/images/0012/001234/123486E.

United States of Tara. Showtime, 2009–2011.

van Dijck, José. "Medical Documentary: Conjoined Twins as a Mediated Spectacle." *Media, Culture & Society* 24.2 (2002): 537–556.

Virzi, Juliette. "30 Fictional Characters People with Depression Relate To." 28 July 2017. *The Mighty.* 15 June 2019. https://themighty.com/2017/07/depression-fictional-characters-relatable/.

Vogel, David L., Douglas A. Gentile, and Scott A. Kapalan. "The Influence of Television on Willingness to Seek Therapy." *Journal of Clinical Psychology* 64.3 (2008): 276–295.

Wahl, Otto F. "Mass Media Images of Mental Illness: A Review of the Literature." *Journal of Community Psychiatry* (1992): 343–352.

_____. *Media Madness: Public Images of Mental Illness.* Piscataway: Rutgers University Press, 1995.

Wahl, Otto F., and Rachel Roth. "Television Images of Mental Illness: Results of a Metropolitan Washington Media Watch." *Journal of Broadcasting* 26.2 (1982): 599–605.

Waldman, Alison. "Come Up with a New Theory: Sheldon Does Not Have Asperger's." 14 August 2009. *TV Squad.* 29 September 2016. https://web.archive.org/web/20090817125113/http://tvsquad.com2009/08/14/come-up-with-a-new-theory-sheldon-does-not-have-aspergers.

The Walking Dead. Netflix, 2010.

Whitehead, Rachel. "*Homeland*'s Depiction of Mental Illness has been a Step Forward for TV." *The Guardian* (2012). http://www.theguardian.com/commentisfree/2012/may/07/homeland-mental-illness-bipolar-tv.

Wilcox, Rhonda V. "There Will Never Be a 'Very Special' Buffy: Buffy and the Monsters of Teen Life." *Journal of Popular Film and Television* 27.2 (1999): 16–23.

Willey, Liane Holliday. *Pretending to Be Normal: Living with Asperger's Syndrome.* London: Jessica Kingsley, 2014.

Wilson, Claire, et al. "How Mental Illness Is Portrayed in Children's Television." *British Journal of Psychiatry* 176 (2000): 440–443.

_____. "Mental Illness Depictions in Prime-Time Drama: Identifying the Discursive Resources." *Australian and New Zealand Journal of Psychiatry* 33 (1999): 232–239.

Wortmann, Fletcher. "Why *Monk* Stunk." 16 May 2013. *Psychology Today.* 28 June 2019. https://www.psychologytoday.com/ca/blog/triggered/201305/why-monk-stunk.

Yellow Peppers. Channel 2, 2010–2014.

Young Sheldon. CBS. 2017–.

You're the Worst. FX-FXX, 2014–2019.

Zuckerman, Esther. "Desmin Borges Breaks Down *You're the Worst*'s All-Edgar Exploration of PTSD." 28 September 2016. *The AV Club.* https://tv.avclub/desmin-borges-breaks-down-you-re-the-worst-s-all-edgar-1798252535. 17 June 2019.

Index

171